D1505323

Residence Hall Assistants in College

*A Guide to Selection,
Training, and Supervision*

M. Lee Upcraft

with the collaboration of
Guy T. Pilato

Residence Hall Assistants in College

Jossey-Bass Publishers

San Francisco   •   London   •   1986

RESIDENCE HALL ASSISTANTS IN COLLEGE
A Guide to Selection, Training, and Supervision
by M. Lee Upcraft with the collaboration of Guy T. Pilato

Copyright © 1982 by: Jossey-Bass Inc., Publishers
433 California Street
San Francisco, California 94104
&
Jossey-Bass Limited
28 Banner Street
London EC1Y 8QE

Library of Congress Cataloging in Publication Data

Upcraft, M. Lee.
    Residence hall assistants in college.

    Bibliography: p. 260
    Includes index.
    1. Dormitories—Staff.   2. Residence counselors.
I. Pilato, Guy T.   II. Title.
LB3227.U62   1982   378'.112   82-48075
ISBN 0-87589-538-7

Manufactured in the United States of America

The paper in this book meets the guidelines for
permanence and durability of the Committee on
Production Guidelines for Book Longevity of the
Council on Library Resources.

JACKET DESIGN BY WILLI BAUM

FIRST EDITION
First printing: October 1982
Second printing: January 1986

Code 8230

The Jossey-Bass
Series in Higher Education

Consulting Editors
Student Services and Counseling Psychology

Ursula Delworth
University of Iowa

Gary R. Hanson
University of Texas, Austin

Foreword

Riessman (1967) referred to the establishment of over 150,000 paraprofessional positions through antipoverty and related legislation as the "nonprofessional revolution." During the last decade, colleges and universities have experienced a similar, though less dramatic, revolution, as many thousands of undergraduates assumed paraprofessional positions as counselors, advisors, programming personnel, and resident assistants. Although a number of these positions existed prior to 1970, it is only recently that we have seen such roles legitimized and expanded.

Much of this expansion is due to the work of campus professionals who have carefully defined job functions and provided workable models for selecting, training, and evaluating undergraduate helpers. Foremost among these leaders is M. Lee Upcraft. He has worked with a number of paraprofessional programs, including academic advising and residence hall work. The training program presented in this book has been carefully developed, revised, and evaluated over the past several years by Upcraft and his associates. As such, it merits the serious attention of residence hall professionals.

I can think of no arena of the campus in which the need for effective helping persons—playing a wide variety of roles—is more critical. A large number of students still attend residential colleges and the vast majority of these students live in residence

ix

halls for at least part of their college careers. Astin's (1977) research has demonstrated the potential positive impact of residence living. Yet, in large measure, it is up to the staff to make this potential a reality. Well-trained, committed resident assistants are the key to an effective hall environment—one that facilitates student development in both academic and nonacademic domains. Such paraprofessionals are usually "made and not born"; their success mainly depends on student affairs professionals providing effective training and supervision. For many professionals, the role of trainer is new; few learn the role in graduate school and few have the opportunity to work with experienced trainers as mentors and guides. Upcraft and his associates recognize this "state of the art," and have therefore developed a structured, clear text that allows a neophyte trainer to produce an effective program for paraprofessionals. More experienced trainers will also, I believe, find this practical, well-delineated approach highly useful in their work.

This book and the accompanying manual represent one ingredient for a successful training program, but motivated, hardworking professionals are needed to make it all work. Together, these materials and the trainers who use them can make an important difference in the lives of college students.

June 1982   Ursula Delworth
                                       Director
                                       University Counseling Service
                                       University of Iowa

Preface

Most residence hall programs rely on paraprofessionals to deliver all or part of their services and programs. These front-line troops are typically part-time employees and full-time graduate or undergraduate students whose titles range from residence counselor to proctor to head resident. (We prefer the title "resident assistant," or "RA," because it is the most commonly used and understood.) Resident assistants are responsible for developing the educational potential of residence halls; this is a very big responsibility, considering all the ways students' lives are affected by living in residence halls. Thus, RAs must be effectively selected, trained, and supervised if institutions' residence hall programs are to contribute to students' academic and personal development.

We wrote this book because of what we learned over the past ten years as we struggled with the problems of selecting, training, and supervising residence hall paraprofessionals. Almost every time we reached an impasse or a seemingly irresolvable problem, we were frustrated by the lack of any helpful research, existing models, or relevant literature. Furthermore, we generally found that the persons hired to select, train, and supervise these paraprofessionals—and these persons are the key element in an effective program—could *not*, without extensive training, handle that part of their job. They lacked knowledge of selection models, student development theory, residential impact, interpersonal skills theory, leadership and small group theory, and supervisory models. In short, they lacked a conceptual basis and the refined skills necessary to select, train, and supervise RAs.

Through trial and error and with the help of many people, we developed a workable selection-training-supervision model. We learned that if instructors are given the appropriate theories, models, and supervised experiences, these people can be highly effective. We devised a training program that is highly structured, based on the reality that most people using it need such structure to make it work. Our experience has borne this out, as literally hundreds of relatively untrained and inexperienced instructors have made the training program work the first time they used it.

We had the advantage of working in a large university with many resources, but our program will work in any institution of higher education, regardless of its size, purpose, or location. We provide a rich blend of theory, existing literature and research, and practical advice. We do not merely present a program we think might work; we present an effective one that we tried, worked with, revised, and fine-tuned, within a research design, based on several years of experimentation.

To begin the proper preparation, selectors, trainers, and supervisors of resident assistants must understand the historical context within which they operate in the residence halls and the purposes and goals of the modern residence hall program. Chapter One provides such a proper perspective.

Prospective selectors, trainers, and supervisors of RAs must also know and understand the problems and issues of selection and training. Chapter Two outlines several such problems and issues and suggests a selection and training program that has increased the competence level of resident assistants. The recommended program evolved from detailed feedback provided by students regarding our first attempts. The students' specific suggestions and complaints and our subsequent "solutions" led to a workable and proven model.

Chapters Three to Seven give the theory and concepts necessary for providing resident assistants with effective leadership. Prospective instructors should know the basics of student development theory and how to apply this knowledge. They should be familiar with student development and residential theory (Chapter Three), the impact of residence halls on students' personal and academic development (Chapter Four), and how that impact develops on a residence hall floor. Finally, they should also know something about interpersonal skills theory (Chapter Five) and leadership development theory and practice (Chapters Six and Seven, respectively). Readers must study and understand these chapters if they are to successfully implement the training program.

Chapters Eight to Ten provide the necessary information for effectively training resident assistants. Chapter Eight focuses on how to teach the training program and shares our experiences, advice, and mistakes. Chapter Nine is the actual training program, including the rationale, goals, and methodology for each of the twenty sessions. Chapter Ten is an extensive experience-based elaboration of the evaluation problems and pitfalls in a training model.

Chapter Eleven is devoted to the issue of supervising resident assistants. We strongly believe that much of the impact of training is lost if it is not followed up with effective supervision. We suggest a supervisory process that is continuous, frequent, and fair to the RA, the supervisor, and the institution.

This book is intended to be used with a companion manual for participants in the training program. *Learning to Be a Resident Assistant: A Manual for Effective Participation in the Training Program.* Having conducted the selection-training program both with and without this manual, we found that the manual adds a significant dimension to RA learning: RAs finish training with a much stronger conceptual base and by using the manual are better prepared for each section and session.

We wish to acknowledge the invaluable support and assistance of Raymond O. Murphy, Patricia C. Peterson, Betty L. Moore, Roger Stimson, Calvin Symons, Andrew Mozenter, Donald Adams, and Leila Moore. Special thanks must go to Dan Peterman, an original collaborator in the development of the training program, and to Ursula Delworth, consulting editor of the Jossey-Bass Series on Student Services, without whose help and support our book would never have been completed. We are also deeply indebted to the many people who have served as instructors in the training program and helped revise and improve the model. Susan Doran and other typists were extremely helpful in preparing and reading the manuscript.

We dedicate this book to our wives, Lillian Upcraft and Grace Pilato; to our children, Kirsten and John Upcraft, and Thomas, Mark, Michael, Natalie, and Lisa Pilato; and to our parents, Milton and Mabel Upcraft, and Connie Pilato.

August 1982   M. Lee Upcraft
University Park, Pennsylvania

                                                 Guy T. Pilato
State College, Pennsylvania

Contents

The Authors

M. Lee Upcraft is director of Residential Life Programs and a member of the faculty of the Pennsylvania State University. He is responsible for administering and supervising one of the country's largest and most comprehensive residence hall programs. Upcraft received his B.A. degree in social studies in 1960 and his M.A. degree in guidance and counseling in 1961, both from the State University of New York at Albany. He received his Ph.D. degree in student personnel administration and higher education in 1967 from Michigan State University.

Upcraft has extensive experience in education—in public schools as a teacher and counselor and experience in higher education as an academic administrator, student affairs administrator, and undergraduate and faculty member. He has authored several journal articles and research monographs and presented papers at numerous professional meetings. He has served as a consultant and conducted several workshops on training residence halls staff. He has extensively researched such topics as student retention, alcohol education, academic achievement, and personal development. He is currently conducting research into improving the intellectual climate of large universities.

Guy T. Pilato is a psychologist in private practice in State College, Pennsylvania. Formerly, at the Pennsylvania State University, he served as a psychologist in the Mental Health Center and as an affiliate associate professor in the Department of Psychology. He received his B.A. degree in biology in 1958 from St. John Fisher College, his M.A. degree in guidance and student personnel administration in 1960 from Teachers College, Columbia University, and his Ph.D. degree in counseling psychology in 1968 from Columbia University.

Pilato has wide experience in higher education as a faculty member, counselor, therapist, and supervisor of graduate training in clinical settings. He has extensively trained paraprofessionals in residence halls and a variety of other settings and has authored several journal articles.

Residence Hall Assistants in College

A Guide to Selection, Training, and Supervision

1

⎍⎍⎍⎍⎍⎍⎍⎍⎍⎍⎍⎍⎍⎍⎍⎍⎍⎍⎍⎍⎍⎍⎍⎍⎍⎍⎍⎍⎍

Residence Halls and the Educational Process

Because it is of interest for persons with responsibilities in residence halls to know and understand the context within which they work, this chapter provides a historical perspective of residence halls, gives evidence of the halls' educational impact, and discusses the goals of a residential education. It focuses on how human resources can be mobilized to fulfill the educational potential of residence halls; specifically, we argue that the key ingredient in this effort is the resident assistant, but *only* when the resident assistant is carefully selected, properly trained, and effectively supervised.

History and Impact

From the very beginnings of higher education in America, colleges sought to develop the total person, not merely the mind. Godbold (1944) reported that colonial colleges were founded to provide a supply of clergymen and to ensure "that youth . . . (were) piously educated in good letters and manners" (p. 5). Morison (1936) reported that Henry Dunster, the first president of Harvard, charged the new fellows to the board of overseers by stating, "You shall take care to advance in all learning, divine, and humane,

1

each and every student who is or will be entrusted to your tutelage, according to their several abilities; and especially to take care that their conduct and manners be honorable and without blame" (p. 19). In fact, some historians argue that the development of the students' "character" was substantially more important to early colonial educators than the development of their intellect. For example, Rudolph (1965) reported there was great concern in the 1760s that Harvard was "developing a dangerous liberality of spirit, which might be useful in the sharpening of the intellect, but which was unquestionably damaging to true and holy character" (p. 65).

Early American colleges attempted to develop character primarily through the concept of *in loco parentis,* whereby colleges acted on behalf of parents for the good of the students. The curriculum stressed traditional religious values that reinforced a Christian concept of good moral character. Outside the classroom, strict rules and regulations were enforced by rigid discipline. "At Harvard, students were forbidden to lie, steal, curse, swear, use obscene language, play at cards or dice, get drunk, frequent inns, associate with any person of bad reputation, commit fornication, fight cocks, call each other nicknames, buy or sell anything, or be disrespectful or tardy or disorderly at public worship" (Leonard, 1956, pp. 26–27). Punishments for violating such rules included flogging, public confessions, public whippings, boxing the ears, extra assignments, fines, suspensions, and expulsions (Rudolph, 1965).

Nowhere was it easier and more efficient to enforce all these character-developing rules than in college dormitories. Besides providing much needed housing for students (earlier attempts at having students stay with faculty or townspeople had failed), the establishment of dormitories made possible "the all inclusive supervision of the lives of students" (Leonard, 1956, pp. 108–109). The "dormitory rationale," as Rudolph (1965) called it, "held young men to a common experience. It took them from the bosom of a sheltering home and placed them under the same roof, where they might share the experiences which made men of boys. The dormitory made possible, or so the argument went, the supervision and parental concern of the faculty for the well-being of their young charges. The dormitory brought to bear the sense of common decency and the sense of self-respect which taught responsibility. In the dormitory young men talked *into the* night about *deep matters....* So the argument went, and everywhere dormitories went up—because it was tradition, because students had to be housed and finally because people actually believed the dormitory rationale" (p. 96).

The supervision of dormitory life was the responsibility of the president, the faculty, the tutors, the priest-seminarians, or other persons. Sometimes presidents insisted on living with their families in a suite of rooms within the dormitory, and some presidents, notably Caldwell of the University of North Carolina, were particularly relentless in keeping students in order and within the college quadrangle. Faculty and other people patrolled the halls frequently and forced entrance into rooms into which they were not admitted by knocking. Penalties for offenders included those mentioned, as well as rustication, by which the offending student was farmed out to the home of a nearby clergyman for a period of time (Leonard, 1956).

In the first half of the nineteenth century, dormitories continued to grow and remain a significant part of the collegiate environment. However, by 1850, some institutions began to have serious doubts about the "dormitory rationale." Francis Wayland of Brown University described dormitory life as "unnatural" and pointed to such evils as the spread of disease by epidemics, the tendency of students to exercise too little, the exposure of many young men to the vice and habits of evil leaders, and the isolation of the college from the life of the community and the world (Rudolph, 1965). During the 1850s, Henry Tappen of the University of Michigan inspired the abandonment of dormitories, and President Eliot of Harvard tried unsuccessfully to kill off dormitories there (Rudolph, 1965). However, between 1896 and 1915, Columbia University, the University of Minnesota, Cornell University, the University of Illinois, and the University of Michigan all initiated dormitories (Rudolph, 1965).

By the first part of the twentieth century, strict supervision still prevailed, and the enrollment of women introduced new rules designed to keep men and women apart, particularly in their residences. However, over the years, faculty supervision gave way to persons who were hired strictly to keep students in line. Hardee (1964) described these people as retired military officers, discarded football coaches, elderly housemothers, and others with "scoutlike" qualities. These supervisors were loyal to the institution, enforced university policy, and maintained the status quo. They also enlisted paid or volunteer students to help supervise other students (although students had served in this manner since colonial times, not until the twentieth century was extensive use of students to supervise residents initiated).

The 1960s brought a real revolution to residence hall living. Students began questioning the concept of *in loco parentis* as a basis for a college-student relationship and successfully killed off most of the rules and regulations they considered offensive to their individual freedom. In residence halls, rules that infringed upon students' privacy in their rooms were eliminated, and freer association of the sexes was permitted, including continuous visiting rights and coeducational residence halls. Concurrently, the dormitory rationale began to change. Development of "character" was no longer possible through strict rules and regulations, but colleges were still committed, at least in their catalogs, to the education of the person as well as the intellect. Character was redefined as "student development," and rules and regulations were replaced by programs, services, and activities that promoted student development. According to Delworth, Sherwood, and Casaburri (1974), residence hall life has become even more significantly aligned with the overall objectives of higher education. "The philosophical base of operations for many residence hall systems has changed from a pure business-economic position to written assumptions about educational value" (p. 48).

As the nature and purpose of residence hall living changed, so did the role of the people responsible for supervising residence halls. As an educational rationale developed, housemothers and retired military personnel gave way to professional residence educators who had graduate training in student affairs or related fields. Many of these persons worked part-time while pursuing graduate work, and residence hall supervision was often their first job in the student affairs field. But they were professionals and they were educators, and they sought to develop the educational potential of residence halls. The role of the undergraduate resident assistant (RA) began to change also. As *in loco parentis* passed from the scene, so did the parietal rules that RAs traditionally enforced. So with a changing philosophy and fewer rules to enforce, RAs could now concentrate on helping students maintain a good living environment and could be seen as a source of help and referral. They could also help develop activities and programs and the educational potential of residence halls.

Nevertheless, in spite of the freer atmosphere of residence halls, students migrated to off-campus housing in large numbers. In the early 1970s, many institutions had trouble filling their halls, and some were forced to close them or convert them to other uses. But the migration was short-lived. As economic conditions worsened, and students discovered that colleges were more benevolent landlords than private entrepreneurs, on-campus housing became popular again. It was cheaper and more convenient to return to residence halls, and most of the rules that students found offensive were gone. By the end of the 1970s, most institutions had overflowing residence halls, and were turning away students who wanted to live on campus.

However, hard evidence of the educational impact of residence halls was still lacking. Administrators believed that residence halls were a good place for students to grow and develop—both personally and academically—and besides, they had to live somewhere if they were to enroll. Not until the 1970s did real evidence of the educational advantages of residence halls emerge. Astin (1973) found that students living in residence halls were less likely than commuters to drop out and more likely to attain a baccalaureate degree in four years. Chickering (1974) conducted a highly controlled study, involving nearly 170,000 students in one analysis and 5,400 in another. He concluded that even when background variables and other student characteristics prior to attending college were taken into account, students living in residence halls had all the advantages. More specifically, students who lived in college residence halls (1) exceeded the learning and personal development predicted when their advantages in ability, prior education and extracurricular activities, and community and family backgrounds were considered; (2) were more fully involved in academic and extracurricular activities and social activities with other students; (3) earned higher grade point averages, even when differences in ability were taken into account.

Chickering further concluded that the gap between commuting and residential students widened as their collegiate experiences increased. "Access, discovery, and encounter occur much less for commuters and they continue in circumstances that add weights to their preexisting handicaps. Thus, a major consequence of American higher education as it currently functions for commuters and residents is to increase the distance between them. 'Unto them that hath is given. From them that hath not, is taken away'" (Chickering, 1974, p. 85).

Chickering's study was followed by Astin's (1977), which involved more than 225,000 students from 1961 to 1974. Astin concluded that the most important environmental characteristic associated with finishing college was living in a residence hall during the freshman year. After students' entering characteristics and other environmental measures were controlled, students living in a residence hall, compared with those living with their parents or in private rooms, added about 12 percent to their chances of finishing college. Astin concluded that students in residence halls (1) expressed more satisfaction than commuters with their undergraduate experience, particularly student friendships, faculty-student relations, institutional reputation, and social life; (2) were more likely to achieve in extracurricular areas, particularly leadership and athletics; (3) were, among men, more likely to earn higher grades; (4) showed slightly greater increases in artistic interests, liberalism, and interpersonal self-esteem.

The relationship between residential living and colleges' and universities' educational goals has been articulated and evidence of impact demonstrated. (This evidence is completely reviewed in Chapter Four.) Leading student affairs educators have discussed, within the context of the larger campus, assumptions and goals for residence halls. Brown (1974) identified three basic assumptions about residence halls and their potential for educating students: (1) students' living environments can have a profound impact on their personal and educational development; (2) residence hall environments can be structured to enhance personal and educational development; and (3) residence hall personnel must be skilled in structuring such environments. Based on those assumptions, Riker and DeCoster (1971) offered five general objectives for college student housing, catalogued into five levels: (1) providing satisfactory physical environment through new construction and renovation, (2) adequate care and maintenance of the physical facilities, (3) establishing guidelines that provide structure for compatible and cooperative community living, (4) developing an interpersonal environment that reflects responsible citizenship and a concern for others and an atmosphere conducive to learning, and (5) opportunities for individual growth and development. These objectives are organized into a hierarchy, with success at any one level depending on how well student needs are fulfilled at lower levels. For example, if students are preoccupied with excessive noise in the residential unit, it is unlikely that much support for educational or cultural programs will be achieved. More specifically, Riker (1980) believed residence halls can help residents: (1) understand and follow through on their developmental growth requirements; (2) better understand themselves and others; (3) improve their competence in relating to others; and (4) create and maintain an environment in which they and others can experience feelings of identity, security, and stimulations.

Human Resources

The objectives just discussed cannot be met without two key human resources: the students living in residence halls and the residence hall staff. DeCoster and Mable (1974) pointed out that all too often the lack of an educational environment in residence halls is falsely attributed to students themselves. "How often have we heard staff members maintain that students in a particular community are not interested in having the professor 'follow them home' from the classroom; that they prefer a residence environment that provides them a relief or an escape from formal academic pressures?" (p. 31). DeCoster and Mable argued, and we agree, that such attitudes can be overcome if residence hall staff make a concerted effort to (1) make students aware of their living unit's objectives, (2) provide enthusiastic support for these objectives, and (3) actively participate in achieving these objectives. In other words, the staff cannot simply react when students want or need something; if they take seriously their responsibility of educating students in residence halls, they must take the initiative and the responsibility for such education.

The staff consists of professionals and paraprofessionals. Professional staff are known as resident directors, head residents, area coordinators, or by other titles. Typically, they live in a residence hall, and are responsible for the supervision of both students and resident assistants. They select and train resident assistants, help plan programs for students, assist students with their problems and concerns, and may even be responsible for the maintenance of the building. Some have advanced graduate preparation and work full-time; others work part-time and are obtaining graduate preparation.

Unfortunately, these professional staff members are often the least experienced and least prepared members of the total student affairs staff. That does not mean that they do not have the potential for developing into fully experienced and knowledgeable professionals with a basic, acceptable level of professionalism, commitment, and skill. However, their initial limitations and strengths must be recognized when developing their selecting, training, and supervising skills.

It is the paraprofessionals in residence halls, however, that are the most critical people for creating a good educational environment. These front-line troops interact daily with students and are typically part-time employees (at the worst, volunteers) pursuing an academic career full-time. They are not true professionals, particularly when one considers their age, experience, the amount of time they have available, and the training they receive. But they are typically very enthusiastic, eager to learn, and filled with potential. With proper training and supervision, they can become effective counselors, advisers, programmers, disciplinarians, and leaders on their residence hall floors. More than any other staff, they are attuned to students' needs, interests, issues, and problems. And that unique perspective contributes greatly to the professional staff's ability to develop the educational potential of residence halls. We are certainly better off then when college presidents and priest-seminarians roamed the corridors of residence halls! With proper training and supervision, residence assistants can get the job done, but without such support, they may not, and residence halls will be just places for eating and sleeping.

Realistically, in an era of limited or declining resources, most institutions will continue to operate their residence halls within the limitations and strengths of the professional staff and resident assistants. However, if resident assistants are trained to be *paraprofessionals,* there will be more hope for realizing the educational potential of residence halls. As defined by Delworth, Sherwood, and Casaburri (1974), a paraprofessional is "a person without extended professional training who is specifically selected, trained, and given on-going supervision to perform some designated portion of the tasks usually performed by the professional" (p. 12). The authors pointed out that paraprofessionals work in a specific area for which they are qualified because of their specific skills and are members of the indigenous population or the population being served.

If colleges use paraprofessionals in residence halls, they cannot ignore the most critical aspect of the definition: Paraprofessionals must be "specifically selected, trained, and given on-going supervision." Too often, these persons, by definition with limited experience and time commitment, are put in authoritative positions without careful selection, proper training (or no training at all), and very little effective supervision. In other words, RAs are left to their own devices, which may or may not benefit students or fulfill residence halls' educational potential. An outside observer of the residence hall scene, trained in organizational behavior, once remarked to us that residence halls were the only organization managed from the bottom up because of the lack of training, supervision, and accountability of resident assistants. Yet schools entrust a great part of the entire educational potential of their halls to these people. Do we really have such little regard for students? Are we that indifferent, or worse, skeptical of the powerful impact of the residential environment?

Our opinion, based on years of working with residence hall staff, is that we must first accept the fact that RAs and professional staff supervisors will continue to lack the necessary experience to implement the educational potential of residence halls when they enter the system. However, what can be improved is the selection, training, and supervision of RAs. We found that residence halls professional staff, in spite of their limited backgrounds and experience, can be trained to carefully select, properly train, and effectively supervise resident assistants *if* they use a highly structured system. Such resident assistants can then help the residence halls become compatible, cooperative communities that develop positive interpersonal environments where students can grow and develop.

The RA's Duties. Delworth, Sherwood, and Casaburri (1974) argued that the starting point for selecting and training RAs should be an accurate description of the job they are expected to do. Although job definitions vary from one institution to another, RAs are typically expected to (1) provide personal help and assistance; (2) manage and facilitate groups; (3) facilitate social, recreational, and educational programs; (4) inform students or refer them to appropriate information sources; (5) explain and enforce rules and regulations; and (6) maintain a safe, orderly, and relatively quiet environment.

RAs provide personal help and assistance as students come to them with their problems concerning roommates, academic difficulties, parental relationships, career decisions, or the opposite sex. Although they are not trained to counsel or provide therapy (nor should they be encouraged to do so), RAs are frequently the first persons in the institution to learn about a student's problem. Thus they should be skillful in solving minor problems and referring major ones to professional sources.

But RAs do not only work with students seeking help. Frequently, RAs must, based on direct observation or information from other students, initiate contacts with students who need help. Unfortunately, most counseling training models assume the client has initiated the contact, not the counselor, and so these models are not that useful when training RAs. For example, the RA must deal with students who drink too much and subsequently harm themselves, others, or the institution's physical facilities. These students may not realize that they have a problem, yet most RAs would initiate contact with those students and try to help. Many times these students may not be all that interested in the RA's help, or they may deny that a problem exists and resist such help.

RAs manage and facilitate groups, typically a group of students living on a floor in a residence hall building. The RAs are formal leaders of that group when they organize programs or conduct group meetings. At other times the RAs must facilitate the group by assuming informal leadership and helping students organize themselves. At still other times, the RAs must assume direct authority with groups of students by enforcing rules and regulations. In all cases, the RAs must know how to deal with groups of students and be able to distinguish the different types of leadership roles required.

RAs facilitate social, recreational, and educational programs. Social programs are easy to organize because students are usually very interested in their own activities and events. Likewise, formal and informal recreational activities, such as intramural sports or throwing a Frisbee, require little effort from the RA. But so-called educational programs are usually not initiated by students and thus require extensive efforts by the RA. Programs which involve intellectual substance, such as seminars led by faculty, require that the RA do much more planning and promotion. Similarly, programs focusing on student development, such as sexuality, career decision making, or interpersonal relationships, may require the same extensive efforts.

RAs are an information source. If students do not know the answer to a question and it is ten o'clock at night, the first place they go to is the RA's room. The breadth of information required to answer these questions is so great that most RAs will settle for knowing where to find the answer if they do not know themselves. And referring students to the right source is not easy. The RA who gains a reputation of *not* knowing a lot about the institution, or even worse, not taking the time to find the answer or make the referral, will soon be out of business.

All RAs are called on to explain and enforce institutional rules. The rules that students agree with are easy to enforce; the difficult ones are those they disagree with, universally violate, or ignore. The best example is rules about alcohol. Many schools are located in states that prohibit the possession or use of alcohol by persons under twenty-one and so the school feels obligated to enforce the law. The problem is that the law is no deterrent, and drinking among underage college students is almost universal. Thus most institutions try to eliminate alcohol in their residence halls or, short of that, attempt to limit or control its use. Underage students who drink think that both the state and the institution are naive, and so the RA is caught in the middle. Even in states where the drinking age is eighteen, RAs must control alcohol abuse and are still caught between the institution's expectations and student norms. The problem of having to enforce rules on the one hand and helping students on the other hand is an age-old dilemma. The so-called cop-counselor conflict of the RA role has been heatedly debated and discussed by RAs and their supervisors since the RA position was originated. We think it is a much overrated problem, too often used as an excuse for poor performance or inadequate supervision. If RAs are properly selected, trained, and supervised, the dilemma can be minimized. Generally, the RA skilled in helping students will also be skilled in enforcing the rules.

RAs are usually called on to keep peace and maintain a safe, orderly, and relatively quiet floor environment. But this is not always easy because residence halls are also students' homes, and studying is but one part of their many activities. There will be parties, loud music, horseplay like water battles, and other activities that may disrupt studying and sleeping. The RA's responsibility is to develop a living environment that (1) provides a study atmosphere and (2) considers students' other residential needs. But RAs cannot do it alone, so to some extent every floor must develop its own time, place, and manner rules.

Obviously, these various roles demand much time, effort, and stress from RAs. Their role in creating compatible, cooperative communities that develop positive interpersonal environments where students can grow and develop cannot be underestimated. But why is it so difficult to carefully select, properly train, and effectively supervise the RAs? What are the key issues and problems that cause these difficulties?

Selection. The students attracted to the resident assistant position have varying degrees of raw talent, experience, maturity, and knowledge. For example, undergraduate students may have the necessary experience and knowledge to do the job but lack the maturity. Graduate students may have the maturity and experience but lack campus familiarity or be more academically preoccupied. In either case, both types of students lack the breadth and depth of competencies to do a very demanding, complex, and stressful job. Second, no two RAs have the same job because floors and buildings can vary greatly according to the differences among students living there. Floors comprised of mostly freshmen differ from those that are mostly upperclassmen. "Study" floors differ from "party" floors, and male floors differ from female floors or male-female floors. Talking with two RAs in the same hall but who have very different floor demographies makes one wonder whether they indeed live within the same residence hall system. The architectural layout of a residence hall is also a factor. Some RAs must supervise more than one floor, and others may have to deal with apartment-type units, both of which limit contact between RAs and students. Finally, typical selection processes lack common understandings of RA role and valid selection criteria. We feel that the interview is an overrated, overused, uncreative, and misused method of screening applicants. At its worst, the interview allows interviewers to exercise their own biases and prejudices arbitrarily. Even if interviews are conducted in an unbiased fashion, there is no evidence to indicate that persons who do well in interviews also do well on the job. Further, there is little or no evidence to suggest that persons who survive the typical selection process will necessarily become successful resident assistants.

Training. Given the differences among resident assistants and the floors they supervise, it is difficult to know what kind of training to offer. What may be appropriate to one individual or setting may not be appropriate to another. Types of training range from a basic nuts and bolts approach—as examples, how to make a disciplinary referral or how to help students who have locked themselves out of their rooms—to highly structured interpersonal relations models—for example, microcounseling, human relations training, or helping skills. Or training may include bits and pieces from all these approaches and thus lack continuity and depth. Even if training models are available (see Meade, 1978, for a description of several different types), they may not be applicable. For a variety of reasons, which we elaborate in the next chapter, pure counselor training models, even those designed for paraprofessionals, rarely work well for training resident assistants. And neither do the "What to do if . . ." cookbooks because they cannot possibly cover all the ifs.

Another problem is that there never seems to be enough time for selecting and training. Many RAs may be new to the campus as well as to the position. Others may have been hired too late in the previous academic year to be trained prior to assuming the job. Offering training at the same time that RAs are coping with a new job does not work well because it creates tension between their immediate needs (adjusting to the position) and their long-range needs (developing the skills necessary to do the job). Tension also builds between time spent on the floor and time spent in training. And most RAs are also full-time students, creating tension between time spent on the job and time spent studying. Even if we know what training we want to offer and find the time to do it, RAs may not accept it. Resident assistants are typically bright but practical individuals who demand a great deal from those who train them. They are sometimes quick to judge the effectiveness of the training they get. Training must be practical yet deep, relevant yet philosophical, immediate yet long-range, current yet universally applicable, and so on. Resistance, either direct ("this training is baloney") or indirect (not fully participating in training sessions), is a common reaction of some RAs.

Supervision. Even if all the selection and training problems are solved, several supervision problems remain. As we stated, too many residence hall systems are governed from the bottom up, usually because the supervisory system is weak, misguided, or nonexistent. First, the people supervising RAs may have limited experience, knowledge, and skill. Many are in their first professional job in student affairs; others are working part-time on a graduate degree and unable to devote full time to the job of supervising. Although they may have had experience as a resident assistant or have even completed a graduate degree, the professionals are not necessarily prepared to select, train, and supervise RAs. And many do not stay in the job long enough to get good at it.

Second, RAs may be as resistant to supervision as they are to training. For many RAs, it is their first job in the human services field, and they may have difficulty adjusting to being a part of an organizational structure. In fact, it may be the first time they have a job description, a supervisor, and most of all, clear accountability for their performance. The adjustment from being just another student to being a part of the institutional structure is also difficult because it requires moving away from the peer group and its support and reinforcement. But most of all, some RAs think that there is no way anyone can supervise or evaluate their job because there is little opportunity for direct observation of job performance. "Only I can really know whether or not I'm doing a good job because I'm the only one who knows what I'm doing" is a typical RA rationalization for resisting supervision.

Third, as with selection and training, very few supervisory models that apply directly to the residential organizational situations are available. Supervision and evaluation of RAs, if done at all, are too often disorganized, subjective, or nonexistent. In many instances, job descriptions are vague or irrelevant, expectations are not specific, and evaluation of performance is subjective. As discussed in Chapter Eleven, supervision can be organized, focused, and more objective if a proper supervisory system is used.

2

ⅉ⅊ⅉ⅊ⅉ⅊ⅉ⅊ⅉ⅊ⅉ⅊ⅉ⅊ⅉ⅊ⅉ⅊ⅉ⅊ⅉ⅊ⅉ⅊ⅉ⅊ⅉ⅊ⅉ⅊ⅉ⅊

Criteria for Selecting and Training Resident Assistants

As we developed this book, we recalled some of the difficulty we experienced trying to find suitable RAs and an effective way of training them. This chapter reviews the literature on selecting and training RAs and describes the experiences that led to our current model of selecting and training. It also elaborates the model's content and methodology and offers evidence of its effectiveness.

Selection Criteria and Techniques

There are probably as many resident assistant selection processes as there are institutions with residence halls, and no one institution selects its RAs the same way from year to year. Three basic issues underlie a selection process: who, what, and how. First it must be decided who will be involved with selection and who will make the final decision. There must then be agreement about what criteria and techniques to use. Finally, it must be determined how prospective RAs will be identified and selected.

Who should be involved in selecting? As we reviewed the literature and looked back on our experiences, we found agreement that program administrators, current resident assistants, and students themselves should be involved. Klockars (1978) found that peer ratings were valuable when selecting RAs. Tibbits (1977) argued for a totally peer-oriented selection process because when he compared peer ratings and professional staff ratings of candidates, he found that they were virtually the same. Current RAs are a source of input because they know the job better than anyone and have an excellent perspective from which to judge candidates. Professional staff who administer residence halls usually have a perspective that transcends the limited view of students and RAs. The staff can take into account institutional goals and needs and what is known about student development, environmental influences, and residential impact. In other words, the staff is in a unique position to exercise a professional judgment based on their past experience and knowledge.

Despite this agreement about who should be involved, there is disagreement about how they should be involved. One argument is that because peer ratings correlate highly with professional staff ratings, peers should select RAs. On the other hand, another argument is that professional staff who administer residence halls and are ultimately accountable for the performance of those selected should do the selecting. The "neutral" argument is for a consensus model, where RAs, students, and professional staff all agree on who should be selected.

Our experience led us to the conclusion that professional staff who train and supervise RAs should make the final decision, based on extensive input from experienced RAs and students. If professional staff are properly knowledgeable about residential environments, student development, and institutional goals, they alone should make the final decision. They clearly are in a better position to judge candidates than students or experienced RAs because the latter groups lack an overall perspective. To us, a peer model or a consensus model assumes that professional staff are equal to, or even inferior to, the inexperienced and partially educated students and RAs. We simply do not believe that that is true, so we encourage extensive input from peers and RAs. But it is the professional staff's responsibility to evaluate that input and make the final decision. When professional staff delegate that decision to students, they are, we believe, admitting that they are less than professional.

As candidates for the position of resident assistant are being selected, their personality characteristics, interpersonal skills, and background and prior relevant experience should be investigated. The following six sections discuss the three selection criteria and the techniques for determining them, review available literature on the effectiveness of the criteria and techniques, and offer our personal experiences and opinions.

Personality. One selection criterion is the personality of potential RAs, on the assumption that certain characteristics correlate positively with successful performance as an RA. This assessment usually starts with a discussion of what these traits are. Several traits have been reported in the literature. For example, Thomas (1979) concluded that RAs who are warm, friendly, and sociable are typically identified by students as effective. McCarthy and Berman (1971) concluded that they were looking for students who could handle stress well, showed evidence of emotional stability and personal integration, and were receptive to learning. In a community college peer counseling program, Pyle and Snyder (1974) looked for candidates with a sincere regard for others, an ability to accept people with different value systems, and warm, empathic, and sensitive feelings.

Assuming agreement can be reached about what these characteristics are and how they are defined (and this is a very big assumption), the next problem is how to identify students who have the characteristics. One way is by using objective personality measures. The idea of finding an instrument that could quickly and easily help us identify suitable RA candidates was very attractive. We were initially encouraged when we learned that several personality inventories were being tried and studied, including the Edwards Personal Preference Schedule (EPPS), the Myers-Briggs Type Indicator, the Personal Orientation Inventory (POI), the Minnesota Multiphasic Personality Inventory (MMPI), the Omnibus Personality Inventory (OPI), and several institutionally developed inventories.

We encountered several problems with the use of such instruments. First, we were never sure which personality characteristics were most conducive to RA performance; when we did agree, we could not settle on common definitions. When we agreed about characteristics and definitions, we could not find an instrument that precisely matched our needs. But most importantly, we found little evidence that these measures correlated with successful RA performance. German (1979), after reviewing several personality inventories, concluded that their use as selection tools for RAs have produced inconclusive results. He also pointed out, and we agree, that although personality inventories can provide useful data for selection processes, program administrators typically like to rely upon more interpersonal skills data when evaluating potential RAs.

Interpersonal Skills. Applicants' interpersonal skills is the second selection criterion, on the assumption that certain interpersonal skills correlate positively with successful performance as an RA. This approach begins with an identification of what these skills are. Several theories have been reported in the literature. The most commonly used model was developed by Carkhuff (1969); others include those of Ivey (1971), Egan (1975), Danish and Hauer (1973), and Brammer (1979). (See Chapter Five for a review of these theories.)

One technique used to identify persons with the appropriate interpersonal skills is the interpersonal skills rating scale. Prospective RAs are asked to perform in situations very similar to the actual helping situations encountered by resident assistants. Such scales include Gazda's Global Scale and modifications of Carkhuff's Index of Communication. Cannon and Peterman (1973) used a modified Carkhuff scale to evaluate prospective RAs as they were involved in a helping interaction with another person. Delworth, Sherwood, and Casaburri (1974) reported that the Carkhuff scales can be good tools for assessing the communication skills of students who want to become paraprofessional counselors.

We found these scales too limiting. The RA is involved in many interactions that are not "helping" or "counseling" in the sense these instruments measure. These instruments assume that a person has initiated a contact with the resident assistant and is willing to work at finding a solution to the problem presented. In fact, most RA interactions are informal and social or involve non-counseling interpersonal interactions. There is also little evidence that high ratings on interpersonal scales correlate positively with successful RA performance. Thus we did not find these scales particularly useful, although we do believe that well-developed interpersonal skills are important to the successful functioning of an RA.

Background and Experience. Evaluating RA candidates' background and experiences to determine their potential as successful RAs involves assessment of such variables as academic average, class standing, and previous leadership experience. There is some evidence that academic average is related to successful job performance. Greenleaf (1974) argued that basic academic achievement is essential if an undergraduate is to serve as a full-time student and assume the responsibility of a resident assistant. Upcraft and Peterson (1980) found a positive correlation between academic average and successful job performance: The higher the candidate's grades at the time of selection, the more successful the candidate was as a resident assistant, as evaluated by students.

Class standing is an influential variable. Most authorities argue that sophomores and juniors make the best candidates, particularly if extensive training is required (Allen, 1974; Delworth, Sherwood, and Casaburri, 1974). Hutchins, Yost, and Hill (1976) compared performance on interpersonal and administrative behaviors of undergraduate RAs to professionally trained (master's degree) RAs and found few differences but recommended using undergraduates. Delworth, Sherwood, and Casaburri (1974) suggested, however, that there are advantages to using seniors, as well as juniors and sophomores, because of their experience within an institution and their ability to help others because of this experience. Upcraft and Peterson (1980) found that students typically evaluate junior resident assistants more positively than sophomores, with seniors earning the least positive evaluation.

Using the variable of prior leadership experience assumes that previous success in a leadership position predicts success in the RA position. Consequently, typical RA applicants have had student leadership positions in residence halls or in campus organizations and governing groups. We could not find any substantive research on this variable in the literature, but our own impression is that prior leadership experience is overrated. Although the RA position is one of leadership, it is very different from being the president of a campus organization or the captain of the football team. The RA position is not democratically elected, and the RA is accountable to the institution, not the residents. The RA also has many other roles, including counseling, programming, and enforcing rules, and these functions are not typically associated with student leadership positions.

Assuming that personality characteristics, interpersonal skills, and background and experience are all important criteria, how is it determined that a candidate possesses these traits? We commented on the limitations of personality instruments and interpersonal rating scales; other selection techniques include the interview, discussions, and role playing.

The Interview. The good old interview is the most frequently used selection technique. In the typical RA selection procedure, each candidate interviews with current RAs and professional staff. The interviewers then get together and make a decision or provide input to the decision makers. Obviously, the interview is a rather quick and easy way to get to know candidates, and interviewers are typically given great discretion in determining topics to be covered, the criteria for evaluating candidates, and the techniques to be used. But in our opinion, the interview is the most widely abused selection technique in residence halls. For an interview to be a successful selection technique, selection criteria must be clearly identified, interviewers must be trained, interviewers' personal biases and prejudices must be minimized, and the content from one interviewer to another must be consistent.

Our experience showed that these conditions rarely exist. Too often, criteria are vague or nonexistent, and the interviewers' personal feelings, attitudes, values, biases, and prejudices take command. Even when the interview is conducted correctly, there is little evidence that performance in an interview correlates with successful RA performance. When interviews are compared with other techniques (Banta, 1969; Bumba and others, 1980), they are clearly inferior. As our selection-training model evolved, we realized how superficial and suspect the interview was, even when executed properly. We discovered again and again that students who did well in an interview did not necessarily do well on the job. Thus we have little faith in the interview as the sole means of selecting RAs.

Discussions. A second selection technique is the discussion group, or candidate seminars. Several candidates interact with one another on selected topics or topics of their own choosing. The groups are observed by those involved in the selection process, and then an evaluation of candidates' performance is made (Bumba and others, 1980). In some instances, the candidates themselves may be asked to rate the other members of the group as to their potential for becoming an effective RA (Klockars, 1978; Tibbits, 1977). Tibbits (1977) concluded that peer ratings result in selection decisions identical to those made by other methods. The Leaderless Group Discussion (LGD) developed by Bass is the best example of the candidate seminar: In this setting, candidates are supposedly less self-conscious and more natural, thus providing a more valid assessment of their potential as RAs.

Our experience with this technique was not all that good, and we have several reservations. First, in the only predictive study of this technique (Haldane, 1973), no significant correlation between seminar ratings and job performance could be established. Second, we have serious doubts about relying too heavily on candidates' ratings of each other. Students indeed have perceptions of other students that should be taken into account, but they are only one piece of the puzzle. Ultimately, we believe decisions about RAs should be made by professional staff, based on their experience, training, and judgment. Finally, as with the interview technique, selecting those students who do well in a seminar setting may or may not relate to doing well on the job.

Role Playing. A third selection technique, designed to determine personal characteristics and interpersonal skills, is role playing. The candidate is presented with a typical situation an RA must face and asked to respond as if he or she were an RA. The other player may be the interviewer, or the role playing may be done in a group of other candidates or current RAs. (We recommend *not* using other candidates because they have a vested interest in the outcome and thus may try to make the role player look bad.) We think role playing is a very positive and effective way of evaluating candidate characteristics and skills, but the method does have limitations. Some candidates have difficulty understanding and playing their roles and some players stick to their prescribed role regardless of the candidate's behavior. Although many research studies on role playing exist in the psychological literature, there is little or no evidence that it is a useful technique for selecting resident assistants. There is no evidence that successful role players are successful RAs.

A Step-by-Step Selection Model

As just discussed, there are no commonly accepted answers to the questions of who, what, and how for selecting resident assistants. There is little evidence that personality characteristics, interpersonal skills, or prior experiences are measurable by current selection techniques, and there is almost no evidence that these criteria indicate successful performance as a resident assistant. There is also little evidence that various selection techniques are related to successful performance. And there is even disagreement about who should make the final judgment regarding candidates. Does this mean that the situation is hopeless? Would it be better to simply hire candidates randomly or to use favorite but unproven selection criteria and techniques?

We do not think so. We agree there is little evidence that current selection procedures are reliable or valid. First, some selection procedures may indeed relate to actual job performance, but very little effort or research has been done to make that correlation. Second, and more importantly, we feel that there is not enough time devoted to staff selection. Discovering people who have appropriate personal characteristics, interpersonal skills, and prior backgrounds simply cannot be done in the two or three hours typically devoted to each candidate. However, we also recognize that, practically speaking, there is not enough time. What is to be done?

Based on our experiences, we suggest the following selection process for resident assistants:

1. Start the whole process at least eight months before the person

will actually assume the position. For example, if you are hiring for September, begin the selection process in January. (This recommendation becomes clearer when we discuss our suggested selection-training model later in the chapter.)

2. Agree on what the job is all about at your institution (see Chapter 1 for suggested functions), and write a clear and unambiguous job description. Both candidates and the persons involved in the selection process should have a common understanding of the position.

3. Agree on selection criteria, and make sure the candidates and other persons involved in the selection process have a common understanding of those criteria. This chapter suggested personal characteristics, interpersonal skills, and prior background experiences as selection criteria; based on the needs of your residence hall system, develop more specificity for each category.

4. On paper, screen out those applicants with a poor record of academic achievement (we suggest at least a 2.75 on a four-point scale) and/or involved in any current or recent disciplinary action (as enforcers of the rules, RAs must be good role models in this regard). Also screen out all freshmen unless there are extenuating circumstances, such as evidence of exceptional maturity or prior experiences. We are also skeptical of graduate students who have no prior experience in residence halls.

5. Conduct a preliminary interview, approximately one hour long, with each screened candidate, focusing on assessment of personal characteristics, interpersonal skills, and prior background experiences. A professional staff member, a student (one who is not a candidate), and a current resident assistant should do the interviewing, with the professional staff member making the final decision. Interviewers should develop a common format for the interview and use the selection techniques identified earlier in the chapter.

This point in the selection process is when to start weeding out candidates obviously not qualified or ready for the RA position.

If there is a reasonable amount of disagreement about a candidate, she or he should be left in the pool. A general rule is to reduce the candidate pool to about twice the number needed to fill expected vacancies. But instead of continuing to narrow the field through further selection procedures, the remaining candidates should participate in a training program before final selections are made.

The best selection procedure actually combines selection and training and is done prior to the candidate assuming the RA position. A comprehensive training program involves at least forty hours of direct contact between instructor and candidate, focusing on student development, self-awareness, and interpersonal and leadership skills development. At the end of the training program, candidates are (1) selected for the RA position, (2) placed in an applicant pool in the event of a vacancy during the year, or (3) completely eliminated from consideration.

Training

There is as much consensus about how to train RAs as there is about how to select them, and there is as much evidence of the effectiveness of training programs as there is for selection procedures: little or none. The evidence to date on the elements of a good and effective training program is inconclusive.

There is substantial agreement that RAs should be trained (Delworth, Sherwood, and Casaburri, 1974; Greenleaf, 1974; Delworth and Yarris, 1978; Powell, 1974; Schuh, 1981; and many others). But there is little agreement about the goals, timing, content, format, and evaluation of training. Here we review the literature on training and then describe our experiences as neophyte trainers of resident assistants.

Goals. There are many goal statements about training RAs. Greenleaf (1974) argued that training should consist of an understanding of the philosophical and educational purposes of higher education, the developmental tasks to be met by young adults, and the relationship of environmental factors to student growth. Training should also create greater self-awareness, skills in human relationships, and grass roots counseling. Powell (1974) identified the four training goals as education for orientation and information, education in mutually cooperative relationships, education in intra- and interpersonal dynamics, and education for contextual integration of students' development. Schuh (1981) identified the four dimensions of training as residence hall operations, institutional support services, human relations, and program advising.

Our experience has been that most or all of these goals are legitimate when training RAs. The practical problem is that there is not enough time to train for all goals, so it is necessary to choose from among them and decide what ones have time and effort priority. We concluded that if the RAs are not interpersonally skillful both individually and in groups and knowledgeable about students, all the other goals are unattainable. (We discuss this subject more fully later in the chapter.)

Timing. There is disagreement about when RAs should be trained. Greenleaf (1974) identified three basic training orientations: spring, preschool, and on the job. Delworth, Sherwood, and Casaburri (1974) argued that preservice training should be brief; their work covered the ideas and skills RAs must have before they begin their work. On-the-job training should cover skill upgrading and teaching new skills. Riessman (1967) recommended that preservice training be short, perhaps a few days, so as not to raise too much anxiety in the RA. Longer training programs, based on human relations training, should be saved for on-the-job experience.

Our experience has been that on-the-job training is overrated and that not enough time is spent training candidates prior to their assuming the RA position. And with little or no preservice training, combining selection with training is impossible. In short, we would rather err on the side of too much preparation before the job rather than not enough.

Content. Everyone agrees that an RA must know about campus-facilities procedures and services. Thus some training programs focus exclusively on how to lock the building at night, how to process a room change, where to go to get help with a financial problem, and how to make a disciplinary referral. But even when there is agreement about the fundamental importance of interpersonal skills training, there is disagreement on content, so many training programs stress crisis intervention training (Schinke and others, 1979; White and Ottens, 1979; Doyle, Foreman, and Wales, 1977), assertiveness training (Layne, Layne, and Schoch, 1977), interpersonal skills models (Carkhuff, 1969; Ivey, 1971; Kagan, 1975; Egan, 1975; Danish, 1973; Brammer, 1979), or other eclectic training models (Mitnick, 1979; Miller and Zoradi, 1977). Our training model incorporates some aspects of all of these approaches.

Format. Some training programs are strictly lecture-discussion in nature, whereas others focus on role playing and other experience-based techniques. Some programs are ad hoc, but others are planned and comprehensive. Recently, many authorities, including Bloland and Siegman (1977), Shilling (1977), and Leventhal and others (1976), have argued the advantages of offering academic credit for training programs. Thus there is much disagreement on the format of training. Our experience led us to conclude that training must be planned and comprehensive and, if possible, offered for academic credit, for the variety of reasons reviewed later in the discussion of our training model.

Evaluation. Unfortunately, in many instances there is no evaluation of training efforts. If there is, it may be very informal, unsystematic, and reduced to asking participants if they liked the training or found it interesting. An improved evaluation practice involves some assessment of trainees' knowledge and skills before and after training. The Carkhuff rating scales are the best and most sophisticated examples of pre- and posttraining ratings. In our opinion, these scales are fine as far as they go. However, we believe that the ultimate evaluation of a training program is how it relates to successful job performance; most training programs lack this evidence (Osterhout, 1977; Shilling, 1977; Bloland and Siegman, 1977).

In the model we will present later in this chapter, we evaluate the RA's performance in training, based upon specific criteria. We then look at this performance in relation to the various functions of the resident assistant position and predict, on the basis of the person's performance in the training program, what we might expect of that person as a resident assistant. (A complete elaboration of the evaluation process is presented in Chapter 10.)

Hart and King (1979) found improvement in telephone counseling effectiveness among students who were trained compared to those who were not trained. Doyle, Foreman, and Wales (1977) found that client satisfaction was greatest for those peer counselors who were trained and supervised. More directly, Peterman, Pilato, and Upcraft (1979) reported that RAs who were trained were more successful on the job, as evaluated by students, than those who were not trained.

Our Selection-Training Model

We would now like to describe our experiences as we developed our model and provide some insight into why we reached certain conclusions.

Problems. We started where most trainers start: with specific demands from resident assistants after they were on the job for training to help them solve their immediate problems. Our first mistake was yielding to the RAs' specific demands for help. To prove that we were really listening to what they had to say, we developed a cookbook of solutions for typical RA problems. We conducted an endless round of how-to training sessions that had little or no connection with each other and no follow-up. We tried to teach RAs how to conduct a house meeting, how to make a referral to the counseling center, how to handle a roommate conflict, how to plan a party, how to break it up, and so on. At first, RAs liked what we were doing, but they (and we) soon grew tired of the time and effort required and the seeming unrelatedness of one issue to another. But more importantly, both we and the RAs did not have the time to cover all the how tos that were required to solve RA problems.

The next mistake we made was doing the wrong thing for the right reason. As a result of our how-to fiascos, we decided that what we really needed was training which helped the RAs develop the underlying skills necessary to deal with the issues covered in the how-to sessions. Thus we conducted sessions on counseling skills using various counselor training models. The problem, of course, was that (1) RAs are not professional counselors, and (2) for the most part, RAs have few counseling interactions with students on their floors. So the training was over their heads, irrelevant, and impractical.

At this point, we were really frustrated and discouraged. First we gave the RAs what they wanted, and then we gave them what we thought they needed. Neither method worked. We were frustrated by our inability to develop training that was relevant, practical, and applicable to the variety of situations an RA must face. Because what we tried had not worked, we ran into a third problem: RA resistance to the whole idea of training. We had in fact regressed; we had gone from a situation where RAs were asking for training to a situation where they did not want it any more, or at least they did not want what we had to offer.

We decided to go back to the drawing boards. We began with the first real effort to listen discriminatingly and perceptively to what RAs were *really* telling us. We expanded our contact with our RAs and worked very hard to draw out their real concerns. When they regressed into rationalizations about what they disliked about our training, we confronted them. When they made sense, we listened and helped them develop more specificity and evidence to support their opinions. Here is what we heard:

1. *Train us for the actual situations we face.* The context for training should *always* be the problems, issues, situations, and dilemmas that we must deal with day to day. Train us for what is absolutely necessary; skip what would be nice to know.
2. *Do not train us to be counselors; it is too limiting.* The reality of our day-to-day existence is that very few students approach us with strictly counseling-type problems. Our initial contacts may eventually lead us to this type of student contact, but students approach us mostly for information or just to shoot the bull. Furthermore, we need help in *initiating* contacts with students, particularly when they are not interested in talking with us.
3. *Teach us skills we can use in all or most situations we face.* Teach us how to confront people. Teach us how to operate effectively in a group situation, and teach us more about how students grow

and develop while in college. Help us mediate roommate conflicts and counsel students with problems.
4. *Develop an organized approach and stick to it.* Show us that you
   know what you are doing and have confidence in it. When you
   are seduced by our rationalizations or apply irrelevant training
   models, you lose credibility with us. Believe in what you are
   doing and convince us that it is relevant to our jobs.
5. *Train us before we assume our job, not during.* We need training
   prior to doing our job; it will build our confidence and make
   our adjustment a lot easier. After we are on the job, we do not
   have the time or energy to devote to training, even though we
   may need it.

Solutions. With this feedback, we developed a training program that fell about halfway between the how-to and the counseling approaches. We considered both the content and the format of
our training and significantly changed both. We went back to the
drawing boards once again, this time armed with a much better
sense of what was needed. The first thing we did was reach a
common understanding about what job we were training for, what
it is that RAs *really* do. As stated previously, every RA job is different, depending on the students on the floor and the type of
environment that develops. But in another sense, every RA job is
the same, so we finally settled on the six different but related roles
identified in Chapter One: (1) providing personal help and assistance; (2) managing and facilitating groups; (3) facilitating social,
recreational, and educational programs; (4) serving as an information source for students; (5) explaining and enforcing rules; and (6)
maintaining a secure, safe, and orderly residence hall building.
    We decided that our training must be based on this common
understanding of the complex roles that the RA position demands.
We felt that regardless of the role, RAs had to know certain things
about themselves and others and possess the interpersonal skills to
deal with a variety of situations. To that end, we determined that an
effective training program must include five factors: (1) an extensive study of students' personal and academic development in the
collegiate setting, (2) an opportunity for participants to explore
their own selves, (3) extensive practice in developing interpersonal

skills, (4) extensive practice in developing leadership and group skills, and (5) application of all four factors to the situations an RA would typically face on a residence hall floor. We also concluded that nuts and bolts training could wait until prefall or on-the-job training.

The training we developed began with a section that taught prospective RAs about students' personal and academic development. One problem in our previous training programs was that RAs assumed their own development (or that of their close friends) was the same as all other students. Background and cultural differences, personality differences, and different levels of academic abilities and maturity make such an assumption very risky. Thus we taught RAs *generalizations* about students' personal and academic development, based not only on their own experiences but on available literature and research.

We began with a history of the RAs' own development and then studied the differences and similarities of that development in relation to the development of others. The RAs looked at their own value system, their academic and intellectual development, their interpersonal relations, their career development, their sexuality and sex-role identity, and their general level of maturity and independence.

The RAs discussed the context within which development occurs in the collegiate setting and the influence of the campus environment, the residence hall environment, peers, roommates, friends, parents, and others. We hoped that the RAs would emerge from this training section with a better understanding of their own development, the development of others, and the environment within which development occurs.

The training then moved from a cognitive look at personal development and the development of others to a more affective and personal look, based on feedback from the rest of the group. The first section on student development gave the group a nonthreatening opportunity to share themselves with each other and a behavioral data base for developing a feedback system within the group. First impressions were identified and explored, and participants had the chance to compare their self-images with the images the group had developed.

The challenge of this section was, of course, the instructor's ability to manage the feedback so it would be positive and constructive rather than destructive. The instructor's role modeling was especially critical in this section. When handled properly, this section was the most meaningful of the whole training program.

Assuming that the candidates now had some insight into their own interpersonal dynamics, we moved to the most critical and central part of the training model: the development of interpersonal skills. Using an eclectic model, we focused on such basic skills as attending to nonverbal behavior; accurate reflection of the content of a message; accurate reflection of the feelings, expressed or unexpressed, behind a message; concreteness; and appropriate self-disclosure. Other skills included summarizing and confronting. The context within which these skills were developed involved both the counseling relationship and the interpersonal interactions an RA has on a floor, such as mediating roommate conflicts, conducting a house meeting, or just plain "shooting the bull" with students.

Resident assistants seemed to have much more confidence in their ability to deal with people one-to-one than in a group. Yet much of the interaction between RAs and their floor is a one-to-group relationship, such as a party, a program, an athletic event, or a water battle. In previous training efforts, we had assumed that the RA who was interpersonally skillful on a one-to-one basis would *automatically* be able to translate those skills to a group situation. We quickly learned that this was not at all the case.

Thus we developed a section on leadership and group skills. Our past experience told us that no other topic would give us as much trouble. We had tried theoretical approaches (models of group process, for example) and practical approaches (how to run a house meeting). We finally looked at these skills for the actual *group* situations an RA must deal with and divided them into the following categories:

1. The RA is the formal leader (such as a house meeting) and must accomplish certain tasks.
2. The RA is a facilitator of the group, such as working with a floor to plan an activity.

3. The RA is clearly the authority figure enforcing a residential expectation, such as ending a water battle, breaking up a rowdy party, or enforcing quiet hours.

We then isolated specific skills needed in each category. We built upon the RAs' basic one-to-one interpersonal skills but added leadership skills necessary to work with groups. We developed all the above units within the context of the actual situations RAs must deal with on their floor. For example, when teaching one-to-one interpersonal skills, the context was not only helping students who asked for help but approaching students who needed help but were not asking for it. When teaching leadership skills, we tied our designs to conducting house meetings, facilitating activities, and enforcing rules. We concluded this section with some opportunity to deal with conflict situations, students in crises, and discipline.

With these content revisions, we felt we had solved some of the strong criticisms of previous training attempts and had incorporated what we learned from our own experiences in training RAs. We now attacked the problem of the training format. Our past attempts at training RAs had been one- or two-shot programs after they were already on the job. Because of the breadth and depth of content we were requiring, we decided that major changes in format were needed.

First, we trained RAs *before* they assumed their job responsibilities rather than after they started working. We felt that they would be better prepared to do their job right from the beginning if they were trained in advance. We also felt that they would have more confidence in themselves and their ability to do the job. It also gave our residence hall professional staff an opportunity to observe potential RAs' skills. This change in format enabled us to (1) make better placement, (2) develop subsequent training programs to compensate for weaknesses, and (3) eliminate persons clearly not ready to assume the position. And because once RAs get on the job time becomes a real problem, we started our initial screening of RA candidates earlier and allowed for a ten-week training period during the spring.

Second, we expanded the amount of time devoted to training. Unfortunately, most institutions limit their training to a few

days before the fall term begins and occasional training sessions
throughout the year. Although this approach may increase RAs'
knowledge level, it probably does little for their *skill level.* The development of interpersonal skills is a much more time-consuming
process. Thus, we expanded the amount of time commitment for
training to forty classroom hours and began the process six months
before RAs assumed their positions. We started training in March,
with two-hour training sessions twice a week over a ten-week
period. Participants then had the summer to think about and work
on improving their skills.

Third, successful completion of the training program became a final prerequisite for hiring. After the initial screening process, we sent candidates a letter of conditional appointment subject
to successfully completing the training program. Although we felt
that the number of candidates screened out after training would be
minimal (it actually turned out to average about 3 percent), we
wanted the option of eliminating candidates we felt were not ready
to do the job. Furthermore, it gave candidates an added incentive
to actively participate in the program.

Fourth, we adjusted the format to follow more closely an
academic course for credit. In fact, we eventually did offer the
training program for credit, through the Department of Counselor
Education. We wrote a syllabus, set up required readings and assignments, and judged student performance via letter grades and
written evaluations. We hoped this very familiar learning format
would communicate to participants that (1) there was intellectual
substance to what we were doing; (2) we were serious about evaluating their performance, and there would be academic as well as
job-related consequences for failure to perform; and (3) if they
were not hired, they would have something to show for their
efforts.

Fifth, the training was conducted by residence hall professional staff rather than administrative or counseling staff. We
trained the persons who supervised RAs and gave them very
specific and highly structured lesson plans for conducting the training. We took a very big risk in doing this because most of our
professional staff felt unqualified, unprepared, or untrained to
conduct this type of training. But we predicted that the advantage

of having the same persons train *and* supervise RAs would out-weigh the trainers' lack of preparation. Both RAs and supervisors would have a chance to get to know one another in advance of the supervisory relationship. In a sense, having administrative or counseling staff train RAs would have wasted the staff's time, so the administrative and counseling staff instead trained and supervised the staff who were training the RAs.

Sixth, we approached the training program using experience-based learning techniques. That is, we asked participants to engage in some type of specific behaviors, within some specified context. Members of the group were then given an opportunity to give feedback to each other regarding the effectiveness of the behaviors exhibited. Once the participants learned the impact of their behaviors on others or on the situation, they were in a better position to improve their skills. There is nothing particularly fancy or innovative in this type of learning. The trick was to develop designs that (1) were relevant to the RA job, (2) were relevant to the RAs' stage of skill development, and (3) moved RAs along in a logical sequence of skills and situations.

These format changes involved much time, effort, and risk. We were not sure that we could find enough time to train RAs before they started working. We were not sure that we could find enough staff time, given everything else they had to do, to increase training time. We were worried about tying training to hiring because some participants, in a situation where they were being evaluated, might not want to take the risks necessary to improve themselves. We were not sure we could convince an academic department to offer the program for credit. And as stated, we took a big risk in assuming that with proper supervision and structure, relatively untrained and inexperienced professional staff could do the training job.

Evidence of Effectiveness. Were these content and format changes successful? If so, what was our definition of "successful?" The overall goal of the training was to raise participants' skill level so that they could perform their jobs more effectively. A related goal was to reduce RAs' traditional resistance to this type of training. Thus, our definition of "successful" was measured by (1) student reaction to the course content, methodology, and overall learning; and (2) participants' actual job performance as perceived by students.

At the end of the training program, participants were asked for their reactions to the training. The response was highly favorable, particularly when compared to the resistance to this type of training we had previously encountered. All aspects of the training were highly rated. For example, four out of five participants rated the sections on leadership development, student development, interpersonal skills, and self-awareness as positive. Course methodology was also highly rated, as were the instructors' participation, knowledge, interpersonal skills, and group facilitation skills. But the strongest endorsement was that 98 percent of the participants recommended that the course be offered again the next year to prospective RAs.

Even though it was a new experience for us to implement a training program that was well received by the participants, it was not enough. Unless the skills developed were translated into effective job performance, we felt that the training could not be considered successful. So at the end of the first term of the RAs' employment, we asked students on the RAs' floors to evaluate the RAs' job performances. We used an evaluation instrument, developed over the past several years, that was based on the RA job description, including the following six factors:

1. *Availability.* Do students perceive their RA to be available during the evening hours?
2. *Approachability.* Do students perceive their resident assistant as someone to whom they could go to discuss a social or personal concern? Is the RA effective when called on to respond to a social or personal concern?
3. *Information and referral.* Do students perceive the RA as someone from whom knowledgeable information about the school's facilities or procedures can be obtained?
4. *Student conduct.* Do students perceive the RA as having explained school rules and regulations and the discipline system? Does the RA enforce rules and regulations?
5. *Floor atmosphere.* Do students perceive the RA as having de-

veloped a house atmosphere where people respect each other's rights and privileges?

6. *Programming.* Do students perceive the RA as promoting the house's educational or cultural programs and social or athletic activities? Have such activities and programs occurred?

The evaluation instrument was administered to all 11,900 students living in residence halls that fall term. Approximately 85 percent of the instruments were returned as usable. Because there were ten resident assistants who were hired but could not schedule the training during the preceding spring term, it was possible to compare student perceptions of their job performance with the sixty-seven first-term resident assistants who did participate.

The RAs who did not participate in the training were not known to differ significantly from those who did participate as to their background, prior experience, class standing, grade point average, or ability to meet selection criteria. Some of this group were unable to participate because of scheduling problems or because they were hired too late to be included in the training. The major known difference between these two groups was participation in the training.

We used a chi square test of significance to compare first-term resident assistants who participated in the training with first-term RAs who did not. *On every criterion (availability, approachability, information and referral, student conduct, floor atmosphere, and programming), the job performance of RAs who participated in the training was significantly better than that of the nontrained RAs.*

From this evidence, we concluded that the training program was an effective method of improving RAs' job performance. Over the past several years, we have made minor changes in the content but almost no revisions in the format. We have added and deleted content areas as students' needs have changed. For example, we have added sections on crisis intervention and discipline. But generally, the strength of the training rests with the experience-based learning format that is part of every session.

Completion of the Selection-Training Process. As we stated earlier, we think the best selection process includes extensively training the candidates prior to their appointments to the RA positions. We

identified five steps in the preliminary selection process: (1) starting
the selection process eight months before the person will actually
assume the position; (2) writing a clear job description; (3) agreeing
on selection criteria; (4) conducting a paper screening of applicants
based on their grades, class standing, and prior disciplinary action;
and (5) conducting a preliminary interview. Two additional steps
that complete the selection-training cycle are:

6. Offer the remaining candidates the opportunity to participate
    in the extensive training program, and inform them that
    successful completion of the program, as judged by the profes-
    sional staff, will result in their appointment as a resident assis-
    tant, or their placement into an alternate pool in the event of
    future vacancies. Unsuccessful completion of the training pro-
    gram will result in their elimination as an RA candidate.
7. Based on the information gained about the personal charac-
    teristics and interpersonal skill level of candidates from the
    training program, decide whether each candidate is to be
    hired, placed in alternate status, or eliminated. This same in-
    formation can also be used to place RAs on particular floors or
    in particular buildings.

These seven steps provide a wealth of data, compared to the
typical selection process. They ensure new resident assistants who
have been trained extensively, and they provide information about
these new RAs that will be helpful when supervising them on the
job. The next task then is to prepare for the implementation of this
selection-training program. The next chapter adds to our knowledge about the model's content and our skill in implementing the
format.

3

⎍⎍⎍⎍⎍⎍⎍⎍⎍⎍⎍⎍⎍⎍⎍⎍⎍⎍⎍⎍⎍⎍⎍⎍⎍⎍⎍⎍⎍⎍⎍⎍⎍

The College Experience
and Student Development

A fundamental assumption of our selection-training program is that students' personal and academic development must be thoroughly understood by professional staff and resident assistants. Unfortunately, our experience has been that these persons usually do not have such a thorough understanding, and too often they infer what they know about students from their own undergraduate experiences. But differences in institutions and variability among students make such inferences narrow, biased, and very suspect. We agree with Blimling and Schuh (1981), who wrote, "There is no justification for professional educators working with students in the residence halls—or in any area of student personnel for that matter not to know and understand the basic principles of student development. The theories of students' intellectual, maturational, and emotional growth should be as familiar to the student personnel professional as algebra to a mathematician, or existentialism to a philosopher. This knowledge is not signaled by the initials after a name, but by a willingness to keep abreast of new development through reading, attending workshops and conferences, and maintaining an open mind to new ideas" (pp. 8-9). A thorough understanding of student development must be based on existing student development theories, research, and practices.

This chapter reviews nine theories of student development, to help build a conceptual base for understanding students. It also presents several generalizations about student development, based on existing research and literature. Finally, an eclectic, working model of student development, based on how students experience their own development, is discussed; this model is also the framework of the first part of the training program.

Theories

What is the definition of student development? How are students developing during the college years? What are the psychological dynamics of young adults? Are there definable stages of development? Do students experience typical developmental tasks while in college? Several different theories explain the development of young adults; we do not present here comprehensive, in-depth descriptions of these theories, just their relevant concepts. We highly recommend that you read original sources or extended summaries such as Lee Knefelkamp, Carole Widick, and Clyde Parker's *New Directions for Student Services: Applying New Developmental Findings,* no. 4. San Francisco: Jossey Bass, 1978.

Erikson's Theory of Psychosocial Development. In our opinion, the father of many current assumptions about youth development is Erik Erikson, who was one of the first people to look at personality development in a social context and define the identity development of youth. His often quoted (and frequently misunderstood) concept of identity crisis has become an accepted part of our thinking about student development. Thus a few of his basic concepts are worth elaborating.

Erikson defined identity as the organized set of images and the sense of self that express who and what we really are. Identity development depends on one's physical stage, one's encounter with society and the social roles one plays, and one's internal ordering of those experiences. Erikson defined eight stages of psychosocial development, of which his fifth stage (youth) is particularly relevant to college student development. He believed that the task of establishing one's identity is especially critical during this stage because of changes in physical maturation and in society's demands on young adults. Youth must redefine themselves, but in the process they may create an identity crisis. For some youth, the questions "Who am I?" and "What will I be?" create a period of uncertainty that passes as a new sense of identity develops. For others, the period of development can be a time of emotional turmoil or even massive personality disorientation (Widick, Parker, and Knefelkamp, 1978b).

Relationships become an important source of information and validation of a new sense of identity for youth. "The sense of ego identity, then, is the accrued confidence that the inner sameness and continuity prepared in the past are matched by the sameness and continuity of one's meaning for others . . ." (Erikson, 1963, p. 261). Stated another way, this new sense of identity is experienced personally, validated interpersonally, and formed within the context of cultural norms (Widick, Parker, and Knefelkamp, 1978b, p. 7).

Erikson emphasizes, however, that the "formation of identity is fostered by an environment which allows for (1) experimentation with varied roles; (2) the experiencing of choice; (3) meaningful achievement; (4) freedom from excessive anxiety; and (5) time for reflection and introspection" (Widick, Parker, and Knefelkamp, 1978b, p. 7). The collegiate environment offers an almost ideal opportunity for experimenting, choosing, reflecting, and achieving, if excessive anxiety can be avoided, creating a "moratorium," as Erikson terms it, that is necessary for full identity development.

Chickering's Vectors of Development. Probably the most widely known theory of student development was expounded by Arthur Chickering. Chickering was the first person to interpret identity-formation concepts specifically within the college context. He was also the first person, in our opinion, to get student development theory into the mainstream of student affairs practices, policies, and programs.

Chickering proposed seven vectors along which development occurs among college students. Each vector is a developmental task to be differentiated and integrated, a concept originally proposed by Nevitt Sanford (Sanford, 1962). According to Chickering, "Increased differentiation occurs when one comes to see the interacting parts of something formerly seen as unitary, when one distinguishes among concepts formerly seen as similar, when actions are more finely responsive to purposes or to outside conditions, when interests become more varied, tastes more diverse, reactions more subtle. In short, as we become more complex human beings" (Chickering, 1969, p. 292).

At the same time, the task of integration is occurring. "Relationships among parts must be perceived or constructed so more complex wholes result. Concepts from different disciplines must be brought to bear on one another and connected in ways appropriate to varied tasks and problems. Consistencies between word and word, deed and deed must be achieved. Impulse and emotion must pull together with conscience and reason. Short-run hedonism must coordinate with long-run purposes" (Chickering, 1969, p. 292).

Chickering's seven vectors are defined as:

1. *Developing competence.* Students must be able to intellectually and interpersonally cope with what comes and do what they set out to do.

2. *Becoming autonomous.* Students must establish emotional independence from parents and peers and break free from the continuous need for reassurance, affection, and approval. They must be able to do things on their own but get help when needed.

3. *Managing emotions.* Students must become aware of their emotions (particularly aggression and sex), learn to control them, and integrate them into ongoing decisions and behaviors.

4. *Establishing identity.* Students must develop a sense of self by clarifying physical needs, characteristics, and personal appearance and by establishing appropriate sexual identification, roles, and behavior.

5. *Freeing interpersonal relationships.* Students must develop an increased tolerance for others, a capacity for intimacy, and relationships based on trust, independence, and individuality.

6. *Clarifying purposes.* Students must develop a sense of purpose in their lives, leading to plans and priorities for their careers, avocations, and life-styles.

7. *Developing integrity.* Students must develop a personally valid

set of beliefs that has internal consistency and provides a guide for behavior.

Chickering suggested that college can accelerate or retard each vector, depending on the (1) institution's clarity of objectives and internal consistency; (2) institution's size, (3) institution's curriculum, teaching, and evaluation; (4) residence hall arrangements; (5) faculty and administration; and (6) friends, groups, and student culture (Chickering, 1969).

Perry's Theory of Intellectual and Ethical Development. William Perry's theory of intellectual and ethical development of college students is drawn primarily from his experiences and research at Harvard University. Perry hypothesizes that students move from a simplistic, categorical view of the world to a more relativistic, committed view through nine stages. In other words, they move from an unquestioning, dualistic framework (right-wrong, good-bad, beautiful-ugly) to the realization of the contingent nature of knowledge, values, and truth. As students move through these stages, they interface their intellect with their identity, resulting in a better understanding of the world and finding personal meaning in the world through an affirmation of their own commitments (King, 1978).

Patricia King summarized Perry's nine stages in the following clusters:

1. *Dualism (stages 1–2).* Students in this stage view people, knowledge, and values through absolute, discrete, and concrete categories. "Right answers" are determined by established authorities, and students learn simple truths without substantiation and without question. Alternative perspectives or multiple points of view are confusing and thus not acknowledged. Truth is self-evident.

2. *Multiplicity (stages 3–4).* Students acknowledge multiple points of view, but they still feel that questions simply have multiple answers. All points of view are equally valid and thus not subject to judgment. Questioning or challenging viewpoints are still avoided. However, toward the end of this stage, students begin to distinguish between an unconsidered belief and a

considered judgment. Authorities tend to be defied or
resisted.

3. *Relativism (stages 5–6)*. Students believe knowledge is contextual and relative. Multiple points of view are now seen as pieces
that fit together into a larger whole. Students who seek the big
picture are able to analyze and evaluate their own ideas as well
as others. Authorities are valued for their expertise, not their
infallibility. Often relativism results in indecision because to
make a judgment would sacrifice one's appreciation for
another's views. Toward the end of this stage, however, students begin to endorse their own choices from the multiple
"truths" that exist in a relativistic world.

4. *Commitment in relativism (stages 7–9)*. Students in this stage (if
they get this far) have made an active affirmation of themselves and their responsibilities in a pluralistic world, establishing their identities in the process. Personal commitments in
such areas as marriage, career, or religion are made out of a
relativistic frame of reference. Identity and life-style are established, consistent with students' personal themes (King, 1978).

Although some students move sequentially through these
nine stages, others may delay in a position, for example, seeking
refuge in relativism and avoiding the responsibility of commitment.
Others may regress to dualistic stages, finding the advanced stages
too challenging, thus creating insecurity and anxiety (King, 1978).

*Kohlberg's Cognitive-Stage Theory of the Development of Moral
Judgment.* Although Lawrence Kohlberg did not develop his theory
exclusively for college students, his ideas are often mentioned in
analyses of student development. In his view, moral judgment is a
progression through various stages of development, each stage
representing a mode or structure of thought. He is concerned
about how and why judgments are made, not their content. In his
view, the structure of moral thought includes the decision-making
system, the problem-solving strategy, the social perspective, and the
underlying logic in making a moral choice (Smith, 1978).

Smith summarized Kohlberg's (1971) six stages of moral development as:

1. *Preconventional level (stages 1–2).* "At this level the child is responsive to cultural rules and labels of good and bad, right and wrong, but interprets these labels either in terms of the physical consequences of action (punishment, reward, exchange of favors) or in terms of the physical power of those who enunciate the rules and labels" (Smith, 1978, p. 55).

    In stage 1 (punishment and obedience orientation), the physical consequences of an action determine its goodness or badness; in stage 2 (instrumental-relativist orientation), right action is that which satisfies one's own needs and occasionally the needs of others.

2. *Conventional level (stages 3–4).* "At this level maintaining the expectations of the individual's family, group or nation is perceived as valuable in its own right, regardless of immediate and obvious consequences. The attitude is not only one of *conformity* to personal expectations and social order, but of loyalty to it, of actively *maintaining,* supporting, and mystifying the order, and of identifying with the persons or group involved in it" (Smith, 1978, p. 55).

    In stage 3 (interpersonal concordance orientation), behavior is evaluated by whether other persons approve or disapprove and by intention. One earns the approval of others by being "nice." In stage 4 (law and order orientation), good behavior consists of doing one's duty, showing respect for authority, and maintaining the given social order for its own sake.

3. *Postconventional, autonomous, or principled level (stages 5–6).* "At this level, there is a clear effort to define moral values and principles that have validity and application apart from the authority of the groups or persons holding these principles and apart from the individual's own identification with these groups" (Smith, 1978, p. 56).

    In stage 5 (social contract, legalistic orientation, generally with utilitarian overtones), right action is defined for general individual rights, based on standards examined and agreed on by society. Relativism of personal values is accepted. Procedural rules for reaching consensus are established, based on laws and the constitution. Outside the legal realm, free agreement and contract are the binding elements of obligation.

In stage 6 (universal-ethical-principle orientation), right is defined by conscience, based on self-chosen ethical principles that have logical comprehensiveness, universality, and consistence. These universal principles include justice, the reciprocity and equality of human rights, and the respect and dignity of the individual (Kohlberg, 1971).

Smith (1978) believed that the college experience may be a very critical period in the development of moral reasoning because students either hold to conventional levels or begin to question them. Kohlberg (1971) argued that confronting moral issues or questions is absolutely essential if moral development is to occur. Smith (1978) agreed that if the college experience is to affect moral development, students must have experiences in their peer groups and the classroom that test their moral judgments and provide an opportunity to reflect on their behavior. There is some evidence (Kramer, 1968) that there may be a regression in moral development during the early college years, but progression in moral development usually is evident by graduation.

Loevinger's Milestones of Development. Jane Loevinger is another theorist who did not speak directly to college students but whose ideas are often discussed in analyses of student development. Central to her theory is the concept of ego development, which she defines as the frame of reference within which one perceives the world (Loevinger, 1976). The structure of the ego determines how one interacts with one's environment. Choices are made based on the demands of the environment. Development is thus a product of the interaction between the individual and the environment, and developmental progress is a series of transformations of the ego structure from less to more complex (Knefelkamp, Parker, and Widick, 1978a).

Loevinger is also a "stage" theorist, and her model consists of the following ten stages:

1. *Presocial stage.* The young infant is unable to differentiate him-

or herself from the surroundings and thus does not have an ego.

2. *Symbiotic stage.* The infant develops a symbiotic relationship with its primary nurturing object and thus is not differentiated from that primary person.

3. *Impulsive stage.* The child affirms personal identity as separate from others and is characterized by impulsive but dependent behavior.

4. *Self-protective stage.* Impulse control is learned, but as a result of short-term rewards and punishments. The child is not yet able to accept personal responsibility for personal actions.

5. *Conformist stage.* Basic trust of others develops, allowing one to identify one's welfare with that of family or close peers. The person is still not able to fully accept responsibility for personal actions.

6. *Self-aware level.* The person moves from the conformist to the conscientious stage, based on increased self-awareness and an appreciation of multiple perspectives. The self, rather than others, becomes the major influence on thinking, feeling, and acting.

7. *Conscientious stage.* The person makes choices based on internalized rules and values. Reason, empathy, and mutuality in relationships characterize this stage.

8. *Individualistic level.* The person moves from the conscientious stage to the autonomous stages, in which one becomes more aware of self and the emotional conflicts involved in the dependence-independence struggle. More tolerance for self and others develops as well as an appreciation of life's ironies and paradoxes.

9. *Autonomous stage.* The person recognizes personal complexities as well as those of the world. There is a high tolerance for ambiguity and an acceptance of inner conflicts. An interdependent relationship is established with others, resulting in progress toward self-fulfillment.

10. *Integrated stage.* The integrated person has transcended the conflicts of stage 9 and achieved an integrated sense of identity (Knefelkamp, Parker, and Widick, 1978a).

Loevinger's contribution to college student development is implicit, but during the early college years, students may be moving from the conformist to the conscientious stage. By the end of the college years, some students may even have moved to the autonomous stage, although they would be exceptions.

Douglas Heath's Model of Maturing. In Heath's view, students move from immature to mature ways of functioning. He suggests a relationship between developmental dimensions that define maturity and personality structures that define the person. Heath identified the following five developmental dimensions that define maturity:

1. *Awareness.* The ability to represent experience symbolically.
2. *Allocentricism.* The ability to socialize and become other-centered.
3. *Integration.* The ability to integrate experience and become open, flexible, and changing.
4. *Autonomy.* The ability to become less manipulated by the environment.
5. *Stability.* The ability to resist disruption by threat and become more adaptable.

Heath also identified four personality structures that define the person during the college years:

1. *Intellect.* Judgment, analytical and synthetic thinking, and logical reasoning.
2. *Values.* Needs, motives, interests, conviction, sense of purpose, and direction.
3. *Self-knowledge.* Sense of self, development of self-concept.
4. *Interpersonal relationships.* Relations with others, impact of others on self (Heath, 1968).

Heath believed that maturity can be explained by the interaction of one's developmental dimensions with one's personality structures. As illustrated in Table 1, the mature personality is defined twenty different ways, depending on the relationship between developmental dimensions and personality structures. For

Table 1. The Mature Personality

Trait	Intellect	Values	Self-Concept	Interpersonal Relationships
Becoming able to symbolize experience	Able to evaluate one's own thought	Awareness of one's own beliefs	Awareness of self; accurate insights and self-analysis	Able to reflect about relationships and analyze why others act and feel certain ways
Becoming allocentric (other-centered)	Thoughts are logical; tied to social reality	Centered around people; tolerant/altruistic	Ability to see self as similar to others; empathy	Caring for others; ability to love; capacity for intimacy
Becoming progressively integrated	Able to problem solve systematically; creative syntheses; coherence in thought	Workable world view; coherence in value commitments	Congruence of self-image; a realistic view of self	More openness; able to be wholly with another; capable of reciprocal, mutual, and cooperative relationships
Becoming stable (resistant to disruption by threat)	Thoughts stay organized; able to function consistently	Clear sustained commitment to set of values	Stable self-view; certainty	Enduring friendships; commitment to specific other
Becoming autonomous	Use of data less imprisoned by bias	Independence of mind; integrity in belief and behavior	View of self as responsible; not overly reliant on others' perceptions	Relationships reflect autonomy; not sacrifice integrity for belonging; nonmanipulative

Source: C. Widick, C. Parker, and L. Knefelkamp, "Douglas Heath's Model of Maturing." In L. Knefelkamp, C. Widick, and C. Parker (Eds.), *New Directions for Student Services: Applying New Developmental Findings*, no. 4. San Francisco: Jossey-Bass, 1978.

example, a person may become autonomous in interpersonal relationships, resulting in relationships that do not sacrifice integrity
for belonging and are nonmanipulative. Or a person's values may
become integrated, resulting in a workable world view and coher-
ence in value commitments.

Generally, Heath sees students during the college years as
becoming more mature, primarily as a result of interpersonal determinants (roommates, peers, and close friends) and intellectual
and academic determinants (courses, faculty, and the general intellectual atmosphere of the college) (Heath, 1968).

Roy Heath's Model of Personality Typologies. Heath's student
development model is based on the interfacing of the individual's
(1) ego functioning or maturity level and (2) style or type or basic
temperamental approach to life (Heath, 1964). He identified three
types of personalities, according to the way one handles the
dynamic tension between the inner, instinctual, feeling self and the
outer, more rational self. Each type moves toward maturity in a
unique way, and each type may achieve the ultimate level of maturity, which Heath calls the "reasonable adventurer" (Knefelkamp,
Parker, and Widick, 1978b). Knefelkamp, Parker, and Widick summarized Heath's three personality types:

1. *Type X.* These persons have difficulty responding to their inner
   selves and being aware of their inner feelings. Low Xs are
   totally unaware of themselves; medial Xs have limited self-
   awareness. Type Xs can cope with the presence of conflict in
   relationships and diversity of opinions. They are learning to
   think and act more independently, but they are still likely to
   avoid taking a stand. High Xs have developed an integrated
   self, can accept their feelings, have begun to use their own
   structures, and are capable of independent thought and
   action.
2. *Type Y.* These persons have a "semiconstricted filter system"
   that enables them to be more aware of their feelings than can
   type Xs. However, this partial awareness results in a distrust of
   these feelings and an intense level of activity designed to avoid
   confronting them. Low Ys strive to become what others think
   they should be, although they may be very insensitive to the

feelings of others. Medial Ys accept the legitimacy of different points of view and therefore no longer hold to dichotomous rules. High Ys are achievement-oriented, but they will risk participating in activities for fun or the newness of the experience. Because rigidity and defensiveness are gone, the high Y can express feelings and empathize with the feelings of others.

3. *Type Z.* These persons have a more porous filter system and thus are often impulsive and moody. Low Zs are aware of their impulses but have no insight into or control of them. They are free spirits who alternate between feeling lonely and misunderstood and unique, original, and creative. Medial Zs have begun to learn how to control their impulses, and thus they perform more consistently socially and academically. They are still subject to wide variations in mood but have more control over them. High Zs have learned to direct their creativity in productive ways. They have also learned to protect themselves from those who are insensitive to their openness and vulnerability.

Roy Heath is probably best known for his concept of the "reasonable adventurer." According to Heath, this is a person who has achieved a high level of maturity and is intellectual, establishes close friendships, has independence in value judgments, a tolerance of ambiguity, a breadth of interest, and a sense of humor. This person is also confident, skillful, reasonable, and interdependent. Reasonable adventurers do not conform to any one behavior model and are highly integrated and individualistic. Heath believes that the reasonable adventurer concept is not an end point but a fluid concept which allows for continuous exploration of new possibilities and new levels of maturity (Knefelkamp, Parker, and Widick, 1978b).

Madison's Reintegration Theory. Peter Madison offers the most clearly psychoanalytic explanation of college student development. His underlying assumption is that a student's response to college is dominated by the past and that there is substantial carry-over of childhood-formed personality structures during the college years. Personality development is thus a function of the student's interaction with the collegiate environment.

The central concept of Madison's theory is reintegration. The present situation arouses responses that were dominant during past similar occasions. This is an unconscious process by which brain-stored traces of past experience are aroused from their latency and interact with the present to influence perception, emotion, memory, association, motivation, and behavior. For example, a roommate relationship might trigger a past association with a sibling. Thus any situation faced by a student must be viewed in terms of similar situations faced in the past. Madison argued that this reintegration process is unconscious and that students have no direct way of knowing what parts of their past are affecting current situations.

Madison argued that students' typical developmental tasks (career choice, establishing identity, achieving academic competence, finding self-respect, achieving independence from parents, dealing with sex drives, developing a value system, and establishing independence from peers) must be viewed as a process of the reintegration of past events with present experiences. A developmental crisis may occur when the pace of change in students exceeds their powers of integration, resulting in confusion, uncertainty, depression, and vacillating moods. In other words, they respond too much as they did in the past, not to the actual present situation. A roommate may not in fact be at all like an older brother, but the student may think he is.

According to Madison, there are several sources of influence in the college environment that act as agents of change. Faculty can have an influence, as can the student culture. Academic success or failure and course content can also have an impact. Madison believes that "developmental friendships" are very powerful and that students tend to develop close, emotional relationships with individuals who differ significantly along personality dimensions that are undeveloped within themselves (Madison, 1969).

Brawer's Functional Potential. Florence Brawer developed a theory of student development that she believes applies to students at both two- and four-year institutions. According to Brawer, student development is best explained by the concept of functional potential, which she defines as "the degree to which a person is able to tolerate ambiguity, delay gratification, exhibit adaptive flexibility, demonstrate goal directedness, relate to self and others, and have a clear sense of personal identity" (Brawer, 1973, p. 34). Brawer thinks that functional potential is comprised of the following six fundamental modes:

1. *Relatedness-aloofness.* The investment of oneself in involvement with others and one's sense of belonging versus one's sense of alienation.
2. *Identity-amorphism.* The sense of certainty about oneself and one's sense of wholeness, sameness, and directedness versus diffuseness and uncertainty of direction.
3. *Flexibility-rigidity.* The openness and closedness of belief systems and authoritarianism, including one's cognitive and affective manner of approach.
4. *Independence-dependence.* The development of autonomy and the readiness to act on one's own, without separation or alienation from others.
5. *Progression-regression.* An orientation toward optimism, which involves activity-passivity, fluidity-immobilization. and flow-fixedness.
6. *Delay of gratification-impulse expression.* An access to one's impulses and an ability to control them when the situation demands.

Brawer identified several variables that influence the development of functional potential in the collegiate setting. Certain demographic variables, such as age, sex, ethnic background, work, military service, religion, and academic major, are important. School directedness, significant others, and group cohesion also have an impact. The student's own orientation or approach to the world is equally important. Brawer believes that the student with low functional potential is at the mercy of the press of the collegiate environment, for good or for ill. The student with high functional potential is less susceptible to the collegiate environment because of greater inner strength, but the person can still be affected both negatively and positively (Brawer, 1973).

Making Sense of All These Theories. We think it is very important for selectors, trainers, and supervisors of RAs to be well schooled in student development theory. We strongly recommend that they strengthen and deepen their understanding by reading original sources and comprehensive summaries. But we also recognize that the diversity of thought about how students grow and develop in the collegiate environment may be very confusing, especially the first time around. And if we are uncertain, surely prospective RAs will be even more confused. A brief description of our experiences in this regard is helpful.

At first we tried to pick one theory and use it when training and supervising RAs: One year we used Douglas Heath, and another year we used Arthur Chickering. But this system did not work; the theories were not inadequate, but we found that students had trouble relating their experiences to the underlying psychodynamics of their development. Students may know that they are having trouble with a career choice, and they may try to understand the reasons why. But they may have some difficulty looking at their experiences in terms of their functional potential or their semiconstricted filter system.

We found it useful to work *from* the student's own experiences *toward* student development theory, rather than the other way around. Frederick Coons (1974) made this point when he developed his "frame of reference" for working with college students instead of a universal, comprehensive theory. He found that his frame of reference, which is based on how students experience their own development, seemed to "make sense to the students themselves" (Coons, p. 19). Our experience paralleled that of Coons, and although we revised his frame of reference, we think his approach is the best way to teach students about their own development and students' development in general.

Student Growth During the College Years

The model (not theory) of student development we found workable has its roots in many of the theories just reviewed. Here we first describe how students see themselves growing and developing in college, and then we review the typical developmental issues that students must deal with if they are to achieve adult maturity and succeed in college.

Recently we conducted research with a group of graduating seniors, asking them what was the most important thing they learned from attending college. Generally, they said "I grew up." When we asked them to be more specific, they replied, "I learned to get along with people" and "I learned more about myself" (Upcraft, Peterson, and Moore, 1981). We think these responses should be the starting point for developing a conceptual basis for explaining student development during the college years. We also believe that the responses are very consistent with the student development theories and research. In other words, growth and development during the college years is a process of maturing by (1) developing autonomy and (2) establishing identity.

Students are establishing themselves as autonomous human beings, achieving independence from childhood influences and assuming responsibility for their own lives. They may vacillate from dependence to independence, but eventually they realize the necessity of an interdependent relationship with parents, peers, and others. Students are also developing a much clearer sense of who they are, or, to use Erikson's term, a sense of ego identity. Students leave college with a greater awareness of themselves, both intellectually and emotionally. Almost all the student development theories reviewed earlier mention autonomy and identity as key concepts; students confirm these concepts from their own experiences.

However, we have found that although most students agree that getting along with people and learning more about themselves are the important learnings of college, they talk about their development more as a series of issues rather than processes. That is, they recall specific issues, concerns, problems, crises, and successes rather than inferred psychological processes. For example, a student might say, "When I first arrived at college, I was really scared to death that I wouldn't get good grades, or worse yet, flunk out." A student does not say, "My sense of self was so undeveloped and insecure that I had not yet achieved a sense of my intellectual self and therefore had great anxiety about college success."

Just what are these issues? We have identified five major developmental issues (similar although not identical to those of Frederick Coons) that students typically must deal with during the college years: (1) formulating a personal value system, (2) developing intellectual and academic competence, (3) deciding on a career and life-style, (4) establishing and maintaining interpersonal relationships, and (5) developing a sex-role identity and capacity for intimacy. These issues may overlap (deciding what sexual behavior is right or wrong, for example), and not all students deal with all these issues all the time. As we have used this model over the years, we have found that it makes sense to students and gives them a framework within which to look at both their own and others' development.

Formulating a Personal Value System. Most students arrive at college with a set of values, defined as the criteria by which the relative worth of various goals, means, and behaviors are determined. These values are rooted in the students' background, home, church, community, and peer group. The students have a varying awareness of, commitment to, and depth of thinking about their own values. They also have varying tolerances for values different from their own. The way their parents presented and taught values to them also varies, from rigid and authoritarian (right is right and wrong is wrong, and no questions asked) to more relativistic (*you* must determine what is right and what is wrong). There may also be great variance between belief and action.

In college, several experiences may disrupt the students' values. Persons with different values and strong feelings about them may be encountered for the first time. The basis for one's values may be challenged in the classroom by exposure to different ideas, concepts, and beliefs. Or students may find that their values do not work for them in the more complex setting of college. Issues that were once simple to deal with become more complex as the multiplicity and relativity of values become evident. Shades of gray enter what once was a world of only black and white. To make matters worse, the old support system of family, church, and community is not there to support and reinforce one's values.

Most students respond to this challenge by rethinking and reformulating their values, based on their experiences in college. There may be periods of experimentation with new ideas, behaviors, and values. There may also be periods when students do not know what, if anything, they believe in or value. According to

Sanford, students are in the process of internalizing values and making them part of their personality structure (Sanford, 1962). In other words, they are converting their externally imposed childhood values to the internally integrated adulthood values.

When students are in the process of reformulating their values, great stress may be placed upon their relationships with parents and peers. Parents may be astonished at new behaviors or new belief systems. For example, when students abandon their families' religious traditions or engage in sexual behaviors that were not tolerated at home, tension between students and parents may arise. New values may also result in disregarding old friendships and establishing new ones. New career patterns may emerge, and new interests develop.

On the other hand, these challenges may result in reaffirming the values students brought with them to college. But if these values are truly internalized and integrated, students will have a much clearer sense of them, a stronger commitment to them, and a much greater understanding of them. Students will also recognize the validity of other values and have a higher tolerance for others' values. Ideally, there will also be consistency between what the students believe and what they do and conceptual consistency among various values. Athough some students may totally escape the challenge and reformulation of values, most will experience it and leave college with a different value orientation than when they entered.

The following autobiographical account relates one student's experiences in formulating a personal value system [all the autobiographical accounts are from actual autobiographies submitted by our students over the years.]

> From childhood I developed a strong affiliation with religion and the church. I never really questioned it since I was required by my parents to attend mass and so forth. In my first few weeks of college I remember realizing, "Hey, I don't *have* to go to church on Sunday." I started to wonder: "Why am I going to church? Does it really mean anything to me? Should I stop?" Also, I became aware that many people I knew and were meeting "used to be

Catholic" and were of many different faiths. I began to realize the universified views of so many different people. Since I was away from parental guidance and restrictions, I realized it was my "personal choice" whether to attend church or generally profess the Catholic faith. At first I felt a little guilty, as if I were questioning the existence of God Himself, but with a little more thought I realized that Catholicism wasn't a "given" anymore, and that if I wanted to continue being Catholic, I'd have to be sure it really meant something to me personally. Over the course of my freshman year, I seriously considered my positions and alternatives. I finally came to the conclusion that I wanted to remain Catholic and attend church. It seems that I am back where I started, but now I really feel comfortable and confident that my religion means something to me personally. Now since I have arrived at my own conclusion after questioning it all, I know it means much more to me.

Obviously this person met the challenges of her value system in college and successfully integrated her beliefs into herself. But such is not always the case, as exemplified in this autobiographical account:

After I arrived at college, . . . I reached the point where I did not believe in God. Apparently, science had the answer to everything. I viewed the Bible as the explanation of men concerning events that could not be explained with the technology of their time. By comparison, our technology was practically omniscient, or so I was led to believe. It was during this time that my morals declined. No longer living in fear and respect of God, I was governed by a new philosophy, which was if it feels right, do it. After all, what difference would it make in 500 years? There were no longer sins, so there was no right or wrong. Since I had no basis for my values, they were changing constantly and caused me to become confused, get into drugs, promiscuous sex, and general rebelliousness. I was a real mess, and almost flunked out in the process.

Developing Intellectual and Academic Competence. The development of a cognitive aspect of self, including reasoning, perceiving, abstracting, creating, understanding, judging, and problem solving, is a primary goal of higher education. But as to what students really experience in college, it is a narrow definition. Although some students may enter college with the expressed purpose of developing their intellect, for most the challenge of college is succeeding in the classroom, which is defined as getting good grades and graduating. Although intellectual development may be a by-product of academic experiences, it is seldom directly focused on by students while they are in college.

Students enter college with a sense of past success in their academic endeavors. They have successfully "played the academic game" in high school and earned good enough grades (or scored high enough on the SATs) to get into college. They may or may not have learned much, developed good study habits, or developed an appreciation for learning. Some students arrive at college with a strong sense of confidence in their ability to succeed in college; others are scared to death that the increased academic competition will destroy them.

Once enrolled in college courses, many students experience the new challenge of getting good grades and succeeding academically. Some have no trouble at all in adjusting to the new academic game and pick up where they left off in high school by getting good grades or even enjoying learning. Others run into difficulty—they may have been able to breeze through high school without working that much, but they find they cannot do so in college. Others work hard without much success because their study habits are inefficient or undeveloped. Still other students find the increased competition too much to handle, and the resulting anxiety blocks learning. And others lack the motivation to do college work for whatever reasons. Many students overcome these initial difficulties and revive themselves academically. Others do not, and so they struggle along at the bottom of the curve, drop out, or change to majors that better suit their interests and abilities.

In the process, students may become more intellectually oriented, although it is possible to succeed academically and totally ignore the intellectual aspects of college life. Many students do in fact learn to appreciate the intellectual side of college and become better problem solvers, abstracters, perceivers, judges, reasoners, and creators. They may also become more esthetic and learn to appreciate art, literature, music, sculpture, and drama. But for many students, college is much more an academic than an intellectual experience, and succeeding academically is much more important than becoming intellectual.

The following two autobiographical accounts illustrate the success, or lack of it, in developing intellectual and academic competence. For the first student, the transition was smooth; for the other student, things went less well.

> My first term at college I tried the same trick every other freshman tries of seeing how little studying I could get by on. I got a 2.00 that term and considered it the end of the world. For the first time in my life, I wasn't a top student anymore, only an average one. So winter term, I cracked down and studied every night. That time I made Dean's list. I went into the spring term with a big head about my abilities and slacked off on studying. I ended up with a 2.5, but for the first time I really learned something. This year I feel I've grown a lot intellectually. For the first time in my life I've been able to remember what I've learned, *and* I can apply it to daily situations. For example, my political science course was tough; I put a lot of work into it. But I also got a lot out of it. I now have an interest in politics and have some understanding of the political environment I live in. Another course I loved was my medieval history course. I worked my butt off and only got a C in the course, but I didn't really care because I learned something.
>
> Another way that college has helped me is with its cultural activities and information centers. Finally, college has given me a lot of practice in using my problem-solving–analysis skills. I think I have a talent for being able to solve problems that arise without warning. This is useful not only in my academic endeavors, but in all aspects of college life and the future.

When I came to college, I was so sure of myself. I came for advising in the summer, and they told me that I would have to reevaluate my thinking because now I would not always be the cream of the crop but that I would sometimes be at the very bottom of the pile. I did not believe them. I had always been told that I was a bright, capable student, but that fact had never really been tested or proved. I would not fail; I could not fail. PSU was quite a shock for me. Large classes were a new experience, and for the first time, I had to depend on my own self-confidence to get me through the rough spots. There was no one around to pat me on the back and give me a gold star because I did all my homework problems. It was a feeling of insecurity that I had to learn to deal with in order to succeed academically. My fall term as a freshman was the first time that I was knocked down off my pedestal of superiority. In retrospect, lack of academic success was the best thing that ever happened to me. I have realized that I will *not* always be on top. What is important is to do what I feel is my best effort. As long as I can say that I have accomplished that, I can be at peace with myself, my parents will not disown me, the world will not come to an end.

Deciding On a Career and Life-Style. Although some students come to college admitting that they do not know what they want to do, most enter with some sense of a career goal. There are varying degrees of commitment to career choice. Some students are pushed into a career by their parents, whereas others choose something just to get rid of the anxiety of not having a career choice. Still others pick a popular or lucrative career, knowing little or nothing of the reality of training for that career or what it is really like to pursue it. But most students attend college with the idea of preparing for some kind of career, no matter how tentative or unrealistic their choice may be.

The college experience is an almost immediate test of a student's career commitment. And the fact that a large percentage of students change their major at least once indicates the instability of career choice upon entering college. Some students find that their choice is stable and have no difficulty preparing themselves for their chosen field. But other students waver and change, for a variety of reasons. Release from parental pressure may allow students to pursue their real interests, based on their real abilities. From courses or contact with faculty, added information about a career may result in discarding an old career choice and selecting a new one. There is also some evidence that the college peer group may influence career decisions (Feldman and Newcomb, 1969). But lack of academic success in a student's initial career choice is a major contribution to career choice instability and is likely to send the student scampering away from one field to another.

Career choice also has implications for a student's life-style after college. From our experience, students seldom put together their career choice with the life-style they would prefer after college, with the exception of women concerned about combining their careers with establishing a home and raising a family. Career choice seldom involves looking at such issues as leisure time, special interests, family commitments, and other nonwork aspects of living. Too often, these issues are faced only at graduation, when it may be too late to do anything about it.

Another issue that has emerged as a student priority is the economic realities of career choice. Choosing a career based on interests and abilities is ideal, but more and more students are thinking about the economic consequences of their career choice. For some students, career choice is *only* a matter of economics, assuming that they have the ability to prepare for the career. Horror stories about college-educated but unemployed teachers, social workers, and linguists discourage students from selecting careers based solely on interests and abilities. Many students note that they may be able to earn more money in careers that do not require a college education, and so they question the value of staying in college.

Although some students fail to develop a stable career choice and either graduate without one or drop out, most students eventually prepare for a career consistent with their abilities, compatible with their interests, and meeting their economic needs. They may even have some awareness of the life-style implications of their career choice and integrate the two in advance as best they can.

Some career choices are stable, but others are not, as illustrated by this autobiographical account:

> When I entered my senior year of high school, I began applying to colleges, but I still wasn't sure what field I wanted to enter. I knew that it would be something along medical lines, so I considered medical technology, pharmacy, and nursing. Med tech and pharmacy seemed so difficult, so I decided upon nursing. It was not a decision I was sure of, by any means, but I thought I'd try it. When I entered college as a nursing major, they immediately began making demands which I was not ready for. They expected me to purchase a uniform, stay at school the following summer, and begin going to clinics. I was not ready for all this and I began to have doubts. I thought a lot about it and even went to see a counselor about it. Basically, the more I thought seriously about it, the less I could see myself doing the things nurses do. But what else did I want to do, if not nursing? I still felt that I wanted to stay in the health field, but where was the question. When I look back on it now, it seems odd that I had never thought of nutrition as an alternative earlier than I did. I guess I just wasn't sure of just what a nutrition major does. . . . I am very pleased today that I made the decision I did, even though I don't know exactly what I want to do in nutrition, and that worries me a bit.

This same woman gave considerable thought to her life-style as well, revolving around marriage, a family, and a career:

> I know I'm not ready for marriage now, and I doubt if I will be for at least three or four more years. I feel the divorce rate is so high in our society, partially because people aren't ready to enter marriage when they do. I don't want to be one of those people. When I enter a marriage, I don't want it to be simply because I'm romantically in love with someone. There are so many other things to think about, such as interests, careers, attitudes on religion, sex, financial matters, and so much more. Economic security is, for instance, important to me, although not something I

work my life around. I don't care if I have lots of status symbols, although I do like some luxuries. I couldn't marry someone who is too concerned with impressing others materially. I also want to keep a career after I have children, but not until they have entered school. I feel that I would owe it to my children to be around when they are small, and in fact, I would certainly want to be around them. But once they reach school age, I want to go back to a career, mostly because I could never stand to sit around a house all day. I hate housework and cooking doesn't thrill me either, and this too will be important when I marry: to have a partner who is willing to share the burden of these things!

For another student, the economic rewards of his career choice are most important:

Logistics (my chosen career) and my desired life-style are compatible. In high school, success to me meant making a lot of money. During my college years, I have become less money hungry and more aware of my own interests, like scuba diving, backpacking, and sports. Success doesn't mean money; it means happiness through a life-style you choose to lead. Naturally, I recognize that it often takes a lot of money to maintain certain life-styles. I seem to have expensive tastes. When I buy something, it can't be just good, it has to be the best. But I am quite confident that a job in logistics will provide an adequate life-style to suit my needs.

Establishing and Maintaining Interpersonal Relationships. More than any other single issue, getting along with people is the most important challenge of college and has the most long-reaching implications. Success in interpersonal relations, as we demonstrate in the next chapter, affects academic success, adjustment to college, satisfaction with college, and general personality development and is a major factor in establishing autonomy and identity. It is also often mentioned by students as the major outcome of college (Upcraft, Peterson, and Moore, 1981).

Students enter college with varying degrees of skill and experience in getting along with people. Some students had no problem in high school with successful interpersonal relationships, and so they developed good social skills. Others were not so fortunate because they lacked opportunity or skill. Some were successful in same-sex relationships but unsuccessful in opposite-sex ones. Other students had successful adult relationships but not with peers. Still others got along with peers but not with adults. Some students did not get along with anyone, and so they come to college with a long history of being loners.

Regardless of past experiences and degree of skill, however, most students coming to college share one trait: They have been uprooted from one interpersonal network and transplanted into another. College is both an opportunity and a curse, but one factor is sure: It is almost impossible to spend four years in college without dealing with this issue. Many students have no difficulty making the transition and are successful because they use the skills they brought with them as a basis for establishing new friendships. For such students, new friendships provide a support system for establishing autonomy and identity and lead to further development and refinement of their interpersonal skills.

But for other students, getting along with people becomes a problem. Some students who thought they were socially skilled find that these skills do not work in the collegiate setting. Some loners no more successfully relate to people in college than they did in high school. Some students have a difficult time adjusting to the new contexts of interpersonal relationships, such as having a roommate or living twenty-four hours a day with fifty other students on a residence hall floor. And for other students, college is an opportunity to start over and do a better job of getting along with people. These students may find that getting along with people with similar abilities and interests is easier than fitting in with their high school peer group.

Students learn to get along with each other and develop their interpersonal skills through their day-to-day interaction with other students, faculty, and other adults in the collegiate community. Roommates and floor members must be dealt with. Mutual activities such as parties and intramural sports require interpersonal skill and cooperation. Advisers, teachers, and staff members must be dealt with successfully if one is to succeed. But perhaps more importantly, students must, perhaps for the first time, relate to persons who have a different cultural background, race, age, sexual preference, and life experience or who are physically handicapped. As a result of encounters with persons different from themselves, students must deal with and successfully resolve such issues as prejudice, stereotyping, and scapegoating.

The following autobiographical account illustrates interpersonal relationships gone wrong in college:

> My interpersonal skills have never been so tested as when I first came to college. When I told my parents I was scared to make new friends, they kept saying, "Be yourself, be yourself." But I wasn't really sure what myself was. I knew that at college I could be anything I wanted to be, and I was tempted to try it. Instead, I just kind of sat back and waited to see what would happen. The first trouble I encountered was with my roommate. We started out being friendly with each other, doing things together, talking about high school and boyfriends, but really we were feeling each other out. She turned out to be very inconsiderate as a roommate; she was loud at night, got a lot of late-night calls, left the light on whenever she left the room, and wouldn't compromise on how far to leave the window open at night (I wanted it closed). I really did try to get along with her, but she refused to compromise on anything. For the first time in my life I became prejudiced because she was Jewish, and I wondered if all Jews were like she was (I've since abandoned that thought). Anyway, we just couldn't get along, so I moved out.
>
> Another difficulty I had was in making friends on my floor. I felt like I just didn't fit in. Granted every girl on the floor was different, but it seemed to me that most of them cliqued together. I was the outcast. I was disappointed in myself for not being able to make friends and angry with others for not paying more attention to me. I thought I at least deserved to be given a chance. But no one seemed interested in me, and I spent many nights crying myself to sleep. . . . In college, so far, relationships with men

have been disasters. It has always been more difficult for me to approach a man I'd like to meet than a woman I'd like to meet because I'm afraid of being rejected.

Developing a Sex-Role Identity and a Capacity for Intimacy. As we stated previously, we agree with Erikson that one's sense of identity is fully developed when one's inner sense of self is consistent with one's meaning for others (Erikson, 1963). An important part of a person's general sense of identity is personal sexual identity. How do I define myself as a man? As a woman? What does that definition mean for my relations with men and women? Traditional sex-role stereotypes used to be benchmarks for such definitions, but today many people in our society are challenging these stereotypes. The result is a freer, less restricted definition of men and women and an unlocking of barriers imposed by rigid sex-role definitions. But it also leaves young adults with a much tougher task of sex-role definition. Old role models do not seem to apply, and societal guidelines are in disarray. Students now must locate themselves on a continuum from unisexuality to traditional sex-role stereotypes. And all this has implications for general identity formation and the ability to establish intimate relationships with others of the same or opposite sex. It also affects career choice, value formation, and behavior.

Students enter college with varying sexual identities, values, and experiences. Many have been raised with traditional sex-role identities, where men are strong and unemotional and women are dependent and emotional. Other students accept differences between the sexes but have been taught more fluid and equalitarian sex-role identities. Some students are trapped between an intellectual sex-role freedom and an emotional sex-role stereotype. Likewise, sex-related behaviors prior to college vary a great deal. Some students have no trouble developing intimacy in a relationship, but others have not had the opportunity or the inclination. Some have been sexually active, while others have been sexually abstinent. Still others are unable to distinguish between physical sex and emotional intimacy.

Upon arriving at college, some students continue their previous patterns of sex-role identity formation and capacity for intimacy. Through their interpersonal relationships, sexual activity, and intellect, they arrive at a sex-role identity comfortable for them and consistent with their values. They also come to know the difference between intimacy and physical sex and decide what is the best sexual behavior for them personally.

But for other students, the transition from home to college may not be so easy as to their sex-role identity and sexuality. Students from homes where traditional sex-role stereotypes were reinforced may end up with a confused sense of themselves as a man or woman and suffer a sexual identity crisis. There may be prolonged periods of questioning that can affect career decisions, friendships, academic success, and values as well as sexual behavior. There may also be a period of experimentation with new sexual behaviors. Some students may even experience the negative consequences of sexual activity, including sexually transmitted diseases, unwanted pregnancies, or abortion.

One thing is certain: College students are sexually active, and there is substantial evidence that they have become more so over the last fifteen years. Thus there are decisions to be made and consequences to be faced concerning sexuality during the college years. In the following autobiography, the woman obviously has some very strong feelings toward society in general, and men in particular, regarding the issue of sex-role identity:

> I believe I should be able to do what I want to and my sex should make no difference. I believe women are capable of doing whatever they want to do and no one, man or woman, can stop them. In high school I was disgusted by the sexual harassment and obvious favoritism displayed by some of the male teachers. Dating also became troublesome because some boys felt they had to play Mr. Macho, protecting the fragile lady. These guys were insulted if a girl offered to pay her way to wherever the date was to be, and they were surprised because they didn't think their date was capable of being so independent. This same type of guy was always shocked when I didn't want to go to bed with him. "What, you're turning *me*

down!" My body has caused me problems since the day it developed. I realize that I'm built fairly well and that I have to be careful about what I wear. But I don't think I should have to put up with the leers and whistling of dirty old men and horny young men. I have a very low opinion of men like that; I definitely feel I am superior to them. During my first term, I was appalled at the number of men who wanted to see how many times they could score in a week. Sex seemed to be *the* number one topic and the only means guys had to assure themselves they could make it socially. I believe men cannot take being beaten by a woman intellectually or athletically. Yet a woman is expected to graciously accept defeat. I think that's ridiculous.

About her sexuality, this same woman describes the moral and interpersonal issues raised by her college experiences:

I am a warm and affectionate person who likes to show it. I can hug a female friend of mine with as little inhibition as I would hug a male friend, and I don't have to think twice about coming across as a lesbian. The implication of the hug is that I love my friend as a friend, not as a sexual partner. I am an impulsive, free spirit not likely to settle down for very long. Therefore, I've been trying to stay away from deep male-female relationships because I have no desire to be tied down. It's hard though because men don't seem to want to accept just being friends.

I like to date, and with some of the guys I've become particularly close to, I've allowed a somewhat physical relationship. The modern world says that's ok, but my religion says it's a no-no. I feel guilty about fooling around, but I'm not sure I should. I'm really torn about what I do and don't believe as far as religion is concerned. The old double standard of "it's ok for men but not for women" doesn't help much either. Frankly, I enjoy making out with a guy I care a lot about, but if I'm not committed to him, is that wrong? I'm trying hard to work this conflict out, but so far I haven't gotten very far.

Collegiate men are having some difficulty adjusting to the newer, less stereotyped sex-role identities of women, as exemplified in this autobiographical account:

> It's confusing as to how men are supposed to act toward women nowadays. Should I hold a door open? Who picks up the bill at dinner? I think the problem of the "new" woman is affecting many women also. I recall a recent encounter when I held a door open for a young woman and stepped back to allow her to enter first. She looked at me and replied, "I'm capable, thank you." After I recovered from the initial shock, I replied, "Yes, you are capable and rude, too." I never thought I'd come out with a statement like that, but her behavior was uncalled for and I felt she should know it. My girl friend, who is also liberated, but in a polite manner, will graciously accept a gentleman's efforts at "playing doorman," although she doesn't approve of it. When this girl was rude to me, I couldn't help but think that if I hadn't held the door for her, she probably would have thought I was ignorant.

This same man describes his own sex-role development:

> In terms of sexual identity, I strongly identified my masculinity with how well I performed athletically, and extended this athletic-masculinity measuring stick to others. I honestly believed that a guy who only played in the band was less of a man than myself. I enjoyed the recognition I received as an athlete in high school, which in turn bolstered my immature viewpoint on what constituted masculine behavior. I've since learned otherwise. I'm now at the point where I can do "unmasculine" things such as show someone all sides of myself without being embarrassed about my weaknesses and inadequacies. I was even able to cry in front of my girl friend, and I hadn't cried at all since I was nine years old.

Finally, this man talks about his current relationship with a woman he has been dating for two years:

Pam and I get along very well. Our outlooks on life are similar and they flow together nicely. Where one of us lacks something, the other one complements. But most important of all, we respect each other as individuals. She has taught me many things about life as well as about myself. She is able to accept me for what I am . . . she has become a precious part of my life.

4

꓄ꓔꓶꓔꓶꓔꓶꓔꓶꓔꓶꓔꓶꓔꓶꓔꓶꓔꓶꓔꓶꓔꓶꓔꓶꓔꓶꓔꓶꓔꓶ

Impact of
Residence Halls
on Student Development

Chapter One reported two landmark studies (Chickering, 1974 and Astin, 1977) that established, based on research, the tremendous influence of the residential environment on students' personal and academic development. We again make the point that too often what we think we know about the residential setting is typically based on our *own* experiences as undergraduates or on our professional experiences in residence halls. However, for an all-encompassing perspective, we must know about the impact of residence halls not only from our own experiences but from existing theories, literature, and research. This chapter reviews several person-environment theories and notes the extensive research on residential impact. It also examines the reasons for this impact and the residence hall staff's role in creating a residential environment conducive to student growth and development.

Parents, students, and faculty are generally ignorant or highly skeptical of this importance of residence halls. Every year when we train prospective RAs, this fact is usually news to these people, and even some of our entry-level residence hall professional staff are uninformed about residential impact. Thus it is worth your while to carefully review the evidence which supports the notion that, generally, residence hall students, particularly freshmen, have an academic and educational advantage over students living elsewhere. More specifically, students living in residence halls, compared to students living elsewhere,

1. Are more satisfied with their living environment (Selby and Weston, 1978).
2. Are more satisfied with their college experience (Astin, 1973, 1977; Rich and Jolicoeur, 1978; Selby and Weston, 1978; Chickering, 1974).
3. Earn higher grades, even when differences in prior achievement are taken into account (Astin, 1973, 1977; Feldman and Newcomb, 1969; Chickering, 1974; Upcraft, Peterson, and Moore, 1981).
4. Are less likely to drop out (Chickering, 1974; Astin, 1973, 1977; Hall and Barger, 1966; Feldman and Newcomb, 1969; Upcraft, Peterson, and Moore, 1981).
5. Have more contacts with faculty (Astin, 1973, 1977; Rich and Jolicoeur, 1978; Selby and Weston, 1978; Chickering, 1974).
6. Have more contacts with other students and a more satisfied social life (Astin, 1973, 1977).
7. Participate more in student and recreational activities (Albrow, 1966; Chickering, 1974; Astin, 1977; Foster, Sedlacek, and Hardwick, 1977).
8. Have fewer emotional problems and greater self-esteem (Sauber, 1972; Lundegren and Schwab, 1979).
9. Have higher educational aspirations (Albrow, 1966; Astin, 1973; Moos and Lee, 1979).
10. Report less conflict with parents (Lundegren and Schwab, 1979).
11. Experience greater changes in values (Nelson, 1971).
12. Have greater artistic interests (Astin, 1977).

Person-Environment Theories

Over the past twenty years, several theories, including those of Barker (1968), Clark and Trow (1966), Holland (1973), Stern

(1970), Moos (1973), and Pervin (1968a, b), have offered explanations of person-environment interactions in the collegiate
environment. These theories are summarized here, based on
Walsh's chapter in the excellent monograph, *Campus Ecology, A
Perspective for Student Affairs,* edited by James H. Banning (1978).
We highly recommend the monograph for those who wish to
explore this issue in greater detail.

   Barker's Behavior-Setting Theory. Barker stated that behavior
settings (a cluster of related behavior-milieu parts) select and shape
the behavior of people who inhabit them. These settings define the
rules for behavior, and people tend to behave in similar ways, depending on the environment, regardless of their personalities. In
this sense, Barker believes that human environments have a coercive influence on human behavior. He downplays an individual's
ability to resist this coercive influence and clearly believes more in
the power of the environment than in an individual's power to
control personal environment. However, Barker does believe that
both the individual and the environment must be taken into account when predicting behavior.

   The Subculture Approach: Clark and Trow. Although several
theorists have offered a subculture approach to explaining
person-environment interactions (Bolton and Kammeyer, 1967;
Coleman, 1966; Keniston, 1966; and Newcomb and others, 1967),
Clark and Trow (1966) are probably the most widely known and
quoted. The subculture approach is similar to the behavior-setting
approach in that both believe in the power of the environment to
overwhelm and influence the individual. However, the subculture
approach is concerned with identifying attitudinal or behavioral
dimensions along which students tend to vary. The term "subculture" implies a collection of people with similar attitudes and behaviors who interact with one another, are mutually attracted to
one another, and are aware of their common differences. Clark
and Trow identified four student subcultures (academic, noncon-
formist, collegiate, and vocational) with which students identify.

   Holland's Theory. In a more balanced view of person-
environment relations, Holland argued that human behavior is a
function of personality and environment. He identified six basic
personality types, based on a cluster of personal attributes: realistic,

investigative, artistic, social, enterprising, and conventional. He also identified six types of environments, corresponding to each personality type; thus for each personality type there is a related environment. Holland theorized that, for example, artistic types search for artistic environments and that when they find them, it is possible to predict and understand better such issues as vocational choice, personal stability, and satisfaction. Holland therefore views behavior as a function of the person and the environment, tending toward the person rather than the environment.

Stern's Need X Press-Culture Theory. Stern assumed that behavior is a function of the relationship between the person and the environment and that the psychological significance of the person may be inferred from behavior. Thus the person is represented by needs, as indicated by self-reported behavior. He further assumed that psychological significance of the environment may be inferred from behavioral perceptions. Consequently, the environment is defined by presses inferred from the self-reported perceptions of the environment. In the collegiate setting, there seems to be a congruence between student needs and environmental presses, and need-press combinations seem to constitute different college cultures.

Moos's Social Ecological Approach. Moos (1973) argued that because environments, like people, have unique personalities, it is possible to describe and characterize an environment as one might an individual's personality. He assumed that the way to describe environments is to ask the people in them. He also assumed that the way people perceive their surroundings influences the way they behave in that environment. Maximum human functioning is related to the environment's ability to facilitate or inhibit behavior. Moos developed the University Residence Environment Scale (Moos and Gerst, 1976) to measure the collective perceptions of students in residence halls of their environment, including personal relationships, personal growth and self-enhancement influences, and system maintenance and change (Insel and Moos, 1974). Moos thus believes that the consensus of individuals characterizing their environment directly influences behavior (Smail, DeYoung, and Moos, 1974).

Pervin's Transaction Approach. Pervin (1967) argued that behavior can best be understood by the interactions between the person and the environment. Individuals tend to survive best in environments congruent with their personality characteristics. When persons are not congruent with their environment, they experience pain and unpleasantness that affect their behavior. People tend to gravitate toward environments that allow their perceived selves to move toward their ideal selves. Pervin's congruency-achievement approach helps individuals match themselves with facilitative environments.

What do all these theories mean for the residence educator who supervises residence halls and the resident assistant who toils in the trenches of residence hall floors? The RA candidate will find little value in reviewing the summarized theories, but they are of use to the professionals who must train the RAs. Several basic principles inferred from these theories challenge commonsense assumptions about life in a residence hall. Most residence hall programs almost exclusively emphasize the individual. The individuals are counseled, advised, disciplined, and referred, as if their day-to-day environment (1) is the same as for all other students and (2) has little or no influence on their behavior. Furthermore, little has been done to encourage RAs to develop an environment in residence halls that is conducive to students' and the institution's personal and educational goals. The basic principles, drawn from the Western Interstate Commission for Higher Education (1973) and from our own analyses, are

1. Students enter residence halls with their own personalities, attitudes, values, skills, and needs, based on their prior experiences in their homes, families, communities, and peer groups.
2. Students enter into an environment never before encountered. It is physically different from anything experienced before, more homogeneous, and more intense.
3. The residence hall environment can have a powerful impact on students and may vary in characteristics and power according to its history, composition, size, and collective attitudes, values, and needs.
4. Students, particularly freshmen, have a high need to identify and affiliate with other students. The residence halls provide

an opportunity to express this need because of optimal physical facilities and students' commonality of purpose.

5. People affect environments, and environments affect people. In residence halls, students develop, influence, and change their environment to meet their needs. Likewise, students' collective norms, values, and needs influence and change the persons in a residence hall environment.

6. Some students are very susceptible to the press of the environment, whereas others seem almost immune. Similarly, some environments are very weak, unstable, and rapidly changing, while others are strong, stable, and less likely to change.

7. When there is congruence between an individual and personal environment, that person is happier, better adjusted, and more likely to achieve personal and educational goals.

8. Residence hall environments can be described, influenced, and channeled by residence hall staff and students to create an optimal personal and academic climate.

Reasons for Residential Impact

RAs need to be taught about not only student development but how residence hall environments influence students. They also need to be taught how to describe and analyze their floors and how to intervene to develop a climate conducive to personal and academic development. In our opinion, this great potential for influencing the residential setting is clearly one of the most underdeveloped roles of the RA.

Why do residence halls so powerfully impact on students' personal and academic development? How does the impact occur, and how might it be influenced? The residential environment gives students maximum opportunity to interact with one another and the collegiate environment. Our review of person-environment theories concluded that persons are susceptible to the press of their environment and that environmental press was a function of the environment's history, composition, physical characteristics, size, collective attitudes, values, norms, and needs. Because residence

hall floors and buildings typically change their composition from
year to year and thus do not develop a history, residence hall
environmental press is a function of architecture and residents'
collective attitudes, values, norms, and needs.

Mable, Terry, and Duvall (1980) identified shared goals,
shared responsibilities, and shared communication as the basic ingredients for interaction between students and their residential
environment. Given the architecture of most residence halls, this
interaction of goals, responsibilities, and communication is
intensified because of the very close proximity of large
numbers of students with each other. Within the residential
environment, this interaction is between the individual and the
peer group, close friends, or roommates. It is especially important
for both residence hall professional staff and resident assistants to
know and understand these influences. As we stated earlier, too
often the selection, training, and supervision of resident assistants
focus exclusively on the individual, without regard for the interpersonal environment within which residents grow and develop.

Peer Group. Studies of peer-group influence are sometimes
difficult to interpret. First, the terms "peer group," "reference
group," "student culture," "membership group," and "friendship
group" are sometimes used interchangeably, and with
different meanings. Peer group as used here refers to a group with
whom an individual identifies and from which the person derives a
frame of reference for evaluating personal norms, attitudes, values, and behaviors.

But even with this definition, it is difficult to sort out the
influence of others as a group versus the influence of others as
individuals. It is particularly difficult if one's friend is also a
member of one's peer group. As a theoretical construct, it is
possible to talk about the influence of the peer group, but as a
practical matter, it is sometimes impossible to separate that influence from one-to-one relationships.

There is ample evidence that the peer group is the most
powerful influence on students' lives once they arrive on the campus. What students learn in college is largely determined by their
fellow students, or as Kenneth Feldman stated, "by the structure of
peer relations that constitutes student society and the configuration

of attitudes, values, and norms that constitute the student subculture" (Feldman, 1972, p. 17). Studies by Appel, Berry, and Hoffman (1973), Bushnell (1962), and many others confirm this fundamental point.

The scope of this influence is enormous, ranging from the students' academic lives to their personal lives outside the classroom. Feldman and Newcomb summarized the eight functions peer groups serve for individual students:

1. Help students achieve independence from home and family.
2. Support and facilitate or impede the institution's academic intellectual goals.
3. Offer students general emotional support and fulfill needs not met by the curriculum, classroom, or faculty.
4. Give students practice in getting along with people whose background, interests, and orientations differ from their own.
5. Provide students support for not changing.
6. Provide students support for changing. Peer groups can challenge old values, provide intellectual stimulation and act as a sounding board for new viewpoints, present new information and new experiences to students, help clarify new self-definitions, suggest new career possibilities, and provide emotional support for change.
7. Offer an alternative source of gratification and self-image and reward a variety of nonacademic interests for students not satisfied academically. Peer groups can also discourage voluntary withdrawal from college for nonacademic reasons.
8. Can help students' postcollege careers by providing general social training and developing personal ties that may be useful later (Feldman and Newcomb, 1969, pp. 236–237).

Given the power and breadth of peer groups, further inquiry into the dynamics of their influence is warranted. The major theorist in this regard is the social psychologist Theodore Newcomb, who pioneered studies of peer-group influence in the collegiate setting. Newcomb argued that peer groups influence because (1) they have the power to reward and punish and (2) human beings want and need each other. According to Newcomb, college student peer groups are especially powerful because their predispositions and backgrounds are similar, they live in close proximity to one another, they are striving for the same goal (a college education), and they are likely to have the same interests (Newcomb, 1966).

A peer group's initial formation is usually based on common interests. Newcomb traced the development of peer groups after their initial formation. As members become more favorable toward each other, they adopt group-shared attitudes or norms. At the same time, they learn to trust each other and accept each other's assessment of things (Newcomb and Wilson, 1966). In other words, peer groups serve both a *normative function* (they reward and punish based on behavioral and environmental norms) and a *comparison function* (the group becomes the basis of comparison for students' attitudes and behavior used in making decisions and judgments) (Cartwright and Zander, 1968). The net result is that students yield some control over themselves to the peer group (Newcomb and Wilson, 1966), or transfer this control from the high school to the college peer group.

Size, homogeneity, and isolation are all important factors in the influence of peer groups. Smaller, homogeneous, and isolated groups are likely to be more powerful, especially if the individuals who form the group come to college predisposed to group influences (Newcomb and Wilson, 1966). Background factors like place of residence, parental income and occupation, religion, education, age, sex, and race also influence predisposition to change, as do position in family, relationships with parents, activity with precollege peers, frequency of moving, and size of school attended. Finally, predisposition to influence by peer groups can be affected by students' personal traits, such as level of anxiety, motivation, aptitudes, values, and self-concept (Newcomb and Wilson, 1966).

The peer group's rewards and punishments create a tendency for students to channel their energy in those directions for which they will be rewarded and to attach a positive value to those directions. Students become attached to those who reward them and alienated from those who punish them and in turn reward and become attached to those who enter into a common effort with them. Because all persons have a need for recognition, respect, and acceptance from others, the net result is that the community, or the peer group itself, maintains the power of reward and punishment (Coleman, 1966).

It is important that residence hall staff understand the specific methods by which the peer group influences its members. Specific rewards can include status, emotional support, economics, or interpersonal relations. Punishments can include isolation, reprimand, withdrawal of rewards, and, ultimately, exclusion. Besides direct rewards and punishments, other methods of influence can be used, such as persuasion, instilling either a sense of loyalty or of guilt, direct authority, or modeling of individual behavior (Cartwright and Zander, 1968).

Thus, because of college students' common background, interests, personality characteristics, their common goals and environment, and their need to be liked and accepted by one another, they are strongly influenced by their own peer group. The group establishes norms and provides behavior guidelines that are enforced through direct rewards and punishments. As a result, students transfer some control over themselves to the group and become subject to its influence; that influence has a pervading effect on students' academic and personal development.

Close Friends. Within the college peer group, friendships develop and become a major source of influence on a student's growth and development. An important aspect of general peer pressure is the influence of close friends: They frequently share one or more important values and affect one another through reinforcement, accentuation, or change of values (Feldman, 1972). A student's close friends during the freshman year are the primary influence on attitudes and values during college. Close friendships have an impact on the same issues as the peer group, but as a function of a one-to-one relationship rather than as the dynamics of a group (Vreeland, 1970).

Both same- and opposite-sex friends have a powerful impact. Friends of the opposite sex are most often mentioned by men and women as the most important influence in their lives (Whittaker, 1970). The most extensive study of same- and opposite-sex influences was Heath's study (1968) of student maturity at Haverford College. Because Haverford is all-male, Heath reported same- and opposite-sex influences only for college men. Close male friends helped these men become more aware of themselves, more allocentric and integrative in their personal relationships, more mature in their values, more insightful about other people, increased their reflective ability, and led to more integrative and autonomous self-concepts.

On the other hand, close female friends had both immaturing and maturing effects on men. Women helped the men improve their self-image, relationships with other women, and values and intellectual skills. But they blocked the men's integration of ideas about themselves and postponed the development of more stable and autonomous relationships (Heath, 1968).

How do students decide who will be their friends? Sometimes new freshmen who are assigned to each other as roommates develop close friendships, so propinquity and opportunity have much to do with the decisions. But beyond that, what is the basis for student friendships? Partham and Tinsley (1980) studied students' expectations of the friendship encounter: They found that students most valued genuine, accepting, confrontive friends in the friendship encounter. Women students, more than male students, valued genuineness, trust, attractiveness, acceptance, openness, concreteness, and nurturance in the friendship encounter.

As mentioned, it is difficult to separate the peer group's influences from those of close friends, particularly in the residential setting, because close friends are frequently a significant part of the peer group. But even long-standing close friends, not a part of the campus peer group, can be influential (Peters and Kennedy, 1970). Close friendships develop in residence halls because of the opportunity and the need to affiliate with others who have the characteristics just identified.

Roommates. Assigning two freshmen students who do not know each other to a residence hall room is a strange practice. Persons who have developed over eighteen or nineteen years in a family environment (they may even have had their own room) are put into the unique situation of a residence hall with total strangers and told to get along. The only other situations where persons are forced to live together this way are the military and prison. The resulting adjustment problems are monumental and can have a very powerful effect on students' academic and personal development.

There is considerable evidence that roommates affect one another. The following generalizations about roommate impact are supported by the literature:

1. Roommates challenge each other's confidence and self-understanding and force each other to become more tolerant and accepting (Heath, 1968).
2. Roommates force each other to express themselves more clearly and sharply (Heath, 1968).
3. Roommates affect each other's attitudes (Vreeland, 1970).
4. A student's grades are likely to deviate from expectancy above or below in the same direction as those of the roommate (Murray, 1961).
5. Highly dissatisfied pairs of roommates have significantly lower academic achievement than do those roommates who have little dissatisfaction with one another (Pace, 1970).
6. Significantly higher levels of academic achievement can be attained by middle and low achievers by assigning them as roommates to above-average achievers, without detrimental effects on those high achievers (Blai, 1971; Ainsworth and Maynard, 1976).
7. Roommates affect each other's study habits (Hall and Willerman, 1963). The odds that a student will study if the roommate is also studying are three in four; the odds drop to one in three if the roommate is not studying (Sommer, 1969).

Obviously, roommates have a significant impact on one another as to self-perception, communication, attitudes, academic achievement, and study habits. The problem is to predict in advance if two strangers will get along, by assigning them according to criteria such as background or birth order. Certain criteria are more effective than others:

1. If roommates choose one another, rather than being randomly assigned, there is less likelihood of difficulty (Hall and Willerman, 1963).

2. Socioeconomic background factors, if considered when assigning roommates, can lessen incompatibility (Lozier, 1970).
3. When students are asked to list least and most preferable characteristics of prospective roommates and the intensity of these preferences, roommates assigned on that basis stayed together longer and expressed more satisfaction than randomly assigned pairs (Roby, Zelin, and Chechile, 1977).

Ineffective criteria are:

1. Roommate self-ratings and ideal ratings were of little help in selecting compatible roommate pairs (Wetzel, Schwartz, and Vasu, 1979).
2. Assigning roommates by birth order and comparing their compatibility with those assigned by conflicting birth order did not yield any differences in compatibility (Schuh and Williams, 1977).
3. Matching roommates according to background variables such as parents' educational level, size of high school enrollment, church attendance, smoking habits, and predicted grades yielded no significant differences in compatibility when compared to randomly assigned roommates (Gehring, 1970).

Assuming that little can be done to accurately predict compatibility, what makes roommates compatible once they have been assigned to each other? Interpersonal similarities are significantly associated with roommate compatibility (Shapiro and Voog, 1969) as well as mundane things like housekeeping and sleeping habits (Cerny, Zax, and Pierce, 1970). Other factors, such as congruent attitudes, are also associated with compatibility, including view of the rewards of honesty, trustworthiness, degree of personal involvement, sharing, and attitudes regarding interpersonal relations (Jones, McCaa, and Martecchini, 1980). On the other hand, value similarity does not seem to play a significant role in explaining satisfaction with living groups (Perkins, 1977).

What can be done to prevent roommate incompatibility before it becomes a problem? Alfred and Graff (1980) studied roommate pairs who received six hours of interpersonal communication training over a six-week period and compared them with a control group of roommate pairs. The group receiving the interpersonal communication training reported a significant increase in affective interpersonal communication, compared to the control group. Peterman, Sagaria, and Sellers (1977) developed the Roommate Starter Kit, which gives new or experienced roommates a structured interpersonal communication format consisting of a series of questions on backgrounds. Freshmen who used the Roommate Starter Kit (1977) earned significantly higher grades than students who did not use it (Upcraft, Peterson, and Moore, 1981). Thus it appears that even if we cannot in advance predict with any great consistency roommate compatibility, we can take steps to enhance compatibility once we have assigned students.

Our experience has been that the peer group, close friends, and roommates account for much of the impact of residence halls on students' personal and academic development. In short, the opportunity for interaction with significant others inherent in residence hall living is much greater than all other living options. The question is now what, if anything, can a college or university do to influence, direct, and structure the residence hall environment to promote opportunities for interactions?

Strategies for Promoting Residents'
Academic and Personal Development

Does the power of the residence halls happen just by chance? Does it result merely from putting students together in rooms strung along corridors? Or can the residence hall environment be structured to create optimal conditions for personal and academic development? Essentially, a college can affect the residential environment three ways: (1) assigning students to residence hall space; (2) the influence of residence hall staff, including resident assistants and professional staff; and (3) implementing educational developmental activities and programs. Here we discuss various strategies within these categories that could affect personal and academic development.

Assigning Students. The decisions made about where students

live and the criteria used to make those decisions have a very powerful impact on students' personal and academic development. We
reviewed roommates' influence on one another and how that influence is determined by the way roommates are assigned. The size
and composition of a residence hall floor, including such variables
as residents' class standing, sex, major, and academic ability, are
also influential. Too often, little attention is paid to these factors, or
the architecture or tradition is allowed to play a predominant role.
Yet these decisions affect students' lives and the quality of the residential environment. What do we know about assigning students to
residence halls?

1. *Assign students by academic major.* Considerable evidence indicates that when students are assigned by major, academic
   achievement is improved (Davidson, 1965; Taylor and
   Hanson, 1971; Schroeder and Freesh, 1978) and scholarly orientation is greater (Morishima, 1966; Schroeder and Freesh,
   1978) when compared with randomly assigned students. However, if a floor is dominated by one particular major, students
   not in that major will be adversely affected as to social interaction and satisfaction with college (Brown, 1968).
2. *Assign students according to academic ability.* There is some evidence that when high-ability students are assigned to the same
   floor, they earn higher grades than high-ability students assigned randomly (DeCoster, 1966). They report their living
   environment more conducive to study, having more informal
   educational discussions, and more desirable accommodations
   (DeCoster, 1968). They also report their environment as more
   stimulating and academically oriented (Kaplan, Mann, and
   Kaplan, 1964).
3. *Assign students to coeducational residence halls.* Generally, coeducational residence halls reveal no differences in academic
   achievement when compared to segregated halls (Linnell,
   1972; Brown, Winkworth, and Braskamp, 1973). However, in
   just about every other way, students in coeducational halls
   were in a better living environment than those in segregated
   halls. Students in coed halls, compared to segregated halls,
   have a higher sense of community and more actively partici-

pate in residence hall programs (Linnell, 1972). They also report greater satisfaction with their social lives and have more informal social interaction in the living environment (Corbett and Somner, 1972). However, they report no differences in frequency of sexual intercourse and little dating among residents.

4. *Assign freshmen with upperclassmen.* Generally, it is not a good idea to create all-freshmen floors or to assign freshmen to floors where upperclassmen are in an overwhelming majority. A mix of freshmen and upperclassmen provides a better living environment (Beal and Williams, 1968; Upcraft, Peterson, and Moore, 1981), but the evidence regarding academic achievement is mixed (Beal and Williams, 1968; Schoemer and McConnell, 1970).

5. *Do not overcrowd floors and buildings.* Every fall, thousands of students are placed in overcrowded conditions, including three-person rooms and common-area space like recreation rooms or study lounges. There is some evidence that this type of assignment is detrimental to students for privacy, roommate relationships, and general satisfaction with the living environment; academic achievement and attrition are negatively affected (McNeel, 1980; Karlin, Rosen, and Epstein, 1979).

Influence of Residence Hall Staff. As pointed out in Chapter Two, most residence hall systems rely almost exclusively on their RAs to implement the living environment's educational potential. But there is very little evidence regarding the effectiveness of RAs doing so. It is known that students are generally satisfied with their RAs, but what impact, if any, do the RAs have on students' academic and personal development? In other words, what evidence is there that RAs help fulfill the educational potential of the living environment?

We found only two cases of evidence in the literature. Upcraft, Peterson, and Moore (1981) looked at RA influence from two perspectives. First, is there a relationship between perceived RA competence and students' personal and academic development? Second, is the perceived quality of the relationship between the student and the RA related to this development? When stu-

dents on floors where the RA was perceived as highly competent
were compared with students on floors where the RA was perceived least competent, no differences in academic achievement,
retention, or personal growth and development were found.
Macdonald (1968) found no relationship between RA task orientation and students' grades. So it appears that perceived RA competence does not relate to students' academic and personal
development.

However, when students were asked to describe their relationship with their RA, the outcomes were different. Students who
described their relationship with their RA as "close" or "compatible" were compared with students who described that relationship
as "incompatible." In this instance, students with a close or compatible relationship with their RA earned significantly higher grades.
Furthermore, these students also reported a greater increase in
social extroversion and personal integration during their freshman
year, compared to those with an incompatible relationship with
their RA. Thus it appears that the quality of the relationship established by the RA with students in residence halls does have an
impact on students' personal and academic development (Upcraft,
Peterson, and Moore, 1981).

Certain types of educational programming positively affect
students' personal and academic development (as we next discuss).
To the extent that RAs are involved in developing these programs,
it is further evidence of their impact on student development.

Influence of Educational Programs. Over the last twenty years,
there has been a considerable emphasis on developing comprehensive or individual programs in the residential environment. The
assumption has been that these programs are a positive thing and
should be encouraged. But is there any evidence that special programs positively affect the residential environment or students'
academic or personal development?

Generally, the answer is yes. For example, living-learning
residence halls, where classes are held and faculty offices are located, appear to have advantages over other halls. Living-learning
residents showed significantly better personal adjustment, intellectual growth, and positive attitudes toward their college experience
(Nosow, 1975; Gordon, 1974). These residents are also more likely to

complete their college programs (Gordon, 1974; Pascarella and Terenzini, 1980). Faculty-student relations are also enhanced by this living arrangement (DeCoster, 1969; Pascarella and Terenzini, 1980).

Unfortunately, most colleges do not have the facilities or the resources to create living-learning programs. Most programs in residence halls are one-shot attempts to educate on a particular subject or create a certain type of social or educational interaction. And there is great skepticism among many people about the value of special programs in residence halls. Do the programs really make a difference? Again, we found little evidence in the literature, with one exception.

Upcraft, Peterson, and Moore (1981) compared the grades, attrition rate, and personal development of students who attended selected educational programs in residence halls with those students who did not attend, controlling for such background differences as academic ability, sex, major, parents' income, and race. Programs studied included social programs, educational programs, intramural participation, programs on sexuality, values clarification, career development, and programs in which faculty participated. Although no differences in academic achievement or retention were noted between attenders and nonattenders, there were some differences in personal development over the freshman year. Generally, social, educational, and sexuality programs had a positive impact, as did intramural participation and programs in which faculty participated. Study-skills, career-development, and values-clarifications programs had little or no impact on personal development during the freshman year.

Thus it appears that comprehensive programs in residence halls, such as living-learning programs, and selected individual programs positively affect students and should be promoted in the residential setting. It is interesting to note that in both types of programs, faculty involvement was a variable. There is considerable evidence that faculty involvement and interaction in the residential setting are very positive influences on students and so should be promoted by residence hall staff (Magnarella, 1979; Pascarella and Terenzini, 1980).

5

꜒꜖꜒꜖꜒꜖꜒꜖꜒꜖꜒꜖꜒꜖꜒꜖꜒꜖꜒꜖꜒꜖꜒꜖꜒꜖꜒꜖꜒꜖꜒꜖

Strengthening Interpersonal Skills of Resident Assistants

From the overview of the training model in Chapter Two, it is evidence that the interpersonal skills section is the central portion of the course. We regard this portion as the meat of the training course. Chapters Three and Four on student development and residential impact form the context in which such skills are used; this chapter starts from the assumption that RAs must have basic interpersonal skills to provide effective group leadership. We believe that much of the work done by RAs involves people, and the RAs' effectiveness is in direct proportion to their skill in relating to others. However, designing an interpersonal skills development model for resident assistants is not easy because of the problems of distinguishing between counseling and interpersonal skills and the problems of time constraints, techniques, and appropriate chronology.

When designing the section on interpersonal skills, we drew from the literature dealing with counseling (helping) skills and interpersonal skills. We recognized that both skills are often treated interchangeably and that a major focus of the RA's job is helping. Yet to confine the RA's duties to within the narrower label of "helping" is misleading. True, the RA is called upon to counsel, but the RA is also expected to maintain residence hall discipline, disseminate information, present programs, and engage in any number of tasks that involve contact with people but that are not usually thought of as helping. A training program that confines its attention exclusively to counseling skills will not prepare RAs for the multifaceted duties of the job. But if the concept of counseling or helping is broadened to "interpersonal skills," all the RA's functions can be included. However, if we do so, we immediately confront a dilemma: Knowing that most counseling or helping skills models require extensive and time-consuming effort, how can a time-limited training program adequately train RAs in all the interpersonal skills they require?

In addition, time constraints force compromises. When developing the training program, we felt that many of the existing interpersonal skills training models provided excellent grounding in the development of skills, but that these models demanded a great deal of time for learning and practicing the various skills. For example, we believed that Carkhuff's Human Relations Training Program (1969) might be a very useful way for RAs to both conceptualize and practice important interpersonal skills. On the other hand, we also realized that training programs which follow a strict Carkhuff format require more hours than we had available for helping RA participants achieve satisfactory levels in each of the basic interpersonal skills. We therefore faced an inevitable question: If there was not enough time to train people thoroughly, should they be trained at all? Ultimately, we decided to proceed, in spite of the time constraints, and discovered that under proper conditions, the development of effective interpersonal skills was possible.

Furthermore, any training program that develops specific skills needs to emphasize the *practice* of both verbal and nonverbal behaviors. Many of the existing training programs are based on research findings that examined the behaviors of successful helpers. The behavioral model underlying these approaches can be considered "elegant" in the scientific sense. Once behavior of effective helpers is evaluated, certain behaviors or techniques can be identified as being used consistently, regardless of the helpers' theoretical orientations. If it is possible to identify and measure those behaviors which appear to correlate with success, it is assumed that the learner of these behaviors will be successful. Without minimizing what can be regarded as objections to the behavioral model, obviously the behavioral skill model has taught us that helping consists largely of skills and that many of these skills can be identified and taught.

Yet training models based on measurable behavioral data may place the cart before the horse. Much of behavioral research ignores the phenomenology of people. In particular, the subjective attitude of caring is difficult to measure. Nevertheless, we make an assumption about caring that is difficult to prove "scientifically": Effective helpers are *caring* people and many of the skills they employ, although teachable, nevertheless flow out of their fundamental attitude of caring. An approach that concentrates solely on behavior skills without attention to phenomenological attitudes is in danger, as Calia (1974) noted, of producing "technicians" who do the "right" things but are not able to spontaneously exercise creative and initiative options. We are impressed by the fact that Carl Rogers (1980), whose pioneering work in theorizing and research about skills underlies almost all the present interpersonal training models, has continued to promote a humanistic view about skills.

An apt analogy of what we are saying is that of strictly behavioral sex therapy. It is possible to teach people sexual techniques, and it seems reasonable to suppose that an improvement in such techniques can improve the quality of their sexual interactions. Yet the question remains, "Can the techniques by themselves have any meaning if they are not flowing from basic attitudes and qualities (which are difficult to measure), such as loving, consideration, sharing, and unselfishness?"

The tension between the behavioral and the humanistic viewpoints will continue, and we do not presume to know all the answers. When designing the section on skills, we attempted to pay attention to both viewpoints. We chose to teach some of the skills that have been identified in the behavioral research, and many of our exercises are designed to help people change behaviors. At the same time, we attempted to promote a more humanistic view, stressing the importance of authenticity in responding, of attitudes of caring and responsibility, and of openness to trying new and spontaneous approaches that may at times transcend the specific skills.

We also believe that interpersonal skills should be taught in some order, based on some logic or purpose. For example, the order of presentation of interpersonal skills may be arranged to roughly approximate the order of what goes on in the helping process. Egan's (1975) "developmental model" sees counseling moving through stages. At first clients present personal problems. The counselor's task is to establish a trusting and caring atmosphere by using "attending" skills that can help the clients feel understood, clarify their own issues, and explore these issues more deeply. As counseling proceeds, and trust or rapport is firmer, the counselor uses genuineness and confrontation skills that involve using more of the counselor's self. The model also encourages clients to even more fully explore the issues and discover aspects of the problems that may have been out of their awareness. Then, as the issues become more deeply appreciated and understood, clients move into a phase of action planning to effect changes in their behavior and outlook. The counselor uses certain new skills to help in this stage also. The model tends to be cumulative or additive; that is, the beginning skills are not dropped at a certain point, to be taken over by the later skills; they continue to be used but are supplemented and enhanced by later skills.

Such a model is very appealing because it makes sense by providing a context within which to teach the skills. However, remember that although the RA's job involves counseling, there are many aspects of the job which do not. Even when RAs are counseling, they may not have the luxury of time to move smoothly through the ideal stages. Sometimes decisions need to be made quickly; sometimes RAs are working with people who have not come to them for help. Sometimes RAs have to be confrontive, even if they have not had time to establish a warm trusting atmosphere, where confrontation will be heard constructively and nondefensively. Therefore, RAs are often called on to use whatever skills best suit the particular situation they are handling.

Again, our model gives attention to both aspects of the problem. On the one hand, we do present skills in an order that approximates an "ideal" counseling process, and we address the issue of order when we are teaching the developmental aspects of counseling. On the other hand, we also continue to stress flexibility and that the real world of the RA does not always correspond to an ideal model.

An Eclectic Interpersonal Skills Model

Our interpersonal skills model is eclectic. It contains elements of many existing models combined with exercises we devised but which are mainly consistent with the main points and emphases of the established models. We used these models as guides, recognizing that none was specifically designed to train RAs. We agree with Meade (1978) that there is no good reason to limit oneself to a particular approach when there is such a variety to choose from, if the choices are based on a particular program's overall goals.

We do not attempt here to extensively review all the models whose ideas we used or which inspired our own inventiveness. Meade (1978) wrote an excellent summary of several of the existing models, and we recommend this reference. Those aspects of existing programs that we found useful for developing this section of the training program include the following.

Human Relations Training (Carkhuff, 1969). Carkhuff's identification and definitions of skills and his methods of teaching are powerful and persuasive. Particularly, we found invaluable his work on the development of empathetic skills (nonverbal attending and accurate reflective listening) of both feeling and content, of the skill of conveying respect, on helping people to become more concrete, and on the importance of genuineness and confrontation.

Egan's Developmental Model (1975). Egan's clear writing style and his ability to place many of the skills identified by Carkhuff in a developmental context helped us to appreciate and include developmental notions in our own model.

Danish and Hauer's Basic Helping Skills Program (1973). Danish and Hauer emphasized the importance of the helper's evaluating personal motivation to help. This respect for the phenomenology of the helper, together with full attention to the practice of skills, makes their program an excellent blending of the humanistic and behavioral approaches. Their program contains excellent advice on using appropriate questions and developing an accurate empathic vocabulary.

Ivey's Microcounseling Training (1971). Ivey's suggestions regarding nonverbal behavior and his emphasis on the reflection and summarization of feeling were very useful to us. Ivey also stressed flexibility (the differential use of skills, depending on goals and situation), which fits in well with the RA's varied life.

Brammer's Model of Helping Relationships Processes and Skills (1979). Brammer's ideas were the primary source for our presentation of what we refer to as initiation skills (summarizing, confronting, and informing). We also found his exposition of the effective use of questioning succinct and readily teachable.

Combs, Avila, and Purkey's Model of Basic Concepts in Helping (1971). This model was a continual reminder of balancing behavior teaching with humanistic perspectives and appreciating the subjective, phenomenological frame of reference. We also used the author's ideas about the use and dangers of self-disclosure.

Our eclectic model of interpersonal skills consists of three dimensions: (1) responding skills (nonverbal attending, reflective listening of content and feeling, and concreteness); (2) self-disclosing skills (self-disclosure of both feelings and similar experiences); and (3) initiating skills (confrontation and summarizing). We introduce participants to the section on interpersonal skills development by presenting an overview of this model. The skills are then taught and practiced in small group sessions. This overview presents the outline of all the skills and concentrates on the first two categories of responding and self-disclosing. The initiating skills are then elaborated in later group sessions. We make this time division for two reasons. First, we do not want to overload the students during this presentation; they will be spending many sessions on responding and self-disclosure, so we believe it is better to reintroduce and elaborate initiating skills later. Second, because responding and self-disclosure can be related to counseling and other interpersonal situations, it is important for students to learn the skills and see how they can adapt them to such situations.

Our lecture will acquaint the reader more fully with the model itself and enable the reader to use it when implementing the training model. Naturally, it can be modified to take into consideration the requirements of a specific residence hall program, and we recommend spicing up this presentation with anecdotes from the presenter's own experiences.

The lecture should start off with a description of situations in which RAs are called on to use their interpersonal skills. We do not present this beginning part of our lecture verbatim because we think you should develop it from your own RAs' anecdotal reports. We do recommend that you choose situations which involve the RA interacting with one person (initiated by both the person and the RA), roommates, groups, other RAs, and supervisors.

Responding and Self-Disclosing Skills: A Sample Lecture

I know you're all looking forward to your jobs as RAs and that you're hopeful of doing a good job. At the same time, now that we've reviewed only a small number of the many types of situations in which you'll be called on to use interpersonal skills, I wouldn't be surprised if you also feel apprehensive. The RA job is, after all, complex and difficult as well as rewarding. Because we appreciate just how demanding the job is, we designed this course to help you practice some of the skills you'll need to get the job done.

So far in this training you've been concentrating on student development, with particular emphasis on the major issues in your own development and the impression you make on others. We regard what you've been doing so far as a preparation for the next section of the training program, which is the development of interpersonal skills.

Please note this listing of interpersonal skills. [Here we show a listing such as the one presented earlier in this chapter.] Notice that the skills are listed under three dimensions: responding, self-disclosing, and initiating. We're going to teach you the skills in that order. Today we'll spend most of our time on the first two dimensions; later in the training, after you've practiced those skills, you'll learn more about the initiating skills.

There's a good reason for the order in which we teach these skills. You see, our knowledge of these skills comes, in large measure, from research that has been done on helping, or counseling. This research has shown that these skills are effective in helping people. Now, effective helping has been shown to go through three sequential stages, which I'll write down: exploration, deeper understanding, and action.

Simply put, the idea here is that people seeking help need to be able to share and explore their problems and feelings. If they are encouraged to do so, they may also be encouraged to dig more deeply into their issues, perhaps into aspects of their problems even they didn't understand before. Then, out of that new understanding, they can form action plans to make changes and solve their problems.

Now here's where the order of the skills becomes important. The researchers have also found that if a helper is using the responding skills during the exploration phase of counseling, the person being helped will be encouraged to sustain his or her exploration and delve into issues more deeply. Then, in the stage of deeper understanding, the helper, while continuing to use responding skills, now begins to utilize the self-disclosing skills. Ideally this will lead to even deeper understanding, and the helper and helpee together can begin to form action plans. When forming action plans, initiating skills become increasingly useful.

Of course, reality is not often as neat or as cut and dried as an ideal model. The model is only a general guide. Sometimes RAs are faced with urgent situations where it would be impossible to go neatly through the three stages, and so they'll have to use initiation skills very early. Also, your ability to move through the stages depends a great deal on the nature of students' problems, on the differences among students in their own ability to confide and trust, and on such realistic issues as how much time and energy you and they have to give to the problems.

One more thought before I begin to tell you more about the individual skills. Helping or counseling is something you will do as RAs, but also remember that many of the interpersonal situations I told you about at the beginning of our talk weren't specifically helping situations. But all the situations did involve interaction and good communication. We're convinced that the skills we're teaching you can be used beyond the helping context—that you'll find good use for them in almost any interpersonal context, whether dealing with friends, roommates, supervisors, parents—anyone.

Responding. Let's begin with responding skills. Responding means being able to focus on really hearing a person in a respectful, nonevaluative manner and being able to say some things that will help people better clarify and specify their issues. First, it involves the skill of nonverbal attending.

A lot of your caring is expressed in nonverbal postures and expressions. For example, I want you to picture yourself listening to the problems of a distressed friend. Chances are you will, out of your caring concern, be doing some things nonverbally that you're not even aware of. You'll probably be looking right into your friend's face. Your own facial expressions will probably register your feelings about what you're hearing; your voice tone will be consistent with your feelings; and your whole body will probably be leaning toward your friend in a posture of alert concern. In our first small group session on responding, we'll try to demonstrate to you how important these nonverbal aspects of caring are. But don't get us wrong: These behaviors are the natural partners of real caring. Being aware of them helps remind us to stay on track with a student when our real caring is lagging because we're tired or grumpy or just having a bad day. We don't want to suggest, however, that simply acting our caring behaviors without really caring is enough; sooner or later students will sense such acting as phony.

When you're being caring, it is important to at first concentrate with intensity on the other person's expressions, both verbal and nonverbal. You're trying to get into that person's shoes to appreciate how she or he experiences the world. To do this, you have to suspend premature judgments and really listen and watch intently. So you begin to notice things, such as the student who is saying she isn't angry but who is clenching her fists and speaking in an annoyed tone.

But simply listening and using appropriate nonverbal expressions are not the only part of good responding. You might call them necessary but not sufficient to get the job done right. In addition, you'll have to do some talking as well. As a matter of fact, effective counselors are often very active, speaking frequently. They don't just sit and nod occasionally. It is true that sometimes a troubled student needs a period of time to unload, so for a while it might be good to just listen, but increasingly you'll need to respond verbally.

Particularly in a helping situation, the RA should attempt at first to limit many verbal responses to what are called reflective statements. This does not mean, as has been commonly supposed, that the helper simply repeats back like a parrot everything the student says. There's an old story about the troubled person visiting a counselor who is a reflective listener. The person says "I want to talk to you." The counselor replies, "You want to talk to me," and the conversation proceeds something like this:

Client:	I'm very depressed.
Counselor:	You're very depressed.
Client:	I don't know what to do.
Counselor:	You don't know what to do.
Client:	Why are you repeating everything I say?
Counselor:	(pause) You seem upset that I'm repeating everything you say.
Client:	This is maddening. If you don't stop repeating me, I'm going to walk over to that window and throw myself out right now.
Counselor:	If I don't stop repeating everything you say, you intend to walk over to that window and throw yourself out.

At which point the exasperated client walks over to the window and throws himself out.

Our reflective listener wasn't very helpful in this case!

Well, it's a rather sick joke, but it illustrates that effective reflective listening doesn't mean just parroting exactly what is being said. It does mean trying to summarize clearly and specifically what the student is saying and particularly what the student is feeling. For example, let's say a student comes to you and says something like "I'm at the end of my rope. My roommate keeps playing loud music until two or three in the morning—the room is always crowded with *his* friends—he doesn't listen whenever I try to talk about what I'm interested in. He's out for no one but himself."

To make a reflective response, you don't have to repeat everything. If you simply said "You sound really angry and exasperated with your roommate because it seems to you that he's damn inconsiderate and selfish," you'd be close to what was being expressed directly.

Let's look at this example a little more closely. It's possible you may feel that there are other feelings or themes going on which the student was not aware of when he made his statements. For example, you might detect jealousy, as well as fear of asserting oneself. Our experience suggests that it's usually not a good idea to reflect these deeper feelings too early—the student may not be ready to hear them until more trust develops between both of you. It's best at first to provide reflections that the student can readily confirm as a good reflection of exactly what was meant. Later, particularly as you sense the student is ready, you can use deeper level reflections more effectively.

By the way, accurate reflections are not as easy to pull off as you might think. It takes a lot of practice. In fact, to really be good at it takes much more practice than we can afford to give in this training. In the sessions where you'll practice reflecting, we hope you'll be impressed enough by the usefulness of reflective listening to be moved to continue to practice your skill at it.

Practicing reflective statements sometimes seems boring to beginning RAs, and you too might get frustrated when we have you do things like go over and over an accurate reflection to a statement. It won't seem real to you, and not at all your idea of what human interaction should be. To me, it's like an orchestra rehearsing a symphony. The director may stop the players many times and have them go over and over certain key passages until they get it right. Anyone listening in on the repetitions of these passages might get bored and even ask "Is this music—is this a symphony?" Of course, by themselves the passages don't necessarily amount to much, but when strung together beautifully within the context of the whole work, they become the symphony.

Similarly, reflective statements, within the context of a helping relationship, become very important helping tools.

Before we turn to the skill of concreteness, I'd like to make a few more random observations about reflective listening. For one thing, you'll be more skillful if you speak on a level similar to that of the other person. What this means is that you talk naturally and don't use psychological jargon and unnecessary intellectual words. At the same time, however, please don't abuse this rule of speaking at the same level by trying to talk an unnatural way. If you're a white middle-class person and your student is a black from an inner-city ghetto, you're pushing my advice too far if you try to talk ghetto talk; the fact is, you'll be picked up as a phony very fast if you do.

It's usually a good idea, again, to the extent that it isn't phony, to respond to a student in a feeling tone similar to his or hers. For example, let's say a female student rushes in and says in an excited joyful voice, "Gee, he finally asked me out. I can't believe it, I'm so happy I could burst," and you respond with a flat and expressionless "that's nice." Well, what a let down! Conversely, if a student comes to you in tears, although you may not be moved to cry too (sometimes you might), you can at least convey your caring by showing a measure of that sadness in your own voice.

A final thought on reflective listening. When you attempt to give a person a good reflective statement, you are really doing two things at once. First, you're conveying your understanding. But you're also finding out if your perceptions are indeed accurate.

We all know how complicated communication can be as witnessed by the fact that the same word, say "love," can mean different things to different people. So when I reflect what you say to me, part of what I'm doing is showing you my authentic desire to understand you accurately. Yet, although I work at becoming skilled at making accurate reflections, I don't want to become so concerned about being right that I remain mute until I'm sure I can reflect perfectly what you say to me. For example, a student complaining to me about a roommate seems to be very angry at his roommate. I make a reflective statement to this effect, and the student replies "No, I'm not angry at my roommate, I'm angry and ashamed at myself, for being so wishy-washy around my roommate." Now, in this example my reflection wasn't strictly accurate. It would have been nice if it were. The more accurate I could have been, the better chance that the student would gain confidence in me. Yet a bit of inaccuracy isn't necessarily a disaster. If the student is picking up genuine concern, in most cases he or she is quite capable and willing to clear up my confusion.

Now, let's discuss *concreteness*. Concreteness is the ability to enable the student you are interacting with to be specific about the feelings and experiences about which she or he is talking. People often talk about their experiences in vague, abstract terms, like "life is a drag," "I'm bummed out," or "I can't get it together." The problem with such statements is that they give us very little information to work with. We need to know more about what is meant by a drag or bummed out. What specifically is going on (or not going on) in the person's life that causes or adds to these feelings? Only when a person can look at these specifics can he or she find something to work on. So if Jane says that she can't get it together, we can use concreteness skills to clarify what she means by that, and in doing so we may find out that she is having difficulty making friends, or studying, or relating to her parents, and then we have something to work with.

Now, before we get to the skill of concreteness, just a few more thoughts to put this dimension into perspective. We're not saying that abstractions are always unhelpful. We all need abstraction to make sense out of life, to place our experiences within some context. There is a danger of getting lost in abstractions and losing sight of our really concrete experiences, but there is also the danger of staying so concrete that we get lost in the minutiae of our experiences, unable to make any sense out of them. Sometimes by gaining insight into the concrete aspects of our lives we can formulate more helpful "abstractions" to make better sense of it all.

And it is an abuse of our concept of concreteness to confuse concreteness with too much detail. Sometimes students, far from being too abstract, will come in and start storytelling, giving painfully detailed descriptions of what they did and said all week. Listening to students, one finds it hard to sort out what's important and what isn't. Being concrete is not a quantitative thing. It doesn't mean being able to give out all the details. What it does mean is being able to relate the most salient and meaningful aspects of an experience.

There are three ways of demonstrating the skill of concreteness. The first is for the RA to act as an example by being concrete in personal reflections. Your own reflective statements are going to be most effective if they are concise summaries of what the student is saying. Often what you're doing is helping the student *label* his or her experience. An example from psychotherapy is instructive at this point. Occasionally, some clients in psychotherapy experience anger, but because of all kinds of repressions going back to childhood, they can't recognize that what they are experiencing is anger. The therapist, in a respectful and caring way, helps the client label these emotions as anger and thereby learn that getting angry is a normal human experience. What psychologists often find is that our ability to label our feelings accurately can help us deal with our feelings more easily.

Of course, there's a limit to how accurately words, which are themselves abstractions, can ever truly label feelings. But we can find words that come closer to the mark, so that even what we label "anger" can be pinpointed more concretely. You'll see what I mean by referring to our Vocabulary of Affective Adjectives in our Training Program Aid E of the manual; it will help you understand how many ways we can talk about, for example, being angry.

The second aspect of the skill of concreteness involves encouraging the student to concentrate on specific instances and details of a problem. You can do this by timing your reflective statements to reinforce concreteness—that is, when the student is moving toward talking about specifics, you can become more active and attentive in your reflections, thus encouraging the student to elaborate.

But what if the student continues to talk very abstractly, and you find that no amount of reflecting back what is being said or felt is helping the student become more concrete? We must speak now about the third aspect of the skill of concreteness: the *discrete* use of questioning.

If you're trying to find out something about another person, asking questions seems to be a natural and direct means of doing so. And indeed, many beginning RAs try to get information by asking a lot of questions. But the first danger of asking questions is that after a while students, rather than taking responsibility for their own explanations, may become less active because all they have to do is *react* to your questions. This can put you in the position of doing all the work, and after a while, RAs who communicate by asking a lot of questions sometimes begin to feel like they're on fishing expeditions, trying very hard to ask just the right questions but often finding that one question leads to another, and another, and another.

A second danger of questioning is that the questions themselves, if not skillfully applied, can determine the subject matter of what's being talked about. If a student mentions she's lonely, I might get curious and begin asking questions about her dating life (maybe because I make the assumption that if she's lonely, it's probably because she's not going out). We can then spend a lot of time with me asking and her answering questions about dating. In short, my questions keep us on the subject of dating. This might be all well and good if my assumption about dating is correct, but what if it isn't? What if what the student means by loneliness is more her relationships with her roommates, classmates, or parents—with her lack of friendships? What if underneath her loneliness are issues about shyness, lack of confidence, difficulty with asserting herself, difficulty with expressing her needs, fear of being disliked, and so on? My well-intentioned questions about dating have actually taken us further and further away from these issues.

Questioning is such a natural thing to do that it's hard for beginning RAs to realize that you can sometimes learn more about a person by reflective listening than by questioning. You might want to try an experiment. Get hold of a friend this week with the intention of learning something new about him or her. Let's say you know very little about your friend's family and want to know more. Now make a rule: You're going to try to learn as much as you can without asking questions, or at least, limiting questions to those moments when a question seems like the only way of keeping the conversation going. Instead of questioning, you're going to try to concentrate on making reflective statements. My suggestion may be a little unfair because you haven't yet been trained in this program to be very skilled at reflective statements, but I'm guessing that you'll still be surprised to learn how much information you can get from a person by simply sharing your respectful, attentive, and active caring. Try it!

Does all this mean that questions are a no-no? Well, remember that a short while ago I said that one of the skills involved in concreteness is the discrete use of questions. A well-timed question, which is based on some understanding through reflective listening, can sometimes be very helpful.

Getting back to the girl who was lonely: If I hold back in my assumption that dating is the problem and use my active listening skills, I might get a better idea of what's really going on. Then, if a question seems like an appropriate and helpful way of getting deeper, I might use a question now, but this time the question, based more on my understanding and less on vague assumptions, might lead us into more relevant material. I'll then find that when the student answers my question, I'll continue to be helpful if, rather than following up immediately with another question, I instead use reflective responses aimed at her response to my question.

The way you word your questions can be very important in minimizing the danger of restricting the subject matter of what is being talked about. Questions can be thought of as close-ended or open-ended. A close-ended question essentially calls for a yes or no response. So let's say, with our lonely student, that I ask the question "Do you get along well with your roommate?" Such a question calls for a yes or no, and that's all the information I might get, and in answering yes or no, the student may not be encouraged to clarify further her feelings about her roommate. On the other hand, open-ended questions are worded so that they free the student to explore, sometimes in directions you might not expect. Using this notion, I might rephrase my question about her roommate to something like: "Could you tell me more about your relationship with your roommate" or "How do you feel when you are with your roommate"? These are open-ended questions because they give the student an opportunity to talk about any aspect of her relationship that seems important to her. In some of your regular small group sessions in the coming weeks, your instructor will help you practice the discreet use of questions as well as the other skills in helping someone become more concrete.

Before we go on to the self-disclosure skills, this is a good time to talk about respect, a quality that underlies all the skills we'll be teaching you. Respect is an accepting, nonjudgmental, and tolerant attitude toward another person. Picture yourself about to talk to someone about a problem. Let's say you don't know this person very well, but you feel you need help. You've done something that you're ashamed of and you know a lot of people would frown on. You're naturally concerned that the person you're seeking help from will also disapprove of you. And indeed, let's say that your fears turn out to be true: This person conveys a lot of disapproval and says, in effect, "you ought to be ashamed of yourself." Now try to imagine how you would feel continuing to talk to this person about your problem. Do you see how difficult it would be to remain open, nondefensive, and trusting? Instead, the chances are that you would feel ashamed, or angry, or hurt—and unwilling to dig deeper into your problems.

Let's take the same situation, but this time with a different helper. You begin to talk about your problem, and immediately you're relieved to see that the person isn't jumping down your throat. In fact, the person isn't making any judgments at all about what you did. It's not that she or he is approving your actions, it just seems that the person seems genuinely interested in you—all of you. Your helper is not reducing you down to a few behaviors you happen to be ashamed of. My guess is that in this case you'll begin to feel more relaxed and trusting. Why? Because this helper has conveyed respect.

Your ability to convey respect starts with your own willingness to suspend critical judgment about what a student is telling you. A man named Erik Erikson (1963) can give us some perspective here. Erikson wrote about the various stages of development we all go through from birth to death. According to Erikson, people during their late teens, in other words, people of college age, are going through a stage called the crisis of identity. They're trying to find out who they are, to develop a coherent picture of themselves. And it's pretty common for people who're attempting to define a suitable identity to get pretty confused at times about what they're really like. So as part of their search, they're likely to try out different roles. You know: The tough-guy role, the sweet little thing, the romeo, the great seductress, the serious scholar, and on and on.

Erikson's thinking helps put respect into perspective because when students are telling you about themselves, it's important to remember not to confuse their roles and behaviors with any real fully developed identity. Fortunately, most of you are nearly the same age as the students you're working with, and I'll guess that you all can identify some roles you've tried on over the last few years that you wouldn't want to be fully identified with by anybody.

Keying into your own experience, therefore, can help you convey respect. Practically speaking, respect is conveyed in three ways, by avoiding evaluative, judgmental statements; communicating in warm, caring tones; and practicing nonverbal responding and reflective listening because these skills contain all the key elements of genuine respect.

Self-Disclosure. Please note that the responding skills we've dealt with thus far have all been student-centered—that is, the skills of nonverbal attending, reflective listening, and concreteness all center on what's going on with the student. They all involve paying a lot of attention to that other person. The next group of skills I want to discuss with you involves bringing more of yourself into the atmosphere. They involve being genuine by using your own feelings and attitudes, which is why we call them *self-disclosure* skills. Generally, these skills are best timed if they begin to appear later in our interactions, after the use of the responsive skills have established feelings of trust and caring, or of what some people call rapport.

Being genuine means being real. As you have been actively listening to another person, that person's story will cause you to have *feelings*. The skill of self-disclosure of feelings is sharing your feelings with another in a manner that will enhance that person's self-exploration. Sometimes such expressions can help confirm and support the student. For example, if a student has been expressing anger at being treated badly by someone, you may find that you also feel some anger. Then you can self-disclose by saying something like "I can appreciate what you're feeling, because when I get treated like that, I get pretty angry too. In fact, I can feel my anger right now just thinking about it." Sometimes genuineness can help the student become aware of other feelings that are important but not in the foreground of his or her experience. You can say something like "I can appreciate your getting angry, yet as you're telling me about it, I also feel sad. I can just picture how alone you must feel sometimes, and that makes me feel sad. I wonder if you feel some of this sadness too."

The skill of self-disclosing feelings is useful when it addresses what is actually going on in the here and now between you and another person. You can use such self-disclosure when you sense that there is something going on right now in the immediate situation which is interfering. Let's say you've been talking with someone who has seemed very involved and open but who for the past ten minutes has turned off. This is both frustrating and confusing you. A genuine response at this moment might be to say "Right now I'm feeling a bit confused and frustrated. When we started talking you seemed so involved, but for the past ten minutes I've noticed you looking out the window and fidgeting in your chair. I'm afraid I may have said something that turned you off. Would you share what's happening with you right now?"

Your open-ended question gives the student the opportunity to talk about what's going on, and the genuineness of your self-disclosure may encourage the student to be equally genuine in return. You may learn that you did indeed do something which bothered the student, and now you can talk about it and hopefully clear it up. Or you might learn that the student suddenly remembered that she or he was supposed to meet a friend ten minutes ago and was sitting there wondering whether to bring this up.

The next skill, self-disclosure of *experience*, is really a special kind of genuineness. In the examples just cited, I was disclosing something of myself when I shared my own feelings of anger or sadness. Self-disclosure of experience is a little more elaborate; it involves telling another person about your own past experiences that seem to resemble what the person has been talking about. For example, you're practicing such self-disclosure when you say something like "I think I can understand how you feel, because I've had some experiences like yours" and then proceed to actually tell about your experience.

Self-disclosure of experiences can be a very potent tool for establishing trust and helping someone feel understood and appreciated. *But,* there is a danger here: Self-disclosure can be a double-edged sword, sometimes causing more harm than good. Let's suppose I'm talking to a student who seems angry with his mother. Ideally, I should use my active listening skills to appreciate the extent and intensity of the anger. However, suppose I'm anxious to let the student know that I care. Without knowing too much about the student's experience, I begin to self-disclose by telling the student about some incidents when I was ticked off at my mother. If my experiences with my own mother were like the student's experiences, my disclosure could be helpful. But what if I'm dealing with someone who is much more continuously enraged and angry than I have been, who has had many hurtful experiences with his mother that are very different from my own? In this case, my self-disclosure, far from making the student feel understood, may actually make him feel more alone and misunderstood.

Let me give you another example from my own experience as a young counselor. I'm a little embarrassed to tell you this, but I think that the story perfectly illustrates the danger of inappropriate self-disclosure. A teenaged boy told me in a counseling session that he was very ashamed that he masturbated. He seemed so tense and afraid while telling me this that I felt sorry for him. So, without attempting by active listening to explore his issues, I broke right into a self-disclosure. I said "Gee, I hope you know that you're not the only person of your age who masturbates, I mean, heck, when I was your age I used to masturbate too—sometimes several times a week." When I shut up, the boy was looking even more forlorn. He wouldn't look me in the eye, and he hardly said another word. Fortunately, I got to see him again, and eventually he began to trust me. I learned that he was masturbating ten to twenty times a day, that he was ashamed and terrified of always living in "mortal sin," and that when I had given him my self-disclosure, he had reacted not by feeling understood but by feeling like a freak.

Mistakes can be undone if there are time and opportunity, and in my case we were eventually able to establish a good helping relationship, but I think the story illustrates that self-disclosing experiences is helpful only to the extent that our own experience *authentically* parallels the other person's experience; we need to know more concretely both what that experience is and the kind and extent of the person's feelings. When we use such self-disclosure, we must not only be aware of timing, but we must be *authentic,* by sharing *real* experiences.

The skills we've been discussing today have been found very useful in situations where you are called on to counsel or help students. During the next several weeks we'll practice and elaborate these skills. Once the entire training program involved teaching you these helping skills, but more and more, largely because of feedback from many of our former students, we've realized that counseling is only one part of your job involving your use of inter-personal skills. Other aspects of your job involve a much more active posture than that of responding to a student coming to you for help. You will sometimes need to inject yourself into situations where no one is asking for help but where you anticipate problems developing unless they're nipped in the bud. After you've had a chance to practice the skills we talked about today, we'll start a new section of the course devoted to initiation skills, designed for situations where you take the initiative to bring about a desired result.

But for now, good luck in learning more about responding and self-disclosure. We're convinced that these skills will help you not only in counseling situations but will go beyond counseling. They are interpersonal skills that will serve you well in your friendships and love affairs and in dealing with teachers, bosses, parents, and supervisors.

Initiating Skills

Rather than introducing the initiating skills to participants in a big block of time, as we did with the preceding skills, we generally take a smaller block of time in small group sessions to elaborate these skills. We teach, and have our students practice, the two initiating skills of confrontation and summarizing. We stress that these skills are useful in the (1) counseling situation, particularly during the stage of action planning, but sometimes in the stage of deeper understanding, and in the (2) various noncounseling situations RAs face.

Confrontation is asking a person to examine inconsistencies among thoughts, feeling, and behaviors. There may be a discrepancy between what the person says and what the person does. Or the person may describe conflicting feelings in the same situation. Or the person says one thing but does another. Any of these inconsistencies must be examined more carefully by the person for greater self-understanding to occur.

The problem is just how to approach a person's inconsistencies. Both RAs and students too often consider confrontation attacking, intimidating, and hostile behavior. So the first step in teaching RAs effective confrontation skills is to reorient their thinking about confrontation from a negative to a positive concept. As Egan pointed out, confrontation can be better viewed as an invitation, "anything that invites a person to examine his or her interpersonal style—emotions, experiences, and behaviors, and its consequences (for instance, how it affects others) more carefully" (Egan, 1977, p. 211).

Confrontation is perceived as an invitation to examine one's interpersonal style if certain conditions are present. First, confrontation is most effective if the parties have had the time to develop a trusting and respectful relationship. It should naturally follow a period of reflective listening and appropriate self-disclosure by the RA. It is most effective when it is nonjudgmental and focuses on the effect of the discrepancy.

For example, suppose a student comes to the RA and says, "Everytime I go out with Sally, I come home feeling just awful. She pays little attention to me, and spends most of her time trying to attract other guys. She doesn't respond to my overtures of affection, and only goes out with me when she can't find anyone else. Although I like her a lot, and enjoy being in her company when no one else is around, I usually come home from a date with her feeling frustrated, angry, and hurt. I just don't know what to do."

Assuming that the RA has a good past relationship with this person and that the RA has done some good reflective listening and appropriate self-disclosure, the RA might move to a confrontation intervention the following way: "On the one hand, you say you care for this person, and in some very few instances you enjoy being with her. On the other hand, for the most part you come home from being with her feeling frustrated, angry, and hurt. I

hear a conflict between two sets of feelings you experience when
you're with her. Maybe you've got to decide which is more important: the pleasurable feelings you experience when you're alone
with her, or the unpleasant feelings you have when you're with
other people."

In this instance, the RA described the discrepancy between
two sets of feelings toward the same person. The RA accurately
reflected both sides of feelings and pointed out the inconsistency
between them in a respectful, nonjudgmental way. Also, the RA
suggested that the person is going to have to decide which sets of
feelings are more important and determine the future of the relationship on that basis. The person may not decide what to do about
the relationship, but the key to helping the student reach this point
was the confrontation by the RA over conflicting feelings.

Summarizing is the skill of tying together several statements
of thoughts and feelings and establishing themes and relationships
among them. It is often used at the student's point of decision
making and typically involves laying out alternatives and discussing
the pros and cons for each one. Again, it should follow a period of
active listening and appropriate self-disclosure by the RA, and only
after the student has had a full opportunity to explore the problem.

To continue with the example of the student who has conflicting feelings about his relationship with his girl friend, the RA
might use the following summarizing statement: "It seems to me
you have basically three choices. You can continue the relationship
as it is, and live with the conflicting feelings you have. Or you can
end the relationship because the unpleasant feelings outweigh the
pleasant feelings, and end your conflicting feelings. Or you can try
to change the relationship by sharing your dilemma with her, and
work toward a relationship that is more satisfying to you."

In this example, the RA summarized the alternatives available to the student and stated the consequences of each alternative.
This summarization now allows the student to more fully explore
each alternative and decide which is best. Before moving on, however, the RA may ask the student if there are other alternatives that
should be identified and explored because the RA may have overlooked some in the summary. In other words, summaries should be
checked out for completeness, clarity, and accuracy.

It is very important to keep summarizing strictly to the facts in the case. RAs are frequently tempted to try their hand at interpreting, or "psychologizing." RAs are not qualified to practice such skills, nor can they be trained in the time available to do so. If the RA cannot help the person by summarizing the alternatives and exploring their pros and cons, the RA should make a referral to persons who are qualified to interpret behavior.

6

⎍⎍⎍⎍⎍⎍⎍⎍⎍⎍⎍⎍⎍⎍⎍⎍⎍⎍⎍⎍⎍⎍⎍⎍⎍⎍⎍⎍⎍⎍⎍⎍

Defining
Leadership Roles
of Resident Assistants

Resident assistants must not only deal with the individuals on their floors but with groups. Of the RA's six functions identified in Chapter One, four (managing and facilitating groups; explaining and enforcing rules; facilitating social, recreational, and educational programs; developing an orderly and quiet atmosphere) require that RAs lead and work with groups of students on their floors.

It has been our experience that leading and working with groups is the least developed skill of typical RAs, for several reasons. First, they have had much more experience dealing with individuals and therefore feel more comfortable and skillful in that context. Second, although they may have been in group leadership positions prior to becoming resident assistants, the carryover is limited. That is, the RA position, with its diverse roles, institutional authority, and accountability, is quite different from being the president of the chess club. Likewise, the chess club is vastly different from a residence hall floor as to purposes, commonality, activities, and dynamics. So neither the prior leadership roles nor prior groups are comparable. Thus RAs need to know a lot more about how to lead and work with groups within the context of their position, the groups on their floors, and the situations they face.

This chapter is a brief overview of leadership development and elaborates our eclectic model of resident assistant leadership. We start from the assumption that RAs have a basic self-awareness and interpersonal skill level that provide a solid foundation for effective leadership. But leadership on a residence hall floor also requires RAs to know and understand their role and the influence and limitations of the position. Furthermore, RAs must know about the students on their floors, both their personal, demographic, and residential characteristics and their group dynamics. Finally, RAs must apply a wide variety of leadership styles, depending on the situation and the maturity level of the floor.

Over the years, the quest to define what makes a leader successful has been long and, until recently, somewhat unfruitful. Early attempts focused on leaders' traits or characteristics. This approach assumed that components of effective leadership were consistent and applied in all leadership situations for all leadership positions. However, when Bird (1940) tested this approach by reviewing studies which compared the traits of leaders to those of nonleaders, he found that only 5 percent of the traits listed appeared in four or more studies. This failure to identify universal characteristics of leaders led researchers, according to Napier and Gershenfeld (1973), to look at other aspects of leadership, including leadership as (1) positional, (2) situational, and (3) functional roles of group members.

Most current leadership definitions focus on these or other aspects of leadership. McGregor (1960) identified four major variables involved in leadership: (1) the characteristics of the leader; (2) the characteristics of the followers; (3) the purposes, structures, and tasks of the organization; and (4) the social, economic, and political milieu. Tannenbaum, Weschler, and Massarik (1961) described leadership as ". . . interpersonal influence, exercised in situation and directed, through the communication process, toward the attainment of specified goal or goals" (p. 24).

Our own eclectic model of leadership development takes into account leadership-development concepts as studied within other organizational contexts and applies them to the RA's leadership demands. We think RA group leadership development depends on four variables: (1) the RA's interpersonal skill; (2) the RA's position, as defined by the institution; (3) floor members' characteristics and attitudes and how they interact with one another; (4) the situations RAs must face and deal with. RAs then decide which leadership styles to apply, given their assessment of these variables. In our experience, this approach makes the most sense to RAs and has helped them define their leadership role on their floors.

The RA's Interpersonal Skill

Our whole approach to this training program assumes that RAs must have effective interpersonal skills to be successful. All the one-to-one skills we identified in Chapter Five apply to the RA's group leadership role. RAs must be attentive to group nonverbal behavior, listen to the content and feeling of group members' messages, and disclose appropriate thoughts and feelings. They must also initiate behavior, summarize what took place, confront discrepancies in the group's messages and behaviors, and lay out alternatives. All the skills necessary for one-to-one effectiveness are absolutely necessary for group effectiveness, but in and of themselves they are not enough: Many RAs who can very effectively deal with individuals fail in group settings.

RAs who are skillful in one-to-one situations may fall apart in group leadership situations for several reasons. First, at least initially, many RAs are more anxious in a group leadership setting, particularly if they have not had much experience. This anxiety may affect their ability to listen and communicate. Second, instead of just one person's thoughts, feelings, and reactions to keep track of, there are several, which is much more difficult. Third, groups develop dynamics of their own, somewhat independent of the individuals within the groups. For example, groups develop communication patterns, power and influence dimensions, norms and values, and other dynamics that affect individuals' behavior, and RAs must keep track of them.

But most importantly, RAs must exercise certain skills in a group setting, if they are to be effective. They must know when to intervene in a group interaction and when to hold back. They must be able to make the group aware of their own dynamics, when doing so will help the group. RAs must be able to suggest strategies to groups to move them along toward their goals. They must be able to mediate conflicts in a group and help groups develop skills, such as feedback, that create better communication among group members. In short, RAs must apply what they know about how to deal with individuals to groups of individuals.

The RA's Position

As we have stressed over and over, the RA position is unique, quite unlike any other position that a student has filled previously or will fill in the future. Also, most likely neophyte RAs are in this position of great responsibility for the first time. Thus it is important that RAs understand the potential and limitations of their positions when leading and working with groups.

Positions grant leaders authority or influence over others. In the RA position, there are times when RAs exercise either authority or influence or maybe both. Many previously mediocre leaders become effective when placed in a position that "fits." And some persons with good skills, high motivation, and good intentions fail in the RA job because they cannot handle the demands of the position. In a sense, the position itself offers the person an opportunity to lead, somewhat independent of that person's skills, characteristics, and abilities. RAs must understand the several sources of their influence, many of which are inherent in the position they occupy. French and Raven (1960) identified five sources of leadership power, which we think apply quite well to the RA position:

1. *Referent power.* RAs influence because of who they are as people. RAs can influence a floor by modeling appropriate behavior. Floor members then emulate and identify with the RA, behaving in specified ways.
2. *Legitimate power.* RAs influence because of the positions they hold. RAs influence the behavior of floor members by the authority given them by the institution. They are given the right to make certain decisions because of the position they hold.
3. *Expert power.* RAs influence floor behavior because of what they know and how interpersonally skillful they are.
4. *Reward power.* RAs influence a floor because of what they can positively reinforce. They have the ability to offer rewards and approval, although this power is limited in the residence hall setting. Generally, RAs' power to offer approval is more influential than their power to reward because RAs have little to offer in the way of rewards.
5. *Coercive power.* RAs can influence a floor because of their ability to punish members of the floor or the whole floor itself. The power to refer persons for disciplinary action is the most typical example of the coercive power of the RA. It is typically used as a last resort or in situations where the institution has not given the RA any choice in the matter.

RAs must understand the expectations, potential, and limitations of their positions, as defined by the institution. They must be comfortable in the position and know and understand the basis for the exercise of their power and influence within the position. Effective RAs combine their skills and abilities with their sources of power. For example, some RAs may be effective modelers, whereas others may rely more on their interpersonal skills or expertise. It is the RAs' responsibilities to know the position they occupy and how their skills and abilities fit with it, to lead and work with a residence hall floor.

Floor Members' Demographic and
Personal Characteristics and Group Dynamics

Most RAs will establish a very high priority for getting to know the students on their floors. Most often this means getting to know individuals one-to-one. But RAs also need to know their floors as collective units, or groups, to provide effective leadership. Our experience showed that RAs seldom do this in any routine or organized way, and their leadership suffers as a result. We think that RAs should view their floors by learning about (1) the collective characteristics and attitudes of their floors and (2) how individuals interact with one another (the floor's group dynamics). The first factor is essential to the second, and both are essential if RAs are to lead and work with their floors.

In many ways, a residence hall floor is a unique group, not typical of the groups discussed in books on group dynamics and organizational development. It is *not* a formal organization with a defined structure, defined roles, and specific tasks. It does *not* have a formal leader with defined functions, in the traditional, organizational sense. It is a temporary group, with a constantly changing membership. But most important, members do not share a common purpose for being there and may have very little in common with one another.

A look at a typical residence hall floor reveals almost as many purposes for living there as there are persons on that floor. Some students are there because they were forced by institutional residency requirements. For others, the floor is strictly a place to eat and sleep—a matter of personal convenience. Some students live in halls because it meets their social and affiliative needs; some see the floor as a place to relax and play, and others want a quiet place to study. There may even be a few students who see the floor as a place to learn more about themselves and to get along with others.

Commonality may also be a problem. Students on the same floor may vary according to class standing, personality, maturity, sex, age, prior experiences, socioeconomic class, cultural background, intelligence, interests, interpersonal skills, self-awareness, and other variables. But somehow they must coexist with one another, regardless of the lack of purpose in being there and commonality among them. It is the RA's job to help the students not only peacefully coexist but develop a positive living environment that helps each person accomplish educational and personal goals.

How does an RA learn more about the individual and collective characteristics of a residence hall floor? First and foremost, the RA must be committed to such a quest and get it done very quickly at the beginning of the year. Although most RAs have a very high priority for "getting to know the students on my floor," many do not know what they are looking for. So their first step should be collecting important information about floor members and looking at that information collectively. Here are the variables we suggest RAs look for as they get to know the floor: (1) demographic variables—age, race, sex, class standing, declared major, probable career, religious preference, type of hometown (urban, suburban, rural), prior noneducational experiences, parents' occupations, disabilities (if any), cultural background; (2) personal variables—reasons for attending college and selecting career and/or major; hobbies; cultural, recreational, and intellectual interests; (3) residential variables—reasons for living in halls; interest in and preference for floor activities; expectations of the floor, the RA, the RA role, and the roommate relationship; tolerance for noise.

Other variables may be added to suit the needs of a particular institution, but the important thing is for RAs to collect this information formally, such as by the use of personnel cards given directly to students, or informally, such as through conversations with students, or both, and then study the implications of the data. Getting a sense of the floor's collective characteristics not only helps the RA's individual interactions but gives the RA vital information about the leadership issue. Our experience has been that commonalities will develop that were not apparent at first glance, and there may be more universality of purpose than previously assumed.

We have found the Floor Characteristics Assessment format shown on pages 122–123 useful for collecting demographic, personal, and residential information about students on a floor.

Knowing the floor's collective characteristics is only half the story; how students on the floor interact with one another is the other half, and RAs must be thoroughly aware of the floor's interactive dynamics if they are to provide effective leadership. Here traditional models of group-process analysis are particularly helpful, including field theory (Lewin, 1951), interaction-process analysis (Bales, 150), systems theory (Homans, 1960; Newcomb, 1962; Simon, 1962), sociometric theory (Moreno, 1953), and psychoanalytic theory (Bion, 1961). However, we have never found any one theory completely applicable to studying the interactions of a residence hall floor. Some of these theories are too advanced for some RAs to understand and use, particularly those whose academic experiences do not include social psychology or sociology.

Over the years, we developed an eclectic model of looking at the interactive dynamics of a residence hall floor. It is a somewhat oversimplified model, but it seems to work with RAs. The model may be presented as a series of questions for RAs to answer, based on their observations and analysis of their floors.

1. *What are the floor's subgroups?* Rarely is a residence hall floor so small or so homogeneous that no subgroups form. Sometimes subgroups are determined by friendships, needs, or interests. Sometimes they form because of shared antipathy to other subgroups, and sometimes the physical arrangements of the floor create them. Subgroups may change within the floor in relation to new tasks, needs, or interests; friendship patterns may change as well. Other subgroups may form on the basis of common ethnic or racial backgrounds. The RA must know what subgroups exist, on what basis they are formed, how they relate to one another, and how to handle any conflicts between them that may develop.

2. *What is the floor's general tone or atmosphere?* RAs describe their floors in a variety of ways: "My floor is really tight," or "Women on my floor are pretty much isolated from one another, and it's difficult to get anything going." There are study floors and party floors. The atmosphere of a floor refers to the degree of informality, freedom, and cohesion that exists among members. The RA must identify the tone of a floor and determine the basis for that tone.

3. *What are the floor's communication patterns?* RAs must know who

Floor Characteristics Assessment

RESIDENCE HALL FLOOR PROFILE   Building _____

Instructions: Please fill out the
following information about yourself   Floor _____
so your resident assistant can get a
better sense of the collective   RA _____
characteristics of your floor and thus
provide better services and programs   Date _____
for you.

1. Age: ____ Under 18 ____ 18 ____ 19 ____ 20 ____ 21 ____ Over 21
2. Race: ____ Caucasian ____ Black ____ Hispanic ____ Oriental ____ Native
                                                                        American
         ____ International ____ Other _____
3. Class Standing: ____ Freshman ____ Sophomore ____ Junior ____ Senior
                   ____ Grad
4. Declared Major: _____
5. College of Enrollment _____
6. Career Goal _____
7. Religious   ____ Roman Catholic ____ Jewish ____ None
   Preference: ____ Protestant: Please identify denomination _____
                    ____ Other: Please specify _____
8. Type of Hometown: ____ Rural ____ Urban ____ Suburban
9. Parents' Occupation: Mother _____ Father _____
10. Status of Parents: ____ Married ____ Divorced ____ Separated
                       ____ Mother deceased ____ Father deceased
11. Parents' Income Level: ____ Under $15,000 ____ $15,000–$25,000
                           ____ $26,000–$35,000 ____ $36,000–$45,000
                           ____ Over $45,000 ____ Don't Know
12. Relationship with Parents: ____ Incompatible
                               ____ Compatible but not close
                               ____ Compatible and close

Comments about Relationship with Parents: _____
_____
_____
_____

13. Siblings: ____ None ____ No. of brothers ____ No. of sisters
14. Reasons for Attending college: ____ To prepare for a vocation
    (check all that apply)   ____ To be a scholar and participate in the
                                           intellectual life of the campus
                                      ____ To enjoy myself and have a good
                                           time
                                      ____ To develop myself as a person
                                      ____ To prepare for graduate school
    ____ Other (please specify) _____
15. Reasons for Living in   ____ Required because I'm a freshman
    Residence Halls: ____ Parents made me
    (check all that apply)   ____ Can't afford to live elsewhere
                             ____ To take advantage of activities and programs
                             ____ To be with my friends
                             ____ To party and have a good time
    ____ Other (please specify) _____

16. General Expectations of the RA: ____ Keep floor quiet and orderly
    (check all that apply)   ____ Provide information
                                       ____ Enforce rules and regulations
                                       ____ Counsel and advise students
                                       ____ Provide educational and recre-
                                       ational programs
                                       ____ Advise and work with floor officers
    ____ Other (please specify) _____

17. Hobbies, Interests, and Activities: _____
    _____
    _____

18. Suggestions for Floor Activities and Programs: _____
    _____
    _____

19. Type of Roommate   ____ Incompatible
    Relationship Established: ____ Compatible but not close
                              ____ Compatible and close
    Comments about Roommate Relationship: _____
    _____
    _____

20. Type of Relationship   ____ Incompatible
    Established with RA: ____ Compatible but not close
                            ____ Compatible and close
    Comments about RA Relationship: _____
    _____
    _____

talks to whom, what they say, and what the effect is. How do RAs *really* know what is going on with their floors? Every RA knows that there are key people in the floor's communication patterns who usually know what is going on. These people become important in getting the word out as well as listening to what is happening. This variable also includes the floor members' skills in communicating with one another, such as clarity of expression, listening skills, and assertiveness. The RA must know what the communication patterns are, who the critical communicators are, and the general skill level of the floor in communicating with each other.

4. *What is the floor's power and influence structure?* The ways floor

members influence one another and the major influencers is very important knowledge to the RA. Stated another way, to influence what is occuring on a floor, who are the key people you need for support? Sometimes these people are formal leaders of the floor, such as the floor officers, and sometimes they are informal leaders with influence because of their status, expertise, or powerful personality. In any event, the RA must know who these people are and the basis for their power and influence.

5. *What are the floor's norms and values?* Every group develops informal rules by which its members are governed, and residence hall floors are no exception. To get into trouble on a floor, how would it be done? On a study-oriented floor, making a lot of noise during quiet hours might be the way. On a very friendly and informal floor, being aloof and distant might be the way. And so on. When norms are violated, there are usually consequences, such as confrontation, isolation, or even physical violence. The RA must know what these informal norms are, what behaviors constitute violations of these norms, and what the punishments for violating the norms are.

6. *How does the floor deal with its problems and conflicts?* Every residence hall floor develops problems and conflicts among its members as a result of daily living together. There are noise problems, personality conflicts, tensions between groups, damage to physical facilities, or chronic alcohol abuse. Sometimes floors ignore a problem, and sometimes they overreact. Sometimes they will deal successfully with a conflict, and sometimes the conflicts remain unresolved, despite efforts to deal with them. The RAs must know how a floor deals with its problems and conflicts and how to help it solve them.

If RAs can gather demographic, personal, and attitudinal data about the students on their floors and correctly observe and analyze their floors' interactive dynamics, they are well on their way to understanding the group with which they work. This in turn helps them provide effective and appropriate leadership to their floors.

Situations RAs Must Face and Deal With

The fourth component of our leadership model is an assessment of the situations in which RAs must provide effective leadership. Situational theory (Barnard, 1938; Cattell, 1951) states that leadership is a function of the situation in which leaders find themselves, rather than what leaders do or the positions they hold. Our own experiences with supervising and training RAs bear out this contention: Some function well in one situation but not in another. An RA having difficulty dealing with the situations presented by one floor may have great success dealing with the situations on another floor.

The problem for RAs is that there is no consistency or predictability in the situations with which they must deal. They literally must be prepared to deal with any and all situations, from life-threatening to the most frivolous. The important principle here is that the type of leadership required is dependent on the *situation,* and before RAs decide how to behave, they must make sure they thoroughly and completely understand the situation. RAs should ask themselves these six key questions before they make decisions about what type of leadership to apply:

1. *Do I have all facts I need?* Have I taken advantage of all possible sources of information?
2. *Do I have a conceptual understanding of the situation?* Are there several ways to organize the facts; if so, which one makes the most sense?
3. *Do others confirm my perception of the situation?* Have I checked out my perceptions with others who would be in a position to know the situation as well as I do? Is there agreement among them?
4. *Have I faced similar situations in the past, and if so, what did I learn?* Have others faced situations like this one? If so, what did they learn?
5. *Who are the people involved in the situation?* What are their characteristics, attitudes, and tendencies in the situation? How well do the people involved know the facts and understand the

situation? How have they behaved in the past in similar situations?

6. *What are my best predictions as to the situation's outcome?* Most situations have several possible outcomes, so what are they in this instance? Which ones can I live with, and which ones are unacceptable?

To review, we think group leadership development depends on four variables: (1) the RA's interpersonal skill; (2) the limits and potentials of the RA position, as defined by the institution; (3) floor members' demographic and personal characteristics and attitudes and their interactive dynamics; and (4) the situations RAs must face and deal with. Based on all these variables, we believe the RA must decide which leadership style to apply, on the assumption that no one style applies in all situations, or with all groups, or in all positions, or with all leaders. Thus, just what various leadership styles are available to the RA?

Leadership Styles

When looking at a given situation, the RA has several leadership-style options. Tannenbaum and Schmidt (1960) developed what has become a classical way of looking at group leadership styles on a continuum ranging from leader to group centered. Figure 1 graphically represents the Tannenbaum-Schmidt model, adapted for a residence hall leadership environment.

RAs must decide which leadership style to use, from RA- to floor centered. Just which style to apply depends on the variables identified and the degree of freedom the institution allows. All RAs operate with some givens established by the institution and about which they have no real choice. For example, if there is a rule that prohibits the use of alcohol in residence halls, and if the penalty for those caught is referral and disciplinary action, there is little point in moving to a floor-centered style of leadership. However, if RAs are given some discretion in enforcing the rule, a floor-centered style may be appropriate.

We have found that RAs consider this way of looking at leadership styles very attractive. The model is understandable and gives

Figure 1. Graphical representation of
the Tannenbaum-Schmidt model.

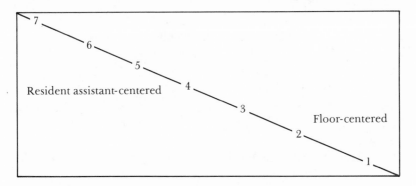

Key: (1) RA decides, announces decision to floor. (2) RA decides, "sells" decision to floor. (3) RA presents decision, invites questions. (4) RA presents tentative decision, invites questions. (4) RA presents tentative decision subject to change, then decides. (5) RA presents problem, gets suggestions, then decides. (6) RA defines boundaries, helps group decide. (7) RA permits floor to function within boundaries defined by institution, group decides.

RAs a great deal of freedom for selecting and choosing appropriate leadership styles as they attempt to lead and work with groups on their floors. But this model does not tell the RA which styles to apply to which situations. Paul Hersey and Kenneth Blanchard developed an approach we found particularly useful for resident assistants making such decisions.

Hersey and Blanchard (1977) agreed that there is no one best style of leadership and that successful leaders adapt their leadership behavior to meet the needs of the group and the situation. In their view, effectiveness depends on the leader, the followers, and situational variables within the environment. They believe that a person's leadership style is a combination of either task behavior or relationship behavior, defined as follows: "Task behavior—the extent to which leaders are likely to organize and define the roles of members of their group (followers); to explain what activities each is to do and when, where and how tasks are to be accomplished; characterized by endeavoring to establish well-defined patterns of organization, channels of communication, and ways of getting jobs accomplished. Relationship behavior — the extent to which leaders are likely to maintain personal relationships between themselves and members of their group (followers) by opening up channels of communication, providing socioemotional support, 'psychological strokes,' and facilitating behaviors" (pp. 104–105).

Hersey and Blanchard combined these two styles on a grid (Figure 2) that helps RAs understand the leadership styles available to them and which style to apply, depending on the maturity level of the followers.

Hersey and Blanchard defined these four leadership styles as:

1. *High task-low relationship leader behavior (S1)*. This style is referred to as "telling" because it is characterized by one-way communication in which the leader defines the followers' roles and tells them what, how, when, and where to do various tasks.
2. *High task-high relationship behavior (S2)*. This style is referred to as "selling" because most of the direction is still provided by the socioemotional support to get the followers psychologically to buy into decisions that have to be made.
3. *High relationship-low task behavior (S3)*. This style is called "participating" because the leader and followers now share in decision making through two-way communication and much facilitating behavior from the leaders since the followers have the ability and knowledge to do the task.
4. *Low relationship-low task behavior (S4)*. This style is labeled "delegating" because it involves letting followers run their own show through delegation and general supervision since the followers are high in both task and psychological maturity (pp. 170–171).

Figure 2. Situational Leadership. Developed by Paul Hersey and
Kenneth H. Blanchard. (© Copyright 1977 by Center for Leadership
Studies. All rights reserved.)

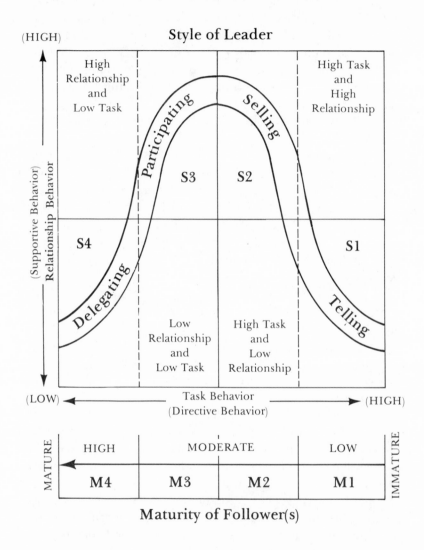

Maturity of Follower(s)

Which leadership style to apply to a given situation depends on the followers' maturity levels. Hersey and Blanchard argued that task-relevant maturity involves two factors: *job maturity*—ability and technical knowledge to do the task, and *psychological maturity*—feeling of self-confidence and self-respect about oneself as an individual. Combining these two dimensions, they developed four levels of maturity: (1) individuals who are neither willing nor able to take responsibility, (2) individuals who are willing but unable to take responsibility, (3) individuals who are able but unwilling to take responsibility, and (4) individuals who are willing and able to take responsibility.

Thus when RAs are faced with a decision about which leadership style to apply, they first determine the level of maturity of the group they are dealing with for the situation they are facing. Then they draw a line from the maturity level to the point at which it intersects with the curve on the grid. For example, suppose a floor has to decide how to maintain a quiet enough atmosphere for studying. It is the RA's judgment, based on the floor's characteristics and dynamics and past experiences with the floor, that the floor could keep a good study atmosphere if it wanted to but just does not want to assume the responsibility. In this instance, the RA might consider applying a participating (high relationship-low task) leadership style, which means raising the issue with the floor, getting communication going among floor members, and helping the floor reach the point where they establish mechanisms for handling quiet hours.

In our experience, this model has proved the easiest and most effective way of teaching resident assistants which leadership styles to apply in which situations. It is *not* an infallible model, and it assumes that the RA can effectively determine the group's maturity level. It also assumes that the RA has the skill to pull off four different leadership styles. Misjudgment about maturity or lack of skill in a particular leadership style will result in ineffective leadership. But among all the models we have tried and looked at, this one has worked best for resident assistants.

7

꜒꜕꜒꜕꜒꜕꜒꜕꜒꜕꜒꜕꜒꜕꜒꜕꜒꜕꜒꜕꜒꜕꜒꜕꜒꜕꜒꜕꜒꜕

Developing Leadership Skills for Difficult Student Problems

Everything we have written so far should give RAs a good basis for dealing with the situations they must handle on the job. If they know and understand student development and have good interpersonal and leadership skills, they are well prepared. But there are three specific situations for which RAs must possess even more knowledge and skill if they are to be handled effectively: crisis intervention, conflict resolution, and discipline. In each instance, RAs need a little more structure and knowledge that have not been included in our training model so far. This chapter focuses on these three situations and offers guidelines for handling them.

Conflict Resolution

RAs must deal with situations in which one or more individuals or groups are in conflict with one another. For example,

RAs are frequently called on to help roommates resolve their differences. Or two groups of students on a floor may need the RA's help to get along with one another. In these situations, RAs must intervene in a way that allows both parties in the conflict to resolve their differences and establish a basis for future interactions.

Unfortunately, simply being interpersonally skillful, knowing students, and knowing groups is not enough. Being a mediator in a conflict situation is a very difficult role, and an RA can end up being seen as ineffective by one or both parties if things go wrong. Even the most skillful RA can mishandle conflict situations by not understanding the nature of the conflict and the role of an effective mediator.

Conflict situations typically arise when two or more individuals or groups disagree about something that significantly affects their lives. Usually the two parties have mutually exclusive wants; that is, if one party is successful in getting what it wants, the other party will be unable to get what it wants. Thus both parties depend on one another and must deal with one another to get what they want. Conflict situations also typically arouse strong feelings in the parties involved. For example, conflicts between roommates can generate strong feelings, disrupt their academic and personal lives, and in general create great distress.

There are many myths about conflict situations. One myth is that all conflicts are bad and should be avoided if possible. The fact is that some conflicts are inevitable, and conflicts become bad only when they are avoided. Another myth is that effective communication resolves all conflicts. Actually, conflict can be very much alive even when the two parties are communicating very effectively with one another. Another myth is that all conflicts are resolvable if the conflicting parties are reasonable. But two parties can be very reasonable and still be in conflict. Yet another myth is that the only way for a conflict to be resolved is for both parties to compromise, or give a little. Compromise is but one of many ways to resolve a conflict. Finally, it is often assumed that both parties are responsible for a conflict, when in fact in some conflict situations one party may be absolutely right and another absolutely wrong.

Our experience has been that untrained RAs believe most of

these myths. Thus RAs need to understand the nature of conflict, the bases for conflicts, and how they, as third-party mediators of conflict, can intervene effectively. They also need to know the many different ways conflicts can be resolved.

Bases for Conflict. One basis for conflict between two parties is a *difference over facts*. That is, the two parties look at the same situation with a different set of facts. They may have incomplete information, or one party may have facts the other does not have. Or they may disagree about the facts of the situation or which ones are relevant.

Another basis for conflict is a *difference over goals*. Although facts and information may be agreed on, the parties may disagree about what is to be accomplished. For example, two groups of students on a residence hall floor may be unable to agree on an acceptable level of noise. The studier's goal may be to reduce the noise level to a point where anyone can study anytime, but the partier's goal may be to have a good time and let off steam, with studying done at the library.

The third basis for conflict is a *difference over methods*. The parties agree on the facts and goals but not on the methods. If the partiers and studiers agree that there should be some noise control, they may disagree about the method. Some may want defined quiet hours, while others may want to simply let people bothered by noise confront those who are making the noise.

A fourth basis for conflicts is a *difference over values*. Fundamental differences over values are the most difficult conflicts to resolve and typically arise in a residence hall situation where residents have cultural, racial, or background differences based on years of conditioning and experience. For example, some ethnic groups have a very high tolerance for noise, while others have a very low tolerance.

Of course, it is possible for some or all of these bases for conflict to be operating in the same situation. So RAs must first determine the bases for the conflict because such information may help them find a resolution of the conflict. Thus the first question RAs should ask themselves when hearing about a conflict situation is, "What is the basis for this conflict? Is it facts, goals, methods, or values, or some or all of these factors?"

Ineffective Ways of Coping with Conflict. Students have many ineffective ways of dealing with conflicts. Some may simply avoid the problem by staying away from situations where conflicts will arise. For example, students having problems with their roommates may spend as little time in their rooms as possible and avoid contact with each other. Others may deny that a conflict exists and cope by giving in every time a conflict occurs. Still other students may appeal to some authority, like the RA, to resolve a conflict. Often students complain about their roommates to the RA and demand that action be taken, without ever having directly discussed their concerns with their roommates. And some students react to conflict situations by getting angry and exploding all over the persons with whom they are in conflict. These confrontations may be angry exchanges of words or even physical violence.

None of these solutions really work because one or both of the parties cannot get what they really want. It has been our experience that confronting a conflict situation directly, person to person and face to face, is the *only* way conflicts get resolved. Sometimes this confrontation can be done by the parties themselves, but sometimes third-party mediation is necessary. Such interactions must allow both parties to freely express their thoughts and feelings and some degree of commitment so an acceptable solution can be worked out.

Possible Outcomes. There are many possible resolutions to conflict situations, a fact that many conflicting parties and neophyte mediators sometimes overlook. According to Blake, Shepard, and Mouton (1964), there are six ways conflicts can be handled. In the *win-lose solution,* one party "wins" all she wanted in the conflict situation, and the other party "loses" everything. For example, roommates are fighting about entertaining guests in their room, and one roommate objects every time the other roommate brings a guest into the room. If the solution is that no guests are allowed, or guests are allowed without restriction, then one roommate clearly wins and the other clearly loses.

In *the do-nothing solution,* neither party does anything, and an unacceptable situation continues. If there is a short time frame involved, parties may be willing to put up with this solution. For example, if roommates feuding over guests know that they will change roommates in three weeks, they may decide to do nothing in the meantime.

In the *someone-else-decides solution,* both parties appeal to an outside authority to solve their conflict. The roommates feuding over guests may approach the RA and demand that he or she decide if guests are allowed, and if so, under what conditions. Sometimes both parties agree in advance to accept this solution; at other times, if one party is not satisfied, it will appeal to the next higher authority.

With *the peaceful coexistence solution,* both parties agree to play down their differences, emphasize their common goals and interests, and live with the situation. The feuding roommates may decide that they share other advantages from living with one another (they have the same major and frequently help each other out with their academic work, for example) that supersede their disagreement about guests. This resolution requires some avoidance of dealing with the guest problem.

The splitting-the-difference solution is probably the most widely used way of handling conflict situations and involves compromise or trading and swapping. In a compromise resolution, both parties agree to budge a little and reduce what they originally wanted for the sake of resolving the conflict. The feuding roommates may agree that guests could be entertained on weekends but not during the week. In trading and swapping, the roommates may decide that the roommate who wants guests anytime can have them, but that roommate must do the other roommate's laundry and clean the room once a week.

In *the mutual problem-solving solution,* both parties agree to explore possible new solutions by engaging in a problem-solving process, such as defining the problem, reviewing the problem, developing alternatives, debating alternatives, searching for solutions, evaluating solutions, and deciding solutions. This resolution requires a high degree of commitment from the conflicting parties, a good third-party mediator to manage the problem-solving process, and much time (Blake, Shepard, and Mouton, 1964).

When RAs are helping students resolve conflicts, they should keep in mind all these possible alternatives. Although win-lose, someone-else-decides, and do-nothing solutions at first glance may seem unproductive, they may be very appropriate in a given situation. For example, if roommates are going to move apart in three weeks, the best solution may be to do nothing. These alternatives should not be rejected just because on the surface they seem like cop-outs.

Most conflict situations that RAs get involved with result in either peaceful coexistence or splitting the difference. Even though mutual problem solving may be an ideal solution, there is typically not enough time, and RAs are seldom skillful enough to manage the process. So RAs typically work toward having the feuding parties minimize their differences and emphasize their commonalities, developing a compromise solution, or arranging a trade-off.

The RA as Mediator. When RAs agree to mediate conflicts, they are entering into a situation fraught with all kinds of difficulties, and they must avoid several pitfalls. If they are not careful, the RAs can end up being hated, distrusted, and disrespected by both sides. If they are good mediators, they can at least bring the feuding parties to the point where they can choose or not choose to resolve their differences and know how to do it. Although each conflict situation is different, the following guidelines help RAs as they mediate conflict situations:

1. *Listen to both parties.* The RA should focus on listening to each party's thoughts and feelings and do much reflective listening. The RA must convince both parties that she or he is a person who understands both sides; the best way to do that is through good reflective listening and good summarizations.
2. *Do not take sides.* The RA should initially suspend all judgment about the conflict and not be seduced into expressing personal opinions too early, particularly if the RA senses that one or both sides have not presented all their thoughts and feelings. The RA should be nonjudgmental, nonevaluative, and as objective as possible.
3. *Define the problem.* After the RA has heard both sides, he or she should help them define the problem. The problem that one or both presented may not be the one that is really bothering them; the RA should help the parties understand the real problem. Part of this definition is to uncover the bases of the problem and help the parties decide if it is a conflict over goals,

methods, values, or facts, or some or all of these factors.

4. *Keep parties talking to one another.* Sometimes the conflicting parties tend to talk to the RA, but not to each other. Although at first it may be necessary for the parties to talk to the RA, the RA should try to move the communication toward each other.

5. *Keep control of the situation.* It is not unusual for one of the parties to try to take control of the mediating situation. The RA should not let that happen, for to be helpful, the RA must establish a good mediating climate, which means playing the game according to the RA's (these) rules.

6. *Spell out alternatives.* When the parties have aired their thoughts and feelings, the RA should spell out the possible solutions to the conflict, including win-lose, do nothing, let someone else decide, peaceful coexistence, splitting the difference, or mutual problem solving. The RA should let the parties mull over and explore the pros and cons of each possible solution.

7. *Let the parties solve their own conflict.* Insofar as possible, the RA should put the burden of resolving the conflict on the parties themselves. The RA should stress that she or he will get involved only if there is an impasse and that she or he does not wish to impose a solution except as a last resort.

8. *Recognize your limitations.* Some parties just will not resolve their differences, regardless of effective communication and good mediation efforts. If the parties cannot agree to a solution, the RA may have to impose one, based on her or his authority as an RA. That could involve one party winning and one party losing. It could also involve doing nothing, on the theory that unless the parties get serious about resolving their differences, they can live with their conflict until it gets better, or worse. If it gets worse, they may have a higher motivation to consider other resolutions.

RAs must be able to help students and groups of students resolve their differences. Our experience has been that if RAs follow these basic guidelines, they will be in a better position to extend the help. We also found that conflicts between two individuals are easier to handle than conflicts between groups. Managing intergroup conflict requires the RA to take into account group-process issues as well, which is much more difficult to do. However, the RA who is a really skillful mediator can do much to help students cope with their floor's interpersonal environment.

Crisis Intervention

RAs sometimes must help students with problems that lead to feelings of depression, anxiety, grief, or frustration. Usually such feelings are generated by situations that students cannot handle on their own, so they seek help. If RAs use the interpersonal skills taught in this training model (active listening, self-disclosure, concreteness, confrontation, and summarization), they can help students deal with these problems by having them talk with a friend, let off steam, or think through the problem. When the problem is solved, the feelings generated by the situation (for example, depression and anxiety) will give way to more positive feelings.

However, once in a while, problems that generate feelings of depression, anxiety, grief, or frustration become crises. According to Aguilera and Messick, "A person in crisis is at a turning point. He faces a problem he cannot readily solve. As a result, his tension and anxiety increase, and he becomes less able to find a solution. A person in this situation feels helpless—he is caught in a state of great emotional upset and feels unable to take action *on his own* to solve his problem" (1974, p. 1).

For example, assume that a female resident seeks help from the RA because she has felt severely depressed for several weeks. She has talked with her friends and even discussed her situation with her parents. She has thought about her problem from every possible angle, but the depression does not go away. She has reached the point where nothing works and hopes the RA can help her feel better. In this instance, the RA may assume that the resident is in crisis because her usual coping mechanism (talking with friends and parents) has not worked, the feelings are chronic, the problems seem irresolvable, and she feels helpless and desperate.

This situation is somewhat different from the female resident who wants to talk with the RA about her boyfriend, who just broke off with her. After a long conversation in which she vents her feelings, she feels better and decides that she can get on with her life. Although her initial feelings (depression) were the same as the first female's, they were situationally generated (being dumped by her boyfriend), and she was able to feel better by simply talking out the situation with the RA. In other words, her usual coping mechanisms (talking with a friend and venting her feelings) worked. Although this person was experiencing a temporary crisis, she was *not* in crisis.

Persons in crisis need more from the RA than just a friendly ear. They need short-term relief from their symptoms and long-term help with their problems. Crisis intervention is defined as the immediate help a person needs to reestablish equilibrium (Aguilera and Messick, 1974). In other words, the RA must get the person out of the immediate crisis so the person can deal with the problems that caused it. As any RA who has dealt with a student in crisis (such as a student who is threatening suicide) can attest, this is not an easy task, especially in life-threatening situations. RAs may have feelings such as anxiety, or even panic, that make dealing with these situations much more difficult. And even if the immediate crisis is handled, there is still the problem of convincing the student to seek professional help.

Short-Run Solution. RAs must know when they are dealing with a crisis situation and how to handle it in the short and long run. They must use their basic interpersonal skills, but they must also be aware that other actions must be taken for the person in crisis to survive. Failure to handle these situations properly may literally result in life or death consequences for the person, so the RA must be prepared to handle them, even though they occur infrequently. Just what can an RA do, in both the short and long run, to handle a student in crisis? In addition to using basic interpersonal skills, RAs should consider the following ten guidelines for dealing with short-run symptoms:

1. *Hear out the person.* The RA should be sure, through good reflective listening, that he or she understands what the person is thinking and feeling. This will help the person, and it will help the RA decide what should be done.
2. *Decide if the person is in crisis.* Based on what the RA has heard,

she or he should decide if this is a situational, temporary crisis or a person in crisis by determining if the person has unsuccessfully used typical coping mechanisms, feels tension and anxiety, feels helpless to solve the problem without help, and has experienced the problem for some time.

3. *Take the person seriously.* Nothing is more likely to drive a person in crisis "off the deep end" than sensing that the RA does not think the problem is serious. No matter how trivial or unimportant the problem may seem to the RA, it is extremely important to the person who is trying to solve it, so the RA must take it seriously as well.

4. *Keep calm.* Even if what the student is telling the RA or doing really scares the RA, the RA should keep calm. What the person needs most is a person who, upon seeing or hearing the problem, does not panic or reach the same emotional state as the person in crisis. The RA must be steady, calm, and rational. It may not be all that easy, especially if the RA is scared to death by the situation. But being calm does not mean being "cool," which can be interpreted as not caring or not taking the problem seriously.

5. *Stick with the person.* The RA's physical presence and willingness to stay with the person will have a powerful impact. The RA should not let the person out of sight until professional help arrives. The RA should keep the person active: talking or walking, or whatever keeps the person involved in the problem.

6. *Get help.* The RA may want to get the person psychological help. In some instances, medical assistance is needed. Severely depressed persons, for example, may be helped by medication prescribed by a physician. The RA should notify the residence hall supervisor and anyone else the RA feels could help. The RA should not try to be a hero and handle the crisis alone.

7. *Avoid interpretation.* The RA is not qualified to provide psychotherapy or help the person solve the causes of the crisis. "Psychologizing" is likely to do more harm than good and elevate the person's extreme emotional state.

8. *Encourage venting of feelings.* Emotional catharsis may be very important for a person in crisis. Crying, shouting, talking, harmless violence (such as punching a pillow), and other cathartic behaviors may help the immediate crisis pass and allow time for help to arrive.
9. *Avoid arguing.* The RA should not argue with the person about some threatened behavior; it will just arouse anger and defensiveness.
10. *Follow up.* Once the person in crisis has received the help needed to get by the immediate crisis, it is very important for the RA to follow up. The RA's job does not end with a referral to the counseling center. It may be very important for the person to continue to rely on the RA for emotional support.

Long-Run Solution. In the long run, persons in crisis need professional help, a supportive environment, and people who care about them. If these conditions are not present following a crisis, chances are the person will simply build up to another crisis, probably one more serious than the first. For example, a student who has threatened suicide may actually try it the next time, if, after the crisis, nothing is done to help. RAs should consider the following five guidelines for helping students in crisis in the long run:

1. *Encourage continued professional help.* Even if a person sees a counselor as a result of the immediate crisis, that person may resist longer-term professional help. The important message here is "you don't have to be crazy to see a shrink." The RA should use personal experiences, if they are relevant.
2. *Work with the counselor.* Sometimes the RA can help the therapeutic process by creating a supportive environment or by being a person who can provide emotional support. Counselors can provide advice on how RAs can be most helpful. However, there are times when the counselor may not see anything the RA can do as helpful. The important point is that the RA should seek the counselor's advice.
3. *Be alert to another crisis.* If the RA sees a pattern emerging similar to the last time the person went into crisis, the RA

should talk to the person or the counselor. People who experience an initial crisis may build up to another one if their problems are not being solved.

4. *Above all, continue the relationship.* After the crisis has passed is when the person may need the RA most. The RA should keep the relationship going and offer general support and help. It may be very important for that person to have such a relationship.

5. *Deal with other residents.* Very rarely do students on a residence hall floor fail to learn about a crisis situation. On the one hand, confidentiality must be maintained; on the other hand, silence may result in misperceptions. RAs, with the help of their supervisors, must decide how the crisis will be handled with other members of the floor. Also, if other floor members are to be helpful later, they may need some information about the crisis and some advice about how to relate to the person. There are no easy answers to this issue, so RAs must be extremely careful about how they handle it.

Discipline

Probably no role gives RAs more initial anxiety than enforcing the institution's rules and regulations. Most neophyte RAs feel uncomfortable with this role and wish that they did not have to do it. They resist playing the heavy or siding with the institution against their fellow students. They may have great difficulty enforcing unpopular rules or ones they disagree with. Thus the whole discipline role must be discussed in any training program, and guidelines for implementing this very difficult role must be outlined.

One problem is that institutions vary a great deal as to the importance of the RA's discipline role. At some institutions, it is *the* role, and little else is expected. At the other extreme, institutions may feel it is up to the students to establish and maintain rules and regulations necessary to provide a good residential environment, and the RA is not called on to enforce rules. But most institutions fall somewhere in between, expecting RAs to enforce rules and do all the other things as well. As we stated earlier, the cop-counselor role conflict is probably as old as the first residence hall, and, we believe, widely overestimated as a problem. The first step in helping prospective RAs deal with the discipline role is *attitudinal.* It is possible, and probable, that RAs can perform their discipline role and function effectively in other roles as well.

Just how does the RA accomplish this? We believe much of what has been written about establishing and enforcing rules in residence halls is rubbish. We think disciplinary counseling is a contradiction in terms and impossible to implement. Our experience has been that student attempts to build community standards on their own, without help from the institution, are doomed to failure. Finally, we believe an institution that does not attempt to impose some standards of living on residents is negligent because such standards are imposed in the real world and because the educational potential of the residence halls will not be fulfilled without such standards.

One reality of most residence hall floors is that there are rules everyone agrees are necessary for maintaining an orderly and supportive environment. There are also rules imposed by the institution (such as limitations or prohibitions on possession and use of alcohol) that many students disagree with and so widely violate when they can. Thus the RA is faced with rules that have community support and those that do not. Obviously, the latter ones are the most difficult to enforce and the ones most likely to get the RA in trouble with the floor. Finally, there are rules that some floor members support but others do not, so the RA may get trapped in a conflict among floor members.

Another reality of most residence hall floors is that occasionally residents are held accountable for their actions in some sort of disciplinary "system." That system may be an internal residence hall's judicial system or an institutional discipline system. It may be student oriented or staff controlled. It could result in dismissal or suspension from the institution. So in addition to dealing with behavior on the floor, RAs and students must deal with a system.

A final reality is that regardless of how an RA handles a disciplinary situation, there is bound to be negative fallout. The person who is involved is certainly not going to like what is happening, and other members of the floor may also feel strongly. Certain persons are going to resent the RA for turning in someone, regardless of how well the situation was handled or the person treated. RAs will never win any popularity contests for enforcing rules, but they may win respect if they handle this role properly.

The following eight guidelines help interpret the RA's discipline role:

1. *State your expectations in advance.* The most important thing for RAs to do at the beginning of the year is to spell out, very specifically, how they will interpret their discipline role. RAs should let their residents know where they do and do not have discretion for enforcing rules. For example, if the institution has a rule that anyone caught possessing or consuming alcohol is referred for disciplinary action, and the RAs do not have any discretion in making a referral, then the floor should know and understand that fact right away.

   RAs should also let their residents know what responsibilities, if any, they have for enforcing rules. If the floor decides on a quiet hours policy, then the floor may have the initial responsibility for enforcing it. The RA may get involved only when floor members are unsuccessful. It is very important for residents to understand which rules they are responsible for, how to enforce them, and what to do if they cannot.

   RAs should also bring home the reality of residence hall living. The hall is not a sanctuary from the laws of the land or the rules of the institution: Residents will be held accountable for their behavior. The RA is an agent of the school and is expected to enforce rules and hold students accountable. In other words, the RA should make sure students understand that the disciplinary role is a valid one, at least as far as the institution is concerned, and the RA, as enforcer of the rules, is a fact of residence hall living, whether students like it or not.

2. *Teach students the rules and the system.* Residents should understand the rules under which they must operate, and it is the RA's responsibility to make sure they know them. That does

not mean that the RA must read every institutional rule at the first house meeting, but these rules should be highlighted and available in written form. Residents should also understand the discipline system, and RAs should help students acquire that understanding.

3. *Be consistent.* Most RAs who have trouble with discipline do so because they are inconsistent. If two situations arise that are virtually identical and the RA handles one very differently than the other, trouble will brew. If one person is dealt with differently than another for violating the same rule in the same way, the RA can expect much criticism. Finally, there should be some consistency from the beginning of the year to the end. We disagree with those people who believe that "RAs should be tough at first, and then ease off later." That approach will get an RA in trouble because it is inconsistent and unfair to students.

4. *Maintain a good attitude.* Nothing gets an RA into trouble quicker than creating the impression that she or he is enjoying applying discipline. RAs who seem to like having authority over students will fail in disciplinary situations because students will resent their attitude.

5. *Be honest.* Some people believe it is a mistake for RAs to admit that they disagree with a rule they must enforce or that they feel uncomfortable with the discipline role. We believe precisely the opposite, so long as RAs have made their expectations clear. If there are rules with which RAs disagree, it is all right for them to say so to students on their floors. If an RA pretends to agree with a rule, it will probably be seen as phony behavior, particularly if residents knew the RA before the RA assumed the position. However, honesty should never be an excuse for inconsistency, ambivalence, or failure to fulfill the RA's discipline role.

6. *Be decisive.* Another way RAs get into trouble in disciplinary situations is by being ambivalent. When action is required, the RA should take it. Doing nothing is almost always a mistake, and most residents will view ambivalence about what to do as a sign of weakness. Anticipating typical disciplinary situations and thinking about how to handle them will help RAs

become decisive, as will seeking advice from other resident assistants and supervisors and acquiring the proper training.

7. *Get help when needed.* If a discipline situation is getting out of hand, RAs must not be afraid to get help from other RAs or from supervisors. Particularly in group discipline situations, it may take more than one person to handle the problem.

8. *Abide by the rules.* RAs are role models and will considerably diminish their effectiveness in the discipline role if they violate the rules themselves. They will have absolutely no credibility with students if they enforce rules they do not themselves abide by. It may also result in a blackmail situation. That is, a student who is referred by an RA for some violation may threaten to turn in the RA for an earlier violation unless the referral is canceled. It is hypocritical for RAs to enforce rules on the one hand and violate them on the other.

Even if RAs follow all these guidelines, they may still mismanage a discipline situation if they do not behave properly on the spot. We agree with the following five-step approach for dealing with discipline situations: (1) collect the facts, (2) approach the student, (3) listen to the student, (4) take necessary action, and (5) follow up (Blimling and Miltenberger, 1981). For example, attempts to take action before knowing all the facts or really hearing out the student will make the student very angry and resentful, and justifiably so. Follow-up is also important because in the heat of the incident, the student may not be thinking too clearly or rationally. Furthermore, because many discipline situations involve intoxicated students, morning-after sessions are usually more effective than trying to reason with drunks.

We believe that the fundamental cause of RA ineffectiveness in the discipline role is not a matter of approach, technique, or attitude; it is the RA's inability to handle the authority role of the position. All other RA roles can be accomplished through other bases of power, including referent (modeling), expert, and reward powers. The discipline role more often than not requires the exercise of legitimate power within the authority granted to the RA by the position. It also may require coercive power or the ability to punish residents for their behavior.

It is a very tall order to expect RAs to assume the mantle of authority for the institution without some unease or ambivalence. RAs are still young adults, with needs to be respected and accepted by other young adults. It is probably the first time the RAs have had to act in an authority role, and the newness creates uncertainty. Some RAs may even disagree with their authority role but live with it because other parts of the job are rewarding. Finally, some RAs may not have fully resolved their own authority problems with parents or other authority figures. It is not easy for RAs to quickly and easily assume a role that requires them to exercise legitimate and coercive power.

However, we believe that if RAs have a chance to work on and think through their discipline role and follow the guidelines we outlined, residents will respect them for the job they must do. It has been our experience that RAs effective in the other RA roles are also effective in the discipline role.

8

꜖ꞈꜛ

Teaching Techniques
for Program Instructors

Even an instructor extensively experienced in the traditional classroom may not be prepared to implement this training model because except for an occasional short lecture, the parallels are almost nonexistent. In a traditional classroom, teachers prepare for what they are going to teach, they deliver their lectures, and they answer students' questions. They give tests and assign a grade. Students finish the course and move on, and whether they have learned anything is their problem, not the teachers'.

Training resident assistants using this program is very different altogether. In an experience-based, small group learning environment, the demands placed on the instructor are very different from those of a more traditional classroom. The instructor must have a different attitude about teaching, be prepared to implement several instructor roles, and use a wide variety of instructional designs and techniques. In short, the instructor must be prepared for an entirely different instructional setting.

The instructor must also be prepared for an active rather than passive response from students, thereby opening up several issues not normally associated with the traditional classroom. This type of learning environment may leave students confused, excited, rebellious, resistant, and/or challenged, and instructors must anticipate and deal with these reactions. Often this means reacting on the spot to what is happening in the classroom and making necessary adjustments in the instructor role or instructional design.

Evaluation also is more complicated. The instructor has to evaluate not only knowledge and understanding but skills and competencies, which is much more difficult to do. In our selection-training-supervision program, performance evaluation is not only an assessment of what was learned in training but a determination of whether participants are hired as resident assistants. Thus there is much more pressure associated with evaluation of performance.

The last, very important difference between teaching this program and a traditional class is that what happens to students after they complete the traditional class is not the instructor's responsibility. If students fall on their faces on the job, it is not the instructor's problem. But in this selection-training-supervision program, the instructor cannot afford to think narrowly; if the instructor supervises someone he or she has trained and problems develop, it is the instructor's responsibility to help solve them. So what does or does not happen in this training program has consequences beyond the classroom, consequences for which the instructor may have to assume some responsibility in the later role of supervisor.

At this point, it may seem that we have trapped ourselves in a logical inconsistency. Early in the book we asserted that this training program took into account the limited experience and training of people who typically train resident assistants. But how can such persons teach in a traditional classroom, much less in a learning environment that demands so much from instructors? As we developed this program, one of our worst fears was that it would fail because our instructors could not handle the demands of the experience-based, small group learning environment. But it did not turn out that way; in fact, some of our staff with prior experience in a traditional classroom had the most difficulty adjusting to teaching this program.

We found that staff with limited teaching experience and background could do a good job with this program because (1) individual training designs were highly specific and structured, (2) a great deal of time and attention was devoted to training and supervising the instructors, and (3) neophyte instructors, out of fear or high commitment (or both), worked very hard at becoming good teachers. More experienced instructors had to unlearn some of their thinking about how to teach and develop new skills. But in the end they too became effective teachers.

During the process of teaching the training program and experimenting with several training programs for instructors, we concluded that several variables contributed to successful, effective teachers: (1) an in-depth, conceptual understanding of the training program's content, (2) a thorough understanding of the training program, (3) the interpersonal and group leadership skills necessary to manage experience-based, small group learning environments, and (4) a thorough understanding of the instructor's role and the instructional issues inherent in such a learning environment.

The first chapters of this book focused on what the instructors should *know* and the skills they should *have* to teach this training program. We also reviewed the conceptual basis for the training program; specific designs are presented later. Here we present a thorough discussion of the instructor's role and the instructional issues instructors must anticipate and deal with while teaching this model.

Instructor Roles

To implement this training program, the instructor must be prepared to assume three different roles: instructor-conceptualizer, facilitator-trainer, and tutor-counselor. Here we define these roles and identify the skills necessary for implementing them.

Instructor-Conceptualizer. In this role the instructor must effectively communicate the knowledge and concepts necessary to accomplish the learning objectives of a training session. This role is most typically implemented by a lecture, followed by questions from or discussions by the participants. Although this particular role occupies a small part of the instructor's total time in most sessions, it is critical. The success of most sessions depends on the instructor's ability to communicate the session's purposes, rationale, and objectives and build group members' knowledge base. Thus an instructor must be concise, organized, and, most of all, interesting and stimulating. You as the instructor can set up the sessions by communicating effectively in the following ways:

1. *Be prepared.* Nothing creates more credibility than instructors who know what they are talking about. You should know both what you are specifically presenting and background information that can enrich discussion and prepare you for questions.
2. *Organize your material.* After you decide what to present, you must organize it to provide an orderly and logical presentation of the information you are trying to get across. Participants should be able to sense your organization of the material.
3. *Be understandable.* Talk in complete sentences and in clear, concise, and hearable voice tones. Avoid filler phrases such as "you know" and "y'understand?" Most of all, present a concept and give examples that RAs can identify with, preferably examples from the RA job. Examples are also an opportunity to inject humor and create interest.
4. *Be self-disclosing.* Give an example for later parts of the session by relating your own experiences, thoughts, and, most of all, feelings. You cannot expect RAs to reveal their thoughts and feelings if you do not set an example early. Self-disclosure is a very powerful teaching tool, particularly for an experience-based learning setting.
5. *Be aware of your own affective state.* This involves the feelings behind what you are saying, the expression of them or the control of them. Ask yourself: Am I bored? Anxious? Enthusiastic? Nervous? Interested? Your enthusiasm and interest should be expressed; your nervousness or boredom should be worked on and overcome. Both can be developed through practice.
6. *Watch personal nonverbal cues closely.* Nonverbal cues can be both enhancing and distracting when you present information. For example, direct eye contact can be extremely helpful, but nervous habits like fidgeting with your fingers can be very dis-

tracting. You may want to consider your posture and whether you prefer to stand or sit when presenting. The whole nonverbal presentation of yourself is important and should be thoroughly practiced.

7. *Be aware of the group.* Keep track of how the group is reacting, and check to see if they understand what you are trying to communicate. What is their affective state? Bored? Interested? Active? You can check the state by noting the group's nonverbal cues or by asking them direct questions. You should be prepared to adapt your style of presentation to their reactions. (This is much easier said than done, but it is essential.)

Facilitator-Trainer. In this role the instructor helps participants understand their group dynamics and behavior. This role is typically implemented by the instructor's direct, verbal interventions, which help the group focus on its communication patterns, influence structure, norms and values, and other group dynamics.

This instructional role is the most difficult one for those of us who train RAs because our prior experience, knowledge, and skill in relation to groups, group behavior, and group dynamics are limited. Instructors who have implemented this training program have felt more insecure about this instructional role than any other. Yet this role is probably the most important because the entire training program takes place in a group setting. By prior training and experience, you can present material to a group (the instructor-conceptualizer role) and work with individuals (the tutor-counselor role). But knowing how to work with a group, as a group, is typically much more difficult, so the skills required to work with groups must be developed and improved.

We start from the assumption that groups have dynamics which should be identified, discussed, and dealt with, just as individuals have intrapersonal dynamics that must be handled. But group dynamics are different from individual dynamics and much more difficult to identify and handle. We first present an eclectic model of group dynamics and then offer some suggestions on what to do with what you learn about group dynamics once you know what they are.

There are many different theories about groups and group

dynamics. Chapter Six identified field theory (Lewin, 1951), interaction process analysis (Bales, 1950), systems theory (Homans, 1960), sociometric theory (Moreno, 1953), and psychoanalytic theory (Bion, 1961). However, we have never found any one of these theories completely applicable to studying the interactions of an RA training group. We have thus developed our own, somewhat abbreviated, way of looking at group dynamics:

1. *Communication.* Do group members skillfully deliver messages to one another? Do they listen to one another, and are they able to reflect a message's content and feelings? Who talks to whom, what do they say, and what is its effect? Do group members feel completely free to communicate openly and honestly? Do some group members communicate better than others?

2. *Power and influence.* Which group members exert the most or least influence on the group, and why? Is the group's influence system based on skills, knowledge, and open communication or manipulation, coercion, and hidden agendas? Is there a subgroup that typically can get its way in the group? Are the rights and opportunities for interaction with the group being infringed on by the more powerful members? Are some group members excluded, and if so, why?

3. *Norms and values.* What are the informal rules by which group members are governed? How did the rules develop, and are they helpful to the group? Are they explicit or implicit? What are the rewards for those who abide by these rules; what are the punishments for those who violate them?

4. *Task level.* Does the group solve its problems effectively? Can it get tasks done? What difficulties, if any, develop when the group has a job to do or a problem to solve? Are there some tasks or problems that are easily handled, and if so, why? Can the group make a decision? If not, why not?

5. *Group atmosphere.* What is the overall tone of the group? Does it fluctuate from session to session, and if so, why? Do members trust one another, and are they free to express their feelings and emotions? Does the group have "flat" times, and if so, why? Do members generally feel good about one another?

6. *Conflict resolution.* How does the group deal with conflict? Do conflicts among members stay hidden, or do they burst out into the open? Can the group identify the sources of its conflict and resolve its differences effectively?

7. *Member roles.* What roles do group members assume, and when do they assume them? Are roles fluid and changeable, depending on the situation, or are group members locked into a basic role regardless of the situation? Who assumes leadership in the group, and why? Are the roles assumed by some group members disruptive or unhelpful to the group, and why?

It is the instructor's responsibility to monitor these group dynamics and to know and understand them. But knowing what to look for is only a beginning for the facilitator-trainer role to be implemented effectively. You must also be able to act on what you know and help the group deal with its issues and problems; here are six tips on how to do just that:

1. *Know when to intervene.* If you spot a group dynamics issue that the group should deal with, know when to intervene. You may want to set aside a specific time at the end of a session to encourage the group to look at its own dynamics or some aspect of its dynamics that you feel should be worked on. Or you may decide to intervene directly during a session to work on an issue blocking the group from accomplishing the session's objectives. You should rely on your own judgment, but the timing of such interventions is very important.

2. *Know how to intervene.* If you identify a group dynamics problem, you must be able to express clearly and concisely your analysis of what is going on so that the group knows what you are talking about. But more importantly, you must be able to communicate *why* you think the group has a dynamics problem and be prepared to give examples. You should be able to remind the group of some past or present behavior that supports your analysis.

3. *After intervening, stop and listen.* Be prepared to listen to what the group has to say about your intervention. They may support what you are saying and add examples, or they may dis-

agree and offer alternative explanations of what is happening. Your role is to help the group clarify how it views itself and be open to revisions of your original hypothesis. Most of all, at this stage, be a good listener.

4. *After listening, reach a consensus with the group.* Be prepared to merge your thoughts and feelings about a group dynamics issue with those of the group. They should confront the weaknesses in your hypothesis, and you should be prepared to point out discrepancies in theirs. But the task is to reach agreement about what the particular dynamic is and how it creates a problem for the group, or how it could be strengthened to further facilitate the group.

5. *Commit the group to resolving the problem.* Discuss various game plans and try new behaviors. For example, if the problem is trust, the group could work on gradually increasing levels of self-disclosure, particularly expression of feelings. Each group member could commit to working on more self-disclosing behavior during the next session. An "I will if you will" approach to group members can very effectively increase trust levels within groups.

6. *Follow up at a later session.* The group may significantly improve on a group dynamics issue, and that should be noted at some future time. Or the group may continue to have a problem, in which case the group should reopen the issue of how to resolve the problem. But follow-up is very important and must be initiated by the instructor.

Tutor-Counselor. This is the role in which the instructor helps individual participants understand themselves, their impact on others, and others' impact on them. This role is typically executed by the trainer's direct, verbal interventions regarding individual behavior in the group, or outside the group on a one-to-one basis. These interventions ideally help individuals gain insight into themselves and others.

This is an easier role for most trainers to execute because by training and experience they are skillful in one-to-one relationships. But when executed in a group setting, a trainer must not only monitor the reaction of the individual involved but that of the

group. The group will make judgments about your level of interpersonal skill and your ability to practice what you preach.

Chapter Five identified the essential interpersonal skills
necessary for conducting effective interactions with people. The
key element in implementing the tutor-counselor role in a training
group is an ability to give and receive useful *feedback*. Feedback is
the exchange of verbal and nonverbal responses among group
members, based on commonly observed behavior. Feedback is a
way of giving help to persons who want to learn how well their
behavior matches their intentions. It is also a means for establishing
one's identity and skill in dealing with others. It is *the* most critical
process for your group to establish and maintain if any learning is
to occur. But such an exchange does not just happen; it must be
governed by strictly defined ground rules. Without such ground
rules, nothing may happen, or worse, the feedback session becomes
a destructive, blood-letting exercise that hinders rather than helps
self-awareness. There are seven such ground rules:

1. *Feedback must be descriptive rather than evaluative.* By describing
    rather than evaluating your own reaction to someone's behav-
    ior, you reduce the chances of a defensive reaction from the
    other person. You also increase the chances of the person ac-
    cepting the feedback and using or not using it as he or she sees
    fit. For example, you may say, "When you interrupt me, I feel
    annoyed at you"; chances are that the person will hear you.
    However, if you say, "You're a rude and obnoxious person
    when you interrupt me," chances are the person will respond
    to your evaluation, not your description of how the behavior
    affects you. State the behavior descriptively, and then state
    how that behavior makes you think and feel.

2. *Feedback must be specific rather than general.* General feedback is
    almost never helpful because it does not give the receiver
    much to work with; it will probably be ignored or result in a
    defensive reaction. For example, you may say, "I think you're a
    very dominating person." "Dominating" has several meanings
    and is of little use to the receiver of the feedback. On the other
    hand, you might say, "When we were discussing imprinting a
    few sessions ago, you kept interrupting me, in a very loud

voice. I felt you weren't listening to me and that I had to accept your point of view regardless of its logic." That statement gives the person a much more definite sense of what her or his dominating behavior is and the impact of that behavior on others.

3. *Feedback must be well intended.* The whole idea of feedback is to help the receiver become more self-aware and improve interpersonal skills. Thus the giver of feedback must offer such feedback for the purpose of helping the receiver, not degrading him or her. When feedback is for the purpose of expressing the giver's hostility or the giver's need to degrade the receiver, it is *not* well intended. For example, if you say, "Interrupters are rude and stupid people who do not deserve my respect and you interrupt me all the time," you have merely expressed your hostility toward the person, not helped her or him. You should always check your feedback before you give it to make sure it is intended to help the other person, not make you feel better.

4. *Feedback must be directed toward a behavior the person can correct.* If you say to someone, "I distrust you because your nose is too big, and I have always distrusted big-nosed people," you really have not helped the person because he or she cannot control the size. All you have done is identify a prejudice of your own. So before you give someone feedback, make sure it is something he can do something about, not just your own bias.

5. *Feedback must be well timed.* Feedback should be given as soon after the behavior as possible and in an atmosphere where the person is ready to hear it. For example, if a person has just heard some very distressing negative feedback, you may want to wait for another time to give the person some additional negative feedback. Try to be sensitive to the other person's ability to handle what you have to say at a particular moment. That is not to suggest you should pull your punches or soften the feedback, but you may want to choose another time.

6. *You must check out feedback.* The receiver must have an opportunity to repeat what the giver said to ensure that there is clear communication between them. Particularly if the message is heavy, the receiver should make sure he or she totally and

completely understands what the sender said. It is often easy to assume that both parties understood the communication, so as a result checking out the feedback is often overlooked. All feedback should be checked out, all the time, to the point where the sender is satisfied that the receiver has heard precisely what the sender said.

7. *Feedback must be checked out with the group.* Is the feedback just the sender's perception, or is it shared by some or all of the group? This is a very important issue for the receiver of the feedback. If the group does not verify the feedback, then the issue is probably just between the sender and the receiver and should be dealt with just by them. However, if the group verifies the feedback, the issue is probably one the receiver must work on, get more insight about, and try to improve. The group check is a way of helping both the sender and receiver of the feedback gain more insight into themselves. For example, the instructor might say after the feedback has been given, "Are there others in this group who feel the same way?"

Instructor Attitude

Knowing what roles to assume and the skills necessary to implement those roles are obviously important, but they are but one aspect of effective leadership in an experience-based learning environment. Your general attitude and the way you present yourself to group members determine your effectiveness within the roles you assume. It is important to communicate what you are *not* as well as what you are. You are *not* just another group member; you are *not* the leader of a democratic group, and you are *not* obliged to seek group consensus about the structure and format of the training program.

What you *are* is a faculty member who has a course to teach. You have interpersonal skills to facilitate group interaction, and you have a program that provides a structure within which learning can occur. But most of all, never forget that you are in charge, and you should act like it. You must maintain control of the learning environment and resist group efforts to determine what shall occur. The primary responsibility for maintaining the learning environment and structuring the interaction belongs to you, not the group. The group's primary responsibility is to actively participate within the structures you have presented.

Of course, your level of interpersonal skill is the chief tool for establishing credibility, building respect, and maintaining control. In addition, your attitude about the training, your role as instructor, and your confidence in yourself and the training program are equally important. Even though you may not feel it at times, you must present yourself to the group as a person who knows what she or he is doing and where she or he is headed. That means carefully preparing for each session and never losing your concentration. Never get overconfident and decide to wing it, even for one session; the price you pay will be the decline of your credibility, respect, and control.

In an experience-based learning environment, all eyes are on the instructor, especially at first. The example you set in terms of your interpersonal skill, willingness to take risks, receptivity to feedback, level of self-disclosure, and enthusiasm for the tasks at hand sets the tone for the entire group. In effect, your behavior determines participants' acceptable and unacceptable behaviors. The pressure is clearly on you at the beginning to practice what you preach and to serve as a role model for everyone else.

Especially in the early feedback sessions, your ability to be self-disclosing, to give feedback constructively, and to receive feedback nondefensively is absolutely essential for group members to develop those skills. Whether or not you like it, you are the role model, and you set the tone for the group. Learn to live with that pressure, and recognize your responsibility to meet this challenge by using exemplary instructional skills.

Structuring the Learning Environment

You should give some serious thought and attention to the amount and type of structure you provide a training group. Too often, instructors provide too much structure, not enough structure, or vacillate between the two formats. In all three cases, the training group's learning environment is impaired.

If you give too much structure and dominate the group, you

are trying to exert too much direct control over the group. Of course, what really happens is that participation drops, little trust develops among group members, and participants disown what is happening. They become spectators in the learning process rather than active participants. Or they may challenge your dominating behavior, diverting the group away from the session's objectives. You may ultimately be in charge, but you will have destroyed the atmosphere necessary to an experience-based learning environment. You will have won the battle and lost the war.

If you do not provide enough structure and are inactive in the group, you are unsure about what is happening in the group and do not know how to exert sufficient control. Of course, what really happens is that the group flounders, becomes confused about what is supposed to happen, and grows disinterested, or the participants attempt to develop their own structure to make things happen. But your inactivity and lack of structure have the same effects as overactivity and too much structure: You will have destroyed the atmosphere necessary to an experience-based learning environment. You will have lost the battle *and* the war.

The trick is to provide enough structure, exercise enough control to make the group develop its own resources, and make individuals active participants in the learning process. Here are four critical guidelines for implementing the process:

1. *Follow the syllabus.* Through our extensive experience with this training program, we learned much about each session and subsequently incorporated improvements and variations. We learned which sessions require extensive structuring and where sticking to the design is absolutely important. We also learned which sessions may be "played with" by the instructors without harming the session's goals. There is a temptation, particularly for neophyte instructors, to vary the design or eliminate it altogether. We strongly recommend that you follow the syllabus fairly closely the first time through, to get a feel for the training program's flow.

2. *Monitor the group.* Some groups take off with little active help from the instructor. The problem with this type of group may be to keep them under control so that all participants have an

equal opportunity to participate. The instructor's role in this type of group is to allow for equal participation and keep the group on track with the session's design. On the other hand, some groups may need all kinds of structure to get going and keep going and may also need some very active interventions by the instructor. You should give the group what it needs to get its own resources going. Sometimes the same group may exhibit both underactivity and overactivity, depending on the design. Sometimes the group will need much structure, and sometimes all you need do is get out of the way.

3. *Get feedback from the group.* Although most groups do not readily recognize the amount of structure they need for a given task, they can usually tell when there is too much or too little. Be tuned to their direct and indirect messages to you regarding this dimension. If there is too much structure, the group will probably be bored, have a very low affect level, and appear to be going through the motions. If there is too little structure, the group is likely to flounder, become confused, and eventually raise questions about the design's rationale. It is up to you to note these symptoms and make the necessary adjustments.

4. *Know yourself.* If you tend to miss on the amount of structure you are providing to the group, it is probably related to the way you typically respond in those situations. Overstructure may be the way you typically respond to anxiety over lack of control. Your past experience may have taught you that the most effective way to control a situation is by imposing structure on it from above. Before you apply a great deal of structure to a design, make sure the decision is based on the group's needs, not your anxiety.

    If you tend to miss in the direction of understructure, it is probably because of the way you typically respond in those situations. Understructure may be the way you typically respond when you do not know what you are doing. Your past experience may have taught you that the most effective way to behave when you do not know what you are doing is to be cautious and restrained. You may believe that it is better the group assumes from your silence you are a fool than to confirm their suspicions by opening your mouth. Again, before you decide to lay back and let the group flounder and develop its own structure, make sure your decision is based on the group's needs, not your own confusion.

Thus, to teach this model you must know and understand the various instructional roles required of you and the skills needed to implement these roles. You also must have a certain attitude which communicates to your group that you are in control of the learning environment. Never underestimate your role-modeling influence, especially in this type of learning environment. Finally, you must continually make decisions about how structured the group should be, to make the most learning occur in the group. In short, we think you should take a major role in creating an effective learning environment by implementing an instructor role that is diverse, confident, and flexible.

Typical Issues

Because this type of learning environment may be unique to both participants and instructors, it is important for instructors to anticipate some typical issues that may arise and be prepared to deal with them. These issues include the evaluation dilemma, deviant behavior, "end run," challenging the leader, and resisting training. For those of you who have led experience-based small groups, much of what follows seems self-evident. But for those of you with little or no experience in this type of learning environment, it is a very important section.

Evaluation. On the one hand, your role is to facilitate learning by encouraging participants to risk new behaviors and get feedback from the group. Developing and refining participants' interpersonal skills depends on your ability to develop a group climate that encourages such experimentation and feedback. For you to develop such a climate, participants must feel they are operating in a nonjudgmental, accepting environment.

On the other hand, the training program is designed to evaluate the participants' interpersonal effectiveness. This means that you as the instructor must make a judgment, at the end of the training, about whether participants should become resident assistants. The consequences of this judgment for participants are very important, considering the job opportunity and compensation involved.

Of course, in the ideal learning environment, the instructor should not have to combine the facilitator and evaluator roles. But the reality of most residence hall programs is that there are not enough competent personnel to separate these roles. Furthermore, it may not even be necessary. It is an issue for the participants, regardless of how it is handled, and can only be minimized, not eliminated. But our experience has been that if properly handled by the instructor, the roles do not necessarily conflict. (Chapter Nine deals more extensively with this issue.)

Deviant Behavior. Almost every group has participants whose behavior is so different that they must be dealt with either to (1) preserve the learning environment of others in the group or (2) teach them more effective ways of relating to the group. Deviant behavior may take several forms. Some participants' behavior may be so obnoxious, overbearing, dominant, and insensitive that they disrupt the ability of others in the group to learn. For example, we had a participant who talked nonstop about herself throughout most of the first two sessions. In spite of subtle hints from participants, and not-so-subtle hints from the instructor, she persisted in this behavior. Something had to be done to allow time for all participants to get air time in the group, not to mention the concern for her ability to succeed as a resident assistant.

Deviant behavior may also take the form of nonparticipation: the very quiet person who says little or nothing, or the more talkative person who reveals little or nothing. For example, we had a participant who said absolutely nothing in the first three sessions. In spite of the group's and instructors' efforts to draw out this person, he hung back. The group quickly gave up, figuring that if he did not want to participate, that was his problem. The instructors, of course, could not give up and allow a prospective RA to sit on the sidelines throughout the training program.

As an instructor, you must do something about deviant behavior. The deviant behavior may be the result of a serious psychological problem, and the person may need therapy to develop more effective ways of relating to people. Or the behavior may be exhibited by a basically healthy person who is experiencing extreme anxiety about participating in a new and possibly threatening situation. How you handle deviant behavior is extremely important, especially in the beginning, and sets the tone for the rest of the training sessions.

Your first task is to determine if the behavior is disruptive to the group or detrimental to the individual involved. Overactivity or complete passivity may be very natural anxiety reactions to a new environment. Once participants become comfortable with the group, the deviant behavior may subside. In fact, it may be very important for the group to deal with their anxiety reactions, with your help and assistance. So be very careful, especially at the beginning, in dealing with individuals who may be overactive or very passive, even if they are mildly disruptive. *It may be a very normal reaction!* Furthermore, if you help the group develop ways of constructively giving feedback to these people, you will have laid the groundwork for future sessions and developed the group's resources to deal with this issue.

If the deviant behavior persists beyond the first few sessions, it may be necessary to deal with it differently. A private, one-to-one session with the participant is an essential first step. In this session, you must establish your good intentions in approaching the subject and have specific behavioral evidence to back up your concerns. The goal is to help the individual see the consequences of personal behavior and help her or him develop new ways of relating to the group.

Sometimes neither the group nor the instructor can help a participant become a productive group member and take advantage of this type of learning environment. If the group has tried and failed, and the instructor has made every effort, both inside and outside the group, it may be necessary to remove the participant from the group. Of course, this eliminates the person from further consideration as a resident assistant. This should be done only as a last resort, and only when it is in the best interests of the group, the individual, and the overall program.

The way an instructor eliminates a participant from the group is very critical. The group could infer from this action that they had better be very careful about taking any risks or exhibiting any behavior that might result in a further reduction of group membership. On the other hand, it may be very obvious that the person could not have survived the training program and that removal was the only thing that could have been done. In either case, the instructor should thoroughly discuss the impact of this action with the group and give them an opportunity to explore their thoughts and feelings about the matter.

The "End Run." An issue that is a variation of deviant behavior is what we call the "end run." The participant may be floating along in the group, very carefully not overparticipating or underparticipating but basically avoiding any kind of real participation. Sensing that time may be running out and that sooner or later the group or the instructor will get after him or her, the participant may seek out the instructor outside the session and attempt to work issues. You should never be seduced into resolving outside the group an issue that should be dealt with within the group. If you do let a participant deal with issues outside the group, you allow the person to cop out of group participation, thereby eliminating a very valuable learning resource.

Of course, there may be very legitimate reasons for discussing an individual issue outside the group, and you should be responsive in such cases. But our attitude is that you really have to convince us, with a very strong argument, that the issue should *not* be dealt with within the group. In most instances, the person will return to the group, deal with the issue, and no longer feel the need to seek out the instructor outside the classroom. You should help that person develop ways of bringing up the issue, and help the group respond effectively.

Challenging the Leader. A fourth issue that may arise in this type of learning environment is a challenge to your authority as the instructor. If you take seriously your responsibility to structure the learning environment and maintain control of what is happening in the group, but the group develops its own resources, there may be a challenge to your leadership. Again, how you handle this challenge is extremely important and has implications for the rest of the training sessions.

Participants will challenge your authority as the instructor for a variety of reasons. They may be overly sensitive about your authority role and rebel not because of you or anything you have done, but because you *are* the authority. They may also rebel because you are too heavy-handed and autocratic in the way you handle the group. Your ability to help the group sort out just what the rebellion is all about and your willingness to admit your part in the situation determine how well you and the group resolve this issue. You can also help the group understand its part and explore constructive ways of dealing with authority.

The challenge to authority takes a variety of forms. Direct, active, and often hostile attacks on your leadership are a common form of rebellion in some groups, but very rare in this type of training. Because the instructor also ultimately decides whether participants become RAs, participants consider this type of resistance very risky, if not foolish. But if such resistance occurs, it is the easiest form of rebellion to handle because it is out in the open and both the instructor and group can deal with it.

Passive resistance is more typical yet more difficult to deal with. This challenge to your leadership may be exhibited by a generally apathetic and lethargic response to group sessions. The participants are tuned out, and they vote no confidence via their closed mouths and minds. This is a difficult challenge because the group may not even understand what is going on. Your task is to not only deal with the challenge but to get the group to recognize the problem in the first place.

As we stated previously, the resolution of a challenge to your authority depends on your ability to help the group sort out the reasons for its challenge and to determine how much of it is your behavior and how much is their own bias about authority. Adjustments on both sides usually resolve the problem. Failure to follow through on these adjustments inevitably results in another challenge. Most often, however, both you and the group will follow through sufficiently to lay the issue to rest once and for all.

Resisting Training. A fifth issue is generalized resistance to either the whole training program or selected sessions. The most typical symptom is an individual's or the entire group's general lethargic and apathetic feeling. A direct challenge may be the question, "How is this relevant?" Again, it is the instructor's responsibility to root out the causes of this behavior and help the group deal with them.

If the group has a fairly consistent pattern of active participation but hits a session where they are uninvolved, the instructor may consider several causes. The group may not understand the session's goals, rationale, or relevance, so it may be necessary for the instructor to go back over them. Also, groups have natural peaks and valleys. If a group has had a particularly intense session, it is not unusual for participants to "let down" for a while, particularly at the beginning of the next session. This may be particularly true after a feedback session. If the instructor helps the group identify this phenomenon, the group can usually make a comeback. Finally, there may be a group issue that needs to be dealt with and is interfering with the topic at hand. The group may be anxious about the task, concerned about a past session, or have unresolved interpersonal issues. Whatever the issue, you must deal with it, either immediately or at an appropriate later time.

Our list of typical issues faced in an experience-based, small group learning environment may not be complete, and you may face other ones equally important. Our best advice is that when you identify an issue, deal with it, even if you are not sure what the issue is or how you are going to handle it. It is better to err in the direction of handling it, even if you muff it, than to err in the direction of ignoring the issue.

The Coinstructor Relationship

We strongly recommend that this training program be taught by two instructors per group; a professional staff member and an experienced resident assistant, for five good reasons. First, more than one perception of what is happening in the group is very helpful. One instructor can set up the session and provide the leadership, while the other can observe individual behavior and group process. It is very difficult to do both things at the same time.

Second, some designs require more than one person to monitor what is supposed to happen, particularly when the group is broken down into smaller groups. In dyads or triads, it is helpful for the instructors to "float" from one group to the next, to provide feedback and to ensure that students understand and are properly carrying out the task. With only one instructor, the coverage of dyads or triads is too thin.

Third, coinstructors can give each other feedback about group performance and generally help each other. In the team that has developed a good working relationship, there are opportunities for improved interpersonal skill development and broadening of one's instructional competencies. It is also helpful to bounce ideas off each other and develop common approaches to the group's problems and issues.

Fourth, participants are given some choice about which instructors can help them. Even the most skillful instructor will not relate well to all participants in an equally effective manner. With two instructors, there is the possibility of stronger participant-instructor relationships because there is a greater variety to choose from. The experienced RA may be particularly helpful to the participant who finds it difficult to relate to adult authority figures.

Finally, without exception, those professional staff who have taught with coinstructors and by themselves much prefer working with coinstructors, for all the above stated reasons. But working with coinstructors can have potential problems if the relationship between the instructors is not open, honest, and, most of all, supportive. Several pitfalls should be avoided when instructors are trying to establish an effective relationship.

First, the instructors must be committed to working on and developing their interpersonal relationship. In most cases, this is something that happens only if there is a real commitment to do so. When preparing for sessions, instructors should anticipate problems that might arise between them in the group. After the session is over, instructors should take some time to debrief what happened, especially noting any problems or issues that arose during the session. Instructors should take the time to strengthen their ability to work together in the training program.

Second, when planning and preparing for a session, the instructors should work together to distribute work equitably, based on each instructor's strengths. Each instructor should have an opportunity to do what he or she does best, as well as the chance to develop areas of inexperience or weakness. Cooperation and teamwork when planning and preparing sessions go a long way toward developing these characteristics in the group itself.

Perhaps the most difficult situation to deal with is a difference of opinion between instructors during the training session itself. For example, suppose you are convinced that your coinstructor is completely mishandling a situation. You feel that unless something is done on the spot, much of what you have been trying to accomplish in the session or in previous sessions will not occur. Furthermore, you feel that without some kind of intervention, future sessions will be more difficult to conduct because of the precedent being set. So you feel you must act. But what should you do?

You may feel that the worst thing to do is publicly criticize your colleague and communicate to the group that you and your coinstructor do not share united goals. You fear that giving your coinstructor negative feedback could disrupt the group and lead to an unproductive confrontation that might not be helpful at all. And there is always the fear that your coinstructor might be right and you might be wrong, and this might become obvious if you intervene.

On the other hand, you may feel that the worst thing to do is just sit there. If you are right, and your colleague is going down the wrong path, it is irresponsible for you to do nothing. We believe your obligation to give the group the best possible learning environment should take precedence over the possible negative consequences of confronting your partner.

It is not an easy decision to make. But almost always, if you are certain you have a point, the best policy is to directly intervene with your coinstructor. This works best if you both have discussed previously how you will do. And you both should be prepared to discuss the issue, once raised, in the group. It will take all the skills you both have, and there is a very high risk to handling the situation in the group. If you fail, you will give the group living proof that you do not practice what you preach. The following example demonstrates an effective resolution of an issue:

> *Setting:* The group is into its first feedback session, and so far things are going well. The group has caught on rather quickly to the rules of giving and

receiving feedback and seems to be enjoying the opportunity to learn from this session. Suddenly, your
coinstructor comes "off the wall" with some feedback
to a participant who has been very quiet in previous
sessions. With very little behavioral evidence to go
on, your partner "attacks" the participant and
accuses her of lack of commitment to the training
program. Although you feel the person should be
confronted about her lack of participation, you feel
an aggressive approach is not helpful. Your approach
would be to probe a bit in a much less confrontive way
about her lack of participation. You might try the
following intervention:

      (To the person confronted): My coinstructor
has a point about your lack of participation, and you
have to agree that, compared to most other group
members, you have been fairly inactive. We have our
own guesses about why you are not participating, but
I find them hard to grasp because there is so little
behavior to confirm or deny our notions. Perhaps you
could share your perceptions and feelings about why
you choose not to participate.

In this example, you began by supporting your colleague in
the basic contention that the person has not participated and that it
is important to find out why. But you have also tactfully reminded
your coinstructor that hypotheses must be backed by behavioral
evidence and that the responsibility for explaining the nonparticipation is the participant's, not the instructor's. By your intervention, you may have extricated your colleague from a situation that,
if allowed to continue, might have been disastrous for the person
and set a very bad example for the group. When you and your
coinstructor debrief the session, you might want to check out how
your colleague felt about your intervention and how such a situation might be handled in the future.

Working with Experienced RAs as Coinstructors

We believe it is important to have an experienced RA as part
of the instructional team. First, an experienced RA has a built-in
credibility with participants who have little or no RA experience.

The RA can add credibility to sessions where relevance to the resident assistant position is not obvious. In this instance, a confirming word from an experienced resident assistant may be much more persuasive than the instructors' explanations.

Second, an experienced RA will probably see what is happening in the group from a different perspective. This perception will lie somewhere between the participants and the professional staff and will be most helpful when planning and implementing class sessions. In particular, the RA can help interpret to the professional staff the participants' reactions and the reasons for those reactions.

Besides helping the group understand the designs and helping the instructors understand the group, the presence of an experienced RA gives participants a chance to communicate with a peer as well as a professional staff member. For some participants, this may be a very important means of communicating their thoughts and feelings.

However, working with experienced resident assistants does involve problems. As with the working relationship between coinstructors, the relationship between experienced RAs and professional staff must be open, honest, and supportive; the same pitfalls as between coinstructors should be avoided. Instructors and resident assistants must work on their interpersonal relationships, distribute work equitably, and learn how to work out differences of opinion. However, additional issues may arise between instructors and experienced RAs.

First, there may be some confusion about the RA's role in the training program. Some instructors may recognize RAs as full partners in the instructional task and consider them equals. Other instructors may consider the RA a valuable assistant in the instructional process, but clearly a subordinate. It is absolutely essential that instructors are very clear in their own minds as to just what the role of the experienced RA is. The most serious problems between instructors and experienced RAs have resulted from unclear role expectations. When RAs expect to be full partners and later learn that they are subordinate assistants, you can expect them to feel frustrated, hurt, and angry.

Second, even if the roles are clearly spelled out initially, the

RA's skill level may call for a change in those roles. For example, an instructor who starts out with an equal partner philosophy may find that the RA is not skillful enough to carry out the full partnership. Or an RA who accepts the role of a subordinate assistant initially may develop skills and begin to assume a stronger, more equal instructional role. In either case, it is important for instructors and the RA to continually discuss their roles and make necessary adjustments.

Third, the RA may have a problem defining herself or himself in the group. On the one hand, the RA is there to provide additional support for the instructors, but on the other hand, the RA represents and advocates for group members. The RA should perform both roles, and it is up to the instructors to recognize the dilemma, reinforce both roles, and help the RA deal with the problem.

Finally, if instructors and the RA agree about a full partnership concept, it may be difficult to pull off, even if both are willing. Professional staff instructors may still see the RA as a subordinate, and the RA may still see professional staff as superiors, because in many contexts outside the group these roles are still operative. All we can hope is that each party can clearly separate their relationship as instructors from other relationships. And we think the responsibility to initiate discussions about this issue rests with the professional staff.

Other General Helpful Teaching Hints

Here is a list of somewhat unrelated bits of advice based on the experience of those who have taught the training model.

1. *Be tough at first.* Make your expectations very clear in the beginning, and enforce them rigorously. For example, use very high standards when evaluating the first homework assignment, and give it back to be redone, if necessary. You will establish your credibility as an instructor who means what you say, and you will get better-quality work in subsequent assignments.
2. *Keep good records.* Your ability to give specific and constructive

feedback regarding participant performance depends on the written records you keep. You should keep not only grades for assignments and attendance records but anecdotal notes on classroom behavior and other written thoughts on participants' progress.

3. *Keep track of the time.* The sessions are very tightly paced, and it is very easy, if you are not careful, to get behind. It is especially difficult if you have got a good thing going and want it to continue. But do not wreck the rest of the design by letting a good thing go too long.

4. *Set up the session properly.* Take a good deal of time preparing to introduce each session. Do not be in such a hurry to get to the "good stuff" that you skimp on the session's goals and rationale. If instructors do not understand what they are doing or why they are doing it, the session will fail.

5. *Do not let the group change the design.* Sometimes the group, for whatever reason, does not want to do what you want them to. They may be apathetic, anxious, rebellious, or in some other state that prevents them from getting to the task. They may even suggest an alternative, such as meeting outside if it is a nice day, doing something different, or canceling the class altogether. Do not compromise! Try to help the group determine the reasons for its reluctance to "get into it"; ideally this insight will help them get back on the track.

6. *Stress attendance and participation.* Never let up on the issue of attendance and participation. Active participation is required not only for participants to learn something about themselves but to facilitate the rest of the group. Be very tough on someone who fails to attend classes.

7. *Keep track of the group.* There are many times when the group will be broken down into smaller groups, such as dyads or triads. Do not just walk away while these smaller groups are operating. The group tends to slide away from the task when the instructor is not directly monitoring the interaction, so keep on the move, and make sure each subgroup is monitored and observed. This also ensures that the subgroups understood the task; if they do not, you can intervene early to correct the situation.

8. *Structure the physical environment.* Obviously, this type of train-
    ing cannot occur in classrooms where chairs and desks are
    bolted to the floor. But neither should it occur in a room full of
    lounge furniture because participants will lounge rather than
    learn. We recommend putting the group in a circle, with chairs
    that do not look like they were meant to be slept in.

The list could go on and on, and as you teach the training
model, you may want to add a few rules of your own. Even if you
have read and absorbed all we have written and recommended in
this book, you may still have a practical problem: How can you fully
benefit from the experience of teaching this training model if you
are operating in isolation? We strongly recommend that instructors
work with a qualified, outside consultant, such as a faculty member,
a counselor, or an experienced residence hall professional staff
member, whose responsibility is to provide you with constructive
feedback on your instructor style, based on direct observation,
taped observation, or your perception of what is happening in your
group. Particularly if you are in a small institution, you will need
such professional advice and personal support.

If you are one of many in your institution who are teaching
this training model, we suggest that you all get together occasionally to share experiences, solve problems, and otherwise help each
other. Joint planning sessions as well as joint debriefing sessions can
be particularly helpful. Over the years we have found ourselves to
be our greatest resource, and the support, encouragement, and
feedback we have received have been to our advantage, improved
our teaching, and strengthened the program.

9

꙳꙳꙳꙳꙳꙳꙳꙳꙳꙳꙳꙳꙳꙳꙳꙳꙳꙳꙳꙳꙳꙳꙳꙳꙳꙳꙳꙳꙳꙳꙳꙳

Implementing
the Training Program
Session by Session

This chapter presents the training program we have found effective for developing competent and successful RAs. Our program assumes that regardless of the RA's role or how the position is defined, RAs need to know certain things about themselves and others and possess the necessary interpersonal and leadership skills to function effectively. To that end, we determined that an effective RA training program should include (1) an extensive study of students' personal and academic development in the collegiate setting, and more specifically, in the residential setting; (2) an opportunity for RAs to learn more about themselves; (3) extensive practice in developing interpersonal skills; and (4) extensive practice in developing group leadership skills. We also concluded that each component should be considered in light of situations that RAs typically face on a residence hall floor.

We present twenty sessions, divided into four basic parts, within a small group format that closely follows an academic course for credit. For each session, we elaborate a rationale, define the goals, describe the design, define time frames, and offer suggestions for instructors. These descriptions assume that participants are using the companion manual, which gives participants information that is necessary to know in advance of each session and describes each session's rationale, goals, and design. We conducted these sessions both with and without the manual and concluded that the manual helps participants develop a much stronger conceptual base and skills.

The training sessions are designed to teach participants in groups of eight to twelve. (With larger groups it is much more difficult to get through each session on time, and larger groups limit each participant's air time and lessen each person's chance to practice skills and get feedback.) Each session is approximately two hours long and begins with instructors' remarks concerning the rationale, goals, and overview of the design. The design is then implemented, and usually at the end of the session, participants are given an opportunity to share their thoughts and feelings. However, recognizing that this format may not be applicable to all situations, the end of this chapter offers two abbreviated formats for implementing this training model: week-long and weekend. These abbreviated formats are better than no training at all, but clearly they are not as effective as the recommended format.

Outline of the Training Model

Part 1: Student Development

Session 1. Introduce training, training requirements, and evaluation criteria. Get-acquainted activities. Elaborate personal and academic development of students. Assign autobiography, part 1, due at session 2.

Session 2. Continue elaboration of student development, including academic development and adjustment to residence halls. Collect part 1 of autobiography.

Session 3. Introduce concept of imprinting and sex-role stereotyping. Assign First-Impression Formation, due at session 4. Assign rewrites of autobiography, due at session 4.

Part 2: Self-Awareness

Session 4. Review First-Impression Formation and introduce the concept of useful feedback. Collect rewrites of autobiography and First-Impression-Formation assignment. Assign autobiography, part 2, due at session 6.

Session 5. Continue First-Impression Formation and feedback exercise begun in session 4.

Session 6. Continue feedback exercise begun in session 5. Collect part 2 of autobiography.

Part 3: Interpersonal Skills Development

Session 7. Introduce interpersonal skills development model, and review nonverbal communication. Rewrites of autobiography due at session 8.

Session 8. Elaborate the concept of active listening, including reflection of content and feeling of a message. Collect rewrites of autobiography.

Session 9. Elaborate the concept of concreteness and the art of asking precise questions. Practice and get feedback on all skills learned so far in the training.

Session 10. Elaborate the concept of self-disclosure, both similarity self-disclosure and immediate self-disclosure in the interaction.

Session 11. Again practice and get feedback on all skills learned so far. Elaborate initiation skills of confrontation and summarization.

Session 12. Practice and get feedback on interpersonal skills learned so far in a counseling relationship.

Session 13. Elaborate the concept of crisis intervention and how RAs should deal with students in high states of distress.

Session 14. Update on feedback and comment on the group interaction so far. Assign Floor Characteristics Assessment, due at session 17.

Part 4: Leadership Development

Session 15. Introduce group leadership development and elaborate leadership styles.

Session 16. Role play various leadership situations the RA must handle on a residence hall floor. Assign Floor Dynamics Assessment, due at session 17.

Session 17. Discuss floor assessment and the exercise of power by the RA. Collect Floor Characteristics Assessment and Floor Dynamics Assessment assignments.

Session 18. Introduce conflict resolution and the RA's role in mediating conflicts between individuals or groups.

Session 19. Present guidelines for handling discipline, and discuss the RA's role in dealing with discipline situations.

Session 20. Final feedback session; evaluate training and instructors.

You must understand the flow of this training program so that you can provide continuity between and among sections of the course. In Part 1, Student Development, we start with concepts of student development and work toward some participant awareness of self-development in college. This not only increases participants' knowledge and awareness of student development but gives them common interpersonal data for sharing impressions of each other in Part 2, Self-Awareness. At the end of Part 2, participants are given an opportunity to look at their own group dynamics, which helps the training process and gives them insight into groups.

Part 3, Interpersonal Skills Development, is a step-by-step development of basic interpersonal skills. One skill is introduced and practiced and then put together with previous skills and practiced. We move from active listening to self-involvement to initiation skills, in each instance working from typical counseling and noncounseling situations RAs must handle on their floors. In Part 4, Leadership Development, we then add group leadership skills and give a model for applying various leadership styles to specific situations, based on an assessment of the residence hall floor. Again, after Parts 3 and 4, participants are given an opportunity to analyze their own group dynamics.

The last session provides closure on the training and gives participants a chance to get some final feedback from the group and to establish several skill-development goals for the future. Participants should end the training with a good idea of their strengths and weaknesses as potential RAs and know much more about how to do the job.

Part 1: Student Development in the Residential Setting

This section gives students key concepts of student development and acquaints them with the powerful influence of the residential setting. Through class presentations, designs, and the autobiography, participants should know more about student development in general, and their own development in particular, in the residential setting. This section is also a basis for sharing impressions of one another in Part 2 of the training model. To prepare for this section, reread Chapters One, Three, and Four here and Chapters One and Three in the manual.

Session 1: Introduction

1. Rationale. During this first session you set the expectations and tone for the class. Your modeling behavior is especially important, and your interpersonal skill level should be exemplary. Now is the first time the group will interact, and group norms will begin to be established that should promote a good learning environment. It is important for participants to begin to understand their own development, in an organized way, and infer from that development some generalizations about the development of others in college. It is very important for you and the group to get off to a good start.

2. Goals. (a) Introduce the training model, instructor expectations, course requirements, and evaluation system. (b) Learn each other's names. (c) Introduce a model of student development, in the residential setting. (d) Provide opportunity for discussion and exploration of selected developmental issues. (e) Assign part one of autobiography (due at session 2).

3. Design. First 20 minutes. Introduce the content and format of the training program. Stress the importance of involvement and participation. Describe experience-based learning.

Review your expectations, including importance of starting on time, getting assignments in on time, and your role as instructor.

Review the evaluation system, including class attendance, class participation, assignments, exams, and the grading basis. Also review the basis for recommending appointment to the RA position. (Refer to Training Program Aids A and B in the manual for specific evaluation forms.)

Next 15 minutes. Conduct the Name Game. State your name and tell something about yourself. The person to your left then repeats your name and in one sentence repeats something about you. That person then states his or her name and tells something about himself or herself. The person on the left of that person then repeats the names and something about each of the first two participants, and states her or his name. This continues until the circle is completed.

Next 10 minutes. Instruct participants to fill out the Student Development, Facts and Myths form in Chapter Three of their manuals.

Next 20 minutes. Go over the items on the form (see the key at the end of the discussion of this session). Elaborate the impact of residence halls and each developmental issue. Give participants an opportunity to discuss their reactions. At the end, ask "What facts surprised you most?"

Next 15 minutes. Introduce the autobiography, giving a brief description of the six developmental dimensions (see Chapters Three and Four in text), and assign Chapter Three in the manual for participants to read for specific instructions before they write the first half of their autobiographies. Assign sections on general background, formulating a personal value system, and developing intellectual and academic competence.

Next 20 minutes. Break the group into dyads, and ask each participant to think about and then share with the other participant a parent-value conflict she had before or after coming to college, based on the following factors:

(a) *What was the value conflict?* Was it over religion, politics, personal behavior, career decisions, or another issue? Focus on specific circumstances of the conflict and the feelings of both parents and participants.

(b) *How was it resolved?* Was the conflict resolved, and if so, how? If it was not resolved, where is it at this time? In retrospect, what did you learn, and how might it have been handled differently, either by you or your parents?

Give each pair about fifteen minutes to share their thoughts and feelings. Offer several examples of parent-student conflicts, such as telling parents about a change in career plans you know will upset them; making friends with someone your parents disapprove of; wanting to go on a weekend vacation with friends, knowing your parents would disapprove. Examples from your own experience are especially powerful.

Next 15 minutes. Within the total group, discuss several generalizations about the types of parent-value conflicts that arise and how they are or are not typically resolved. Catalog the generalizations on paper.

Final 5 minutes. Remind participants to read Chapter Three in the manual and to write part 1 of their autobiography by the next session. Participants should focus especially on the case studies in Chapter Three—as examples of what to write in their autobiographies.

4. Helpful hints. (a) Initial instructor self-disclosure, especially feelings, is the key to getting the group involved in this session. In both the autobiography review and the parent-value exercise, offer examples from your personal experiences. *(b)* Throughout this session, watch out for overactive or underactive students. Try to limit those who run off at the mouth, and encourage participants who are reluctant to jump into the pool. *(c)* Feel free to substitute other exercises for learning each other's names. We suggested but one of many good exercises.

Key to Student Development, Facts and Myths Instrument

1–T	11–F	21–T	31–T
2–T	12–T	22–F	32–T
3–F	13–T	23–T	33–T
4–F	14–T	24–F	34–T
5–F	15–T	25–T	35–T
6–T	16–T	26–F	36–T
7–T	17–F	27–T	37–T
8–T	18–T	28–T	38–F
9–T	19–T	29–T	39–T
10–T	20–F	30–T	40–T

Session 2: Students' Developmental Dimensions

1. Rationale. Students must understand their own development in the context of overall student development. Because the autobiography helps build insight into their own development and forms a basis of comparison to others' development, there should be time to discuss it in class. This session continues this process and focuses on other developmental issues.

2. *Goals.* *(a)* Clarify and discuss part 1 of the autobiography. *(b)* Elaborate students' academic development. *(c)* Elaborate other selected developmental issues. *(d)* Elaborate adjustments to residence hall living.

3. *Design. First 5 minutes.* Introduce the session's rationale and goals.

Next 15 minutes. Review participants' reactions to writing part 1 of the autobiography. What was easy to write about? Where did they experience difficulty or frustration? How did it feel to collect thoughts about yourself and write them down?

Next 25 minutes. Ask each participant to think about and then share with the group initial academic adjustment as a freshman, based on the following two factors:

(a) Was the academic transition smooth or rough? Did you continue to earn good grades, as you did in high school, or did you experience academic difficulty?

(b) How did you feel about the transition? Were you elated over your success? Frustrated and depressed over your failure? How did others (friends, parents) react to your academic success or lack of it?

Give the group about twenty minutes to share their thoughts and feelings. Offer several examples of academic transitions from high school to college: Maybe you had no trouble and continued to earn high grades. More likely you achieved less than you expected, at least initially. Or maybe your first semester was a complete disaster. Again, examples from your own experience are especially powerful, but do not go on so long that you use up valuable group time.

Next 5 minutes. Summarize the discussion, identifying typical transitions and the feelings generated.

Next 5 minutes. Ask the group to identify two typical student problems they might expect to deal with as RAs in each of the following issues: deciding on a career and life-style, learning to establish and maintain interpersonal relationships, developing sexual awareness and a capacity for intimacy. Use this discussion as an opportunity to sharpen participants' understanding of each issue.

Next 15 minutes. Break down the group into triads, assigning each subgroup one developmental issue. Each subgroup should then develop two approaches to solving the three problems identified by the total group.

Next 15 minutes. Ask each subgroup to report their findings to the total group. Use this discussion to help participants understand how knowledge about student development is essential to handling student problems.

Next 25 minutes. Ask each participant to think about and share his initial adjustment as a freshman in a residence hall, based on the following three factors. (If some participants did not live in a residence hall, ask them to share their social and interpersonal adjustment in college.)

(a) Was the adjustment to residence hall living smooth or rough? How did you get along with your roommate? Did you feel accepted as part of the floor? Were you isolated?

(b) What were your feelings about living there? Did you feel good, depressed, frustrated, or just OK?

(c) How did you feel about your RA? Was that person helpful to you or others? If so, why? If not, why not?

Next 10 minutes. Review and summarize this discussion, focusing on the RA's five roles as identified in Chapter One. Review the training program in light of these roles.

Remind participants that they will get back part 1 of their autobiography at the next session and will then be assigned a rewrite.

4. Helpful hints. (a) Give participants plenty of time to share their reactions and feelings about writing an autobiography. *(b)* Use plenty of instructor self-disclosure, and strongly emphasize the labeling of feelings. Refer to the Vocabulary of Affective Adjectives in Training Program Aid E of the manual to expand participants' feeling word vocabulary.

Session 3: Sex-Role Stereotyping

1. Rationale. Thus far participants have been asked to share with each other their thoughts and feelings about *past* events or experiences. This type of self-disclosure is relatively "safe," does not create much anxiety, and is a good way to get participants to share their thoughts and feelings. This session brings the group to a more here-and-now sharing about the important but relatively safe issue (sex-role stereotyping) in terms of self-disclosure.

2. *Goals.* (a) Develop an understanding of sex-role identity. (b) Develop an awareness of sex-role stereotyping and the role of imprinting in that phenomenon. (c) Move the group to a higher level of interpersonal communication and self-disclosure. (d) Return part 1 of the autobiography and assign the rewrites (due at the next session).

3. *Design. First 5 minutes.* Review the session's rationale and goals.

Next 15 minutes. Introduce the concept of sex-role identity based on Chapter Three of the text. Refer to Chapter Three in the manual to introduce the concept of "imprinting" as one way of explaining how sex roles are developed and how sex-role stereotyping results.

Use several examples in your presentation. How do we learn what boys and girls do or do not do? Ask the class to brainstorm sources of the ideas and messages sent ("Girls cook, play with dolls, cry easily, and boys don't." "Boys play rough sports, take out the garbage, and never cry, and girls don't").

Again, talk about your own imprinting experiences, attitudes, and feelings.

Next 30 minutes. Divide participants into same-sex subgroups and have them reach a consensus on the following three questions:

(a) How do we describe ourselves as women or as men?

(b) How do we describe the opposite sex?

(c) How does the opposite sex describe us?

Each subgroup should summarize on paper its answers to these questions.

Next 5 minutes. Post the written summaries, and let each subgroup read what the other subgroup wrote.

Next 30 minutes. Bring the whole group back together and discuss the following:

(a) What did and did not surprise you about the way the other subgroups described themselves?

(b) What did and did not surprise you about the way the other subgroups described the opposite sex?

(c) What imprints remain powerful for you today, and what ones are less powerful or nonexistent?

Next 10 minutes. Assign rewrites of part 1 of the autobiography, stressing the importance of reading the instructors' reactions. Review again the rewrites due at the next session.

Next 15 minutes. Ask participants to share how they think and feel about the group so far:

(a) Do you feel comfortable participating in this group? If so, why? If not, why not?

(b) Are you learning anything so far? If so, why? If not, why not?

(c) How might the group improve the learning environment?

(d) What progress, if any, has the group made since it first started meeting?

Next 5 minutes. Distribute the First-Impression-Formation assignment (see Chapter Three in the manual), reminding participants that it is due at the next class session.

4. Helpful hints. (a) In the imprinting exercise, the group may too easily disown stereotyping behavior and not admit to the lingering effects of imprinting. Try this variation: "Imagine you are ten years old. What imprints or images do you have of the opposite sex?" *(b)* This is typically a lively session, with lots of enthusiasm and activity, so your problem may be controlling the quantity of the interaction. Make sure everyone has an equal opportunity to participate. *(c)* Again, instructor self-disclosure, expression of feelings, and specific examples are extremely important. *(d)* Encourage expression of both positive and negative attributes of the opposite sex. Establish that it is OK to be negative.

Part 2: Self-Awareness

This section gives participants some direct feedback regarding their behavior in the group. Session 4 starts with first-impression formation because it is a bit less threatening and very important for RAs to know what kind of first impression they make on people. When RAs first start working with their floors, first impressions are sometimes lasting, so they need to know how they turn people off or on when they first meet them.

More importantly, this section gives participants the skills necessary for giving and receiving feedback in a way that provides self-insight. Thus the process as well as the product is important in sessions 4 to 6. Also, this section sets the stage for Part 3, Interpersonal Skills Development, because participants will have a fairly accurate and up-to-date perception of their strengths and weaknesses that will be helpful as they develop their various interpersonal skills.

Session 4: First-Impression Formation

1. Rationale. When RAs first assume their responsibilities on a residence hall floor, they are forming first impressions of their residents, and the residents are forming first impressions of the RAs. Thus first-impression formation is an important process for RAs to understand. It is also important for RAs to know specifically just what kind of first impression they create, and they must know and understand how they create first impressions on others. There is a tendency to dismiss first impressions as meaningless. How often have you heard, "I never go by first impressions," or "I don't have first impressions; I withhold judgment until I get to know the person." In our opinion, these views are naive and not at all the way most people deal with first impressions. In fact, first impressions do occur, whether or not we like it, and they may be lasting, if we let them. Even if our own first impressions are subject to change, the other person's first impression of us may not be. So first-impression formation is an important aspect of RA effectiveness. It is also the groundwork for a more meaningful relationship between RAs and their floor members.

2. Goals. (a) Increase participants' awareness of the way they form first impressions of others and how they use or dismiss these impressions. *(b)* Increase participants' awareness of the way others form first impressions of them and what kind of first-impression image is formed by others. *(c)* Review and discuss criteria for useful feedback. *(d)* Review the format for training sessions 5 and 6. *(e)* Assign part 2 of the autobiography.

3. Design. First 10 minutes. Review the session's rationale and goals.

Next 20 minutes. Discuss the First-Impression-Formation assignment, including the following two questions: *(a)* On what bases do you typically form first impressions? *(b)* Are you satisfied with the bases from which you form first impressions? What would you like to change?

Next 20 minutes. Have each participant write a list of words or phrases to describe things most noticed, initially, about each member of the group. Do not use names, just descriptors, for example, "heavy makeup," "giggles a lot," "very quiet," "fantastic body," "really cute," or "very perceptive."

Summarize these phrases on paper and categorize them into verbal behavior, physical characteristics, or nonverbal behavior. Ask participants where their first impressions typically fell for this group.

Encourage acceptance of the idea that we all form first impressions and that the issue is not whether we do, but how we use them. Some participants will resist this exercise because "they don't go by first impressions" or "first impressions are seldom right."

Next 20 minutes. Introduce the concept of feedback and the rules of effective feedback, stressing that

(a) Sharing impressions of one another has two objectives: to learn some things about how we come across to others and to work on skills in sharing impressions of others because there are effective and ineffective ways of giving and receiving feedback.

(b) Refer to the criteria for useful feedback at the end of Chapter Four in the manual. Go over each rule and give examples (develop specific examples in advance and practice them before you preach them).

(c) Receiving feedback is just as important as giving it. Resist the temptation to judge whether the feedback is "right" or "wrong." Instead, decide whether the feedback is useful.

(d) Through giving and receiving feedback, people sharpen their sense of social identity. Feedback is one way of defining who we are or what we are like in the eyes of others.

Next 15 minutes. Participants practice their skill in sharing impressions:

(a) A participant directs feedback to one of the instructors, sharing one of the two following thoughts: "Something I noticed

(or am aware of or react to) about you is _____"; or "I found myself feeling _____ toward you."

(b) Continue until each person has directed one of those two sentences toward one instructor. The instructors should reflect accurately the content of the message.

Next 5 minutes. Ask participants to jot down five things they expect people to say about them in the feedback session.

Next 25 minutes. Begin the feedback session, under the following conditions:

(a) One person at a time receives feedback from all others in the group.

(b) As people share impressions, the receiver speaks only to clarify and help understanding, not to justify or explain behavior.

(c) Encourage receivers to seek clarification from the senders if they do not understand the message.

(d) After everyone has given this feedback, each receiver summarizes what has been said.

(e) Receivers then share with the group what they expected people to say about them, based on what they had earlier jotted down.

(f) Spend about ten to twenty minutes with each participant.

(g) Let participants volunteer when they wish to have their turn receiving feedback.

Last 5 minutes. Assign part 2 of autobiography, including sexuality, career/life-style, and interpersonal development; tell participants assignment is due at session 6.

4. Helpful hints.

(a) Work hard at developing participants' skills in giving and receiving good feedback. Besides your own modeling behavior, make the group stick to the rules of good feedback. Make several interventions early on, to reinforce their importance.

(b) Start the feedback with a participant you think will do a good job of responding and will get a balance of positive and negative feedback. You may want to consider using the experienced RA who is helping instruct the training program.

(c) Do not let the group scapegoat someone with a barrage of negative feedback. Sometimes one or two participants may be particularly obnoxious or offensive, and there is thus a tendency to jump on these people. Make the group consider the positive impressions they have made, even if they are few and implicit.

(d) Likewise, do not let the group give only positive feedback to a participant. The lack of negative feedback may be negative feedback for someone who has tried hard to please everyone in the group.

(e) If a person becomes upset with the feedback given by the group, you must help both the group and the individual deal with that situation. The group's failure to deal with an upset member can seriously limit the group's willingness or capability to continue to give constructive feedback. At the end of each feedback session, you may need to provide some support for participants who had a particularly rough time. However, be careful that support does not lead to erasing the legitimate feedback they have received or discourage participants from continuing to give feedback that may be upsetting to the receiver.

(f) Be very active in giving feedback and take your turn receiving feedback from the rest of the group.

(g) Be sure and let the last person get feedback. Do not continue someone over to the next session.

Session 5: Giving and Receiving Good Feedback

This session continues the feedback process begun at the end of session 4. Briefly review the rules of good feedback and continue with the next volunteer. You should have time for about six participants to get feedback. At the end of this session, summarize how you think the group is progressing in its ability to give and receive constructive feedback, stressing strengths and weaknesses.

Session 6: Giving and Receiving Good Feedback

This session continues session 5; you should have time for the remaining participants. At the end of this session, give the group about fifteen minutes to share their thoughts, reactions, and feelings concerning these feedback sessions. The group must have this opportunity because it is a very necessary catharsis following what are usually very intense and meaningful sessions. You should also be willing to share your own reactions regarding both your personal experience and the group's dynamics. Do not forget to collect Part 2 of the autobiography.

Part 3: Interpersonal Skills Development

This section is the heart and soul of the training program. Most prospective RAs can develop an understanding of student development and the residential context within which such development occurs. And most can learn to give and receive constructive feedback. But not all can develop the interpersonal skills necessary to function effectively as a counselor, adviser, mediator, facilitator, planner, disciplinarian, and leader on a residence hall floor. Session 7 presents an eclectic model of interpersonal skills development (reread text Chapter Five in preparation for that presentation). Sessions 8 to 14 then teach the component skills, one by one and in combination, until they are all put together in a successful interpersonal interaction.

Although much of this section is taught in the context of helping relationships, we recognize that a majority of RA-student interactions are not truly helping relationships, so we use examples that draw upon the wide variety of interpersonal situations an RA must handle.

Session 7: Introduction

1. Rationale. For RAs to develop effective interpersonal skills, they must know what the skills are and why they are essential to interpersonal effectiveness. This session presents an entire eclectic model of interpersonal skill development, specifically designed for the RA position. Emphasis is on the more basic skills of attending to nonverbal behavior, active listening, concreteness, and self-involvement. The initiation skills of summarizing and confronting are mentioned but emphasized and elaborated later in session 11.

2. Goals. *(a)* Present a conceptual model of interpersonal skills development for RAs. *(b)* Give participants an opportunity to discuss and understand this conceptual model. *(c)* Teach participants to attend to nonverbal behavior.

3. Design. First 5 minutes. Introduce the session's rationale and goals.

Next 20 minutes. Review and elaborate the model of interpersonal skills presented in Chapter Five of the text (summarized in Chapter Five of the manual), particularly emphasizing nonverbal communication, active listening, concreteness, and self-involvement. Stress the sequential nature of building interpersonal skills and the initial awkwardness in practicing these skills one at a time. (Refer to manual for additional background in presenting this model.)

Next 20 minutes. Distribute 3 X 5 cards and ask each participant to jot down the three most important things she learned or relearned from Chapter Five in the manual and listening to the presentation just completed.

Have each participant share these three things with the rest of the group; record these responses on paper, without editorial comment. Permit only questions of clarification.

Summarize what the group has learned or relearned, stressing the most important concepts. If the group omits some concepts, emphasize them once again, and note where the group is strong and weak in their conceptual basis for interpersonal skills development.

Next 15 minutes. Set up the Empty Chair exercise:

(a) Place two chairs facing one another, and choose a participant to sit in one chair.

(b) Have the participant talk about a personal matter to the empty chair for at least three minutes.

(c) Ask the participant to share how it feels to talk to an empty chair. What was good about it? What was missing?

(d) Repeat the exercise three more times, with three different participants.

Next 10 minutes. Help the group discuss and understand what happened. Some participants will express mixed feelings. Surprisingly, some may say that talking to an empty chair was more comfortable than talking to a person, perhaps because the chair was not evaluating or judging them. Others will feel uncomfortable because the chair offered no reactions or response. Make the point that if a person had been in the chair, a nonjudgmental, respectful, and caring response probably would have been most helpful.

Next 5 minutes. Briefly summarize to the group the types of nonverbal behaviors that have been found effective in successful interpersonal encounters (refer to Chapter Five). Stress the importance of nonverbal behaviors in the communication process, including eye contact, active facial expression, body rotation and posture, proximity to one another, and body lean.

Make the point that these nonverbal behaviors are not just gimmicks. If a person is genuinely interested in hearing, understanding, and helping someone, these nonverbal behaviors are natural expressions of this concern.

Next 5 minutes. Demonstrate and model these nonverbal behaviors with your coinstructor, with one of you as the listener and one as the speaker. Pick a relatively important and real concern — do not role play an imagined concern. The listener should limit responses to nonverbal ones.

Next 30 minutes. Give the group a chance to repeat the completed demonstration in the following way:

(a) Break participants into triads. Each triad will have a speaker, a listener, and an observer. Ask participants to decide who will take what role, but stress that each person will eventually get to play all three roles.

(b) Ask the speaker in each triad to talk to the listener about some real personal issue. The listener may respond only nonverbally. The observer then gives feedback to the listener about the effectiveness with which he or she responded nonverbally.

(c) Switch roles until each participant has taken each role.

Next 10 minutes. Ask participants to discuss their thoughts, feelings, and reactions to this exercise. They should identify which nonverbal cues were most effective when they were receiving them, and which ones were the most effective when they were sending them.

4. Helpful hints. (a) Make sure the group has a good grasp of the concepts of interpersonal effectiveness. Drive home the missing points if they do not. (b) Choose one of your more skillful participants for the first Empty Chair exercise. Do not rely on a volunteer because the modeling impact of the first participant is important. (c) Remind students that rewrites of Part 2 of the autobiography are due in Session 8.

Session 8: Active Listening

1. Rationale. The next step in developing basic interpersonal skills is active listening. The rationale is simple: If you do not really know or understand the other person, you cannot communicate with or help that person. Most participants are not as good at listening as they think they are, and some cannot even accurately reflect the content of a message, let alone its deeper meaning or the feelings behind the content. Thus participants must learn that active listening is not a skill to be taken for granted and that they probably will need more help in developing that skill than they first assumed.

2. Goals. (a) Introduce participants to the concept of active listening and its importance in effective interpersonal communication. (b) Give participants an opportunity to practice accurate reflection of a message's content. (c) Give participants an opportunity to practice accurate reflection of the expressed or unexpressed feelings of a message.

3. Design. First 5 minutes. Outline the session's rationale and goals.

Next 5 minutes. Review briefly the concept of reflective listening (refer to Chapter Five), and remind participants of its importance in an interpersonal communication.

Next 10 minutes. Demonstrate the Faithful Tape Recorder method of content reflection.

(a) One instructor relates a personal recent happening that was charged with some feelings. The other instructor acts as a "faithful tape recorder" who plays back everything the speaker said, and only what the speaker said, as soon as the speaker finishes.

(b) The first speaker speaks for about two minutes, to demonstrate the difficulty of remembering everything in a typical interaction.

(c) Participants then give feedback on whether the tape recorder faithfully played back everything. The group may have heard something the tape recorder missed.

(d) Instructors then summarize this exercise, pointing out how really difficult it is to accurately reflect just the content of a message.

Next 50 minutes. Repeat the Faithful Tape Recorder exercise with the group in the following sequence:

(a) Ask a participant to share a recent happening charged with feelings. Ask another participant to serve as the faithful tape recorder. Let the speaker talk for three minutes without interruption. The faithful tape recorder should then try to reflect *all* the content conveyed. It should become obvious to the group that a three-minute accurate content reflection is just about impossible. Make the point that more frequent interruptions for content reflection are more effective.

(b) Ask another participant to share a recent happening charged with feelings. This time the faithful tape recorder should reflect content approximately every thirty seconds. It should become obvious that reflection of shorter messages is more effective, but ask the question: Is it really necessary to reflect *everything?*

(c) Ask another participant to share a recent happening charged with feelings. This time the faithful tape recorder should reflect only a *summary* of the main points of the speaker, approximately every thirty seconds to a minute.

(d) Summarize the exercise, again pointing out the difficulty of simply reflecting the content of a message but that it can be done if reflections are done frequently and only the highlights are reflected.

Next 10 minutes. Introduce the importance of reflecting the speaker's *feelings* as well as the content. Refer to the Vocabulary of Affective Adjectives provided in the manual. Distinguish between feeling "domains" (love and affection, elation and joy, potency, depression, distress, anxiety, criticism and scorn, impotency and inadequacy, and anger and hostility). Accurate reflections of feelings must first hit the right domain and then the precise feeling word within that domain. Furthermore, feelings then have to be qualified by *intensity,* with such words as "somewhat," "quite," "very," or "extremely."

Make the point that most of us have a very small feeling word vocabulary and are usually lucky to get the right domain, much less the precise feeling word and exact intensity.

Next 30 minutes. Repeat the Faithful Tape Recorder exercise with the group, in the following sequence:

(a) Ask a participant to share a recent happening charged with feeling for about one minute. Ask the faithful tape recorder to identify the feeling domains, the precise feeling words that reflect the speaker's feelings, and the intensity of those feelings. Do *not* reflect any of the content. Let the group add their reflections. It should become obvious to the group that accurate reflection of the feelings is also more complicated than originally imagined and that it is much more difficult.

(b) Ask another participant to share a recent happening charged with feeling for about thirty seconds. Ask the faithful tape recorder to reflect the main points of the message's content and the expressed or implied feelings. Let the group add their reflections. It should be obvious to the group that the two processes of reflection of content and reflection of feeling, when done together, are very difficult to do correctly and very effective when done properly.

Last 10 minutes. Summarize the session, stressing the importance of the accurate reflection of content and feeling as a basic ingredient in effective interpersonal communication and the difficulty in doing it well. Ask participants to again review Training Program Aid E in the manual.

4. Helpful hints. (a) In the content-reflection exercise, be sure you make participants stick to content *only*. It is very easy for the listener or the group to add interpretations or analyses. (b) In the feeling-reflection exercise, really drive home the point about specificity of feeling words. Do not let participants get away with generalized, nonspecific words like "concerned" or "anxious." And try to get them to add qualifiers that communicate intensity. You may need to be very active at first to get them to be specific and identify intensity. Do not forget to collect rewrites of autobiography, Part 2.

Session 9: Concreteness and Putting It All Together

1. Rationale. Participants have been introduced to three fundamental interpersonal skills: nonverbal responding, reflection of content, and reflection of feelings. We now add one more responding skill: concreteness. In the first part of this session, participants have the opportunity to practice the fine art of asking the right question, so that both the speaker and the listener can completely understand what the speaker is communicating. In the second part, participants have the opportunity to put it all together by practicing attending to nonverbal behavior, reflecting the content and feeling of the message, and being concrete. It should be stressed that in a normal interaction, such specificity and structure is seldom possible, but to learn these skills, it is important to practice them as completely and thoroughly as possible.

2. *Goals.* *(a)* Give participants an opportunity to practice the skill of concreteness. *(b)* Give participants an opportunity to practice all the interpersonal skills learned so far.

3. *Design. First 5 minutes.* Introduce the session's rationale and goals.

Next 5 minutes. Review the concept of concreteness presented in Chapter Five. Point out that the skill of concreteness is not completely distinct from the skill of reflective listening because good reflections are often succinct, concrete summaries in which feelings and experiences are more accurately identified and labeled. In this sense, the students have already begun to practice concreteness.

This exercise concentrates on using a combination of concrete reflections and discrete open-ended questions, to help those who present problems vaguely and abstractly become more concrete.

Before starting the exercise, give some examples of open-ended versus close-ended questions.

Next 40 minutes. Break the group into triads. In each triad designate one person to play an RA, another to be a student, and the third to be an observer. Change this ordering every fifteen minutes, so each member of the triad can get practice in each role.

Within each of the three fifteen-minute sections, the student role plays talking to the RA by presenting problems vaguely and abstractly ("I'm bummed out," "I can't get it together"). The RA's task is to use a combination of accurate reflections and open-ended questions to help shape the student toward more concreteness. After ten minutes of such practice, the observer gives feedback and leads a five-minute evaluation of the process.

Note: After the first fifteen-minute role plays, it is a good idea to remind everyone that questions, even open-ended ones, are best used sparingly and are usually most effective if followed immediately by effective listening than by another question.

Next 70 minutes. Ask two participants to engage in an interaction for about two minutes. The speaker should talk about something important that is strongly felt, and the listener should engage in effective interpersonal skills, including appropriate nonverbal behavior, active listening, and being concrete. The group and instructors then give feedback to the listener, followed by feedback from the speaker. The listener then summarizes the feedback, focusing on strengths and weaknesses.

4. *Helpful hints.* (a) This session has a lot of activity, so carefully keep track of the time. (b) Make sure each participant receives feedback on all four skills being practiced and is able to accurately summarize that feedback.

Session 10: Self-Disclosure

1. *Rationale.* In sessions 8 and 9, the emphasis was on accurately reflecting the *sender's* thoughts and feelings—in other words, accurately reading the other person. Sessions 10 and 11 emphasize the *receiver's* thoughts, feelings and behavior—in other words, accurately reading oneself and determining appropriate responses. As participants become more aware of what is happening in the other person and what is happening in themselves, they form a basis for deciding how to respond.

2. *Goals.* (a) Establish the importance of knowing one's own thoughts and feelings as a basis for responding to another person. (b) Practice disclosing the listener's experiences that are similar to the speaker's. (c) Practice disclosing the listener's thoughts and feelings about the interaction with the speaker. (d) Practice putting it all together by attending to nonverbal behavior, active listening, concreteness, disclosing similar experiences, and disclosing feelings about the interaction with the speaker.

3. *Design. First 5 minutes.* Outline the session's rationale and goals. Review the responding skills covered so far and introduce the concept of self-involvement (refer to Chapter Five). Self-involvement is the listener disclosing those experiences similar to

those of the speaker and disclosing the thoughts and feelings about the interaction with the speaker.

Next 5 minutes. Introduce the self-disclosure exercise.

(a) Select one participant to role play an RA and another to role play a student.

(b) Ask the student to elaborate for about one minute some issue or problem of concern ("I don't have any close friends," "I don't know what I want out of college," or some other issue).

(c) Ask the RA to search personal experiences and disclose those aspects of the issue similar to those expressed by the student.

(d) After this similarity self-disclosure, ask the RA to express a few thoughts and feelings about the interaction so far ("When you told me you didn't have any close friends, I felt great compassion for you.").

(e) Ask the student to comment on the effect of both types of self-disclosure, and then ask the group to do the same.

Next 5 minutes. Summarize the concept of self-disclosure by suggesting the following:

(a) Similarity self-disclosure should occur fairly early after the speaker has revealed something that relates to the listener's experience because doing it then models this behavior and encourages more self-disclosure by the speaker.

(b) Similarity self-disclosure is most effective when the listener's experiences most nearly approximate the feeling domain and intensity of the speaker's experiences.

(c) Similarity self-disclosure should not be competitive in the sense of "You think you've got troubles; I've had troubles that were far worse than those!"

(d) The listener's disclosure of feelings about the interaction with the speaker should be brief, concise, and on target.

(e) Both forms of self-disclosure should not be so frequent as to shift the focus of the interaction away from the speaker to the listener.

Next 50 minutes. Repeat this exercise until each participant has had a chance to practice appropriate self-disclosure. Give each participant about five minutes, and keep moving on schedule.

Next 5 minutes. Review the skills covered so far, emphasizing attending to nonverbal behavior, reflecting the speaker's content and feeling, concreteness, and disclosing of the listener's appropriate thoughts, feelings, and experiences.

Next 45 minutes. Give each participant the opportunity to get feedback on personal skills in responding to another person. Each participant should get about ten minutes of group time, in the following way:

(a) Ask a participant to talk, for no more than one minute, about a recent happening charged with some feeling.

(b) Ask another participant to reflect the content and feeling of the speaker's message; the speaker should confirm that reflection.

(c) When the speaker's message has been confirmed, the listener should then provide an appropriate disclosure of his or her response to the sender, stressing both thoughts and feelings.

(d) The group then gives the listener feedback on nonverbal responding, active listening, concreteness, and self-disclosing skills.

Because the group may have difficulty getting into this exercise, the instructors should demonstrate it to lead it off. Then each class member should have an opportunity to get feedback (both in this class session and in session 11).

4. Helpful hints. (a) Make sure you rehearse instructor role modeling to begin the last exercise. You must do it right or the whole exercise will be ineffective. (b) The group may resist the idea of practicing these skills in such a repetitious manner, so you may have to review once again the reasons for proceeding in such a seemingly tedious manner. Most likely they will demonstrate the need to proceed slowly by their lack of skill as they do the exercise.

Session 11: Summarizing and Confronting

1. Rationale. The first part of this session continues the exercise begun in session 10: Participants are asked to put it all together regarding their responding skills. During the first hour, we complete that exercise, on the premise that participants need practice integrating the responding skills.

Thus far, we have focused on skills that apply to any and all interpersonal interactions. Attending to nonverbal behavior, accurately reflecting a message's content and feeling, being specific and asking appropriate open-ended questions, and disclosing our own thoughts, feelings, and experiences are but first steps in establishing effective relationships. As we move to the "action" phase of interpersonal interaction, things get more complex. How does a person initiate behaviors that help solve a problem, resolve an issue, or bring closure to interaction? What skills are required?

RAs are frequently involved in interactions that are not helping in the traditional sense, such as enforcing rules, providing information, or just plain interacting socially. The RA is also involved in encounters in which the other person may not be all that interested in participating, such as when the RA confronts a student in a disciplinary situation. Finally, the RA may be a third-party mediator in conflicts involving individuals or groups of students. Thus RAs must go beyond basic responding skills and move to initiation skills, or skills that solve a problem, resolve a conflict, or bring some kind of closure to a situation. These skills include summarizing and confronting. This session introduces these skills and helps participants understand their importance in interpersonal interactions.

2. *Goals.* (*a*) Complete the Putting It All Together responding skills exercise. (*b*) Introduce the concept of initiation skills, including summarizing, confronting, and informing.

3. *Design. First 60 minutes.* Review the session's rationale and goals. Continue and complete the exercise begun in the last session, giving participants the opportunity to practice putting together all their responding skills.

Next 10 minutes. Introduce the concept of initiation skills, including elaborating the definitions of summarizing and confronting (refer to Chapter Five).

Summarizing is tying together several statements about the speaker's thoughts and feelings, establishing themes, and offering other ways of looking at the issue presented by the speaker. *Confronting* is pointing out to the speaker some discrepancy between one attitude and another, an attitude and a behavior, a feeling and a behavior, or one feeling and another feeling.

Next 40 minutes. You should role play each initiation skill, based on examples given in Chapter Five. It is very important that you rehearse these roles, to provide exact examples of each initiation skill. At the end of the demonstration of each skill, involve the group in a discussion of the appropriateness and effectiveness of the intervention. Do not move to the second skill until you are sure the group thoroughly understands and recognizes the first skill you are demonstrating.

Next 10 minutes. Summarize initiation skills. Make an assignment for the next session: Each participant should come to class prepared to present a real problem or issue to another participant, one that typically might be presented to an RA, such as roommate difficulties, difficulties with parents, uncertainty about staying in school, uncertainty about career choice, and problems with an opposite-sex relationship.

4. Helpful hints. (a) Make sure you rehearse each initiation skill. The demonstration will make or break the exercise, so spend some time preparing. (b) The next session is critical, so be sure you spend enough time setting it up at the end of this session. (c) Pass out Trainee's Evaluation of Instructor form (pp. 143–145 in the manual), to be filled out anonymously and due at the next session.

Session 12: Using Effective Interpersonal Skills in Counseling Situations

1. Rationale. Participants now have an understanding of all the skills required to be effective in interpersonal relationships. The counseling setting is a useful way to introduce, isolate, and demonstrate the effective use of the skills we presented in our model. Students sometimes go to their RAs for help with personal problems, so it is very important for RAs to know how to help students when asked. Of course, RAs are not psychotherapists and should not perform functions beyond their skills and abilities. But very often they are the first person in the institution that students seek out for help because generally students are more willing to talk with a fellow student than with counselors or staff. In this session, RAs are once again asked to put it all together and practice their responding and initiation skills in counseling situations typical of the ones they will face on a residence hall floor.

2. Goals. (a) Give participants an opportunity to deal with problems typically presented to RAs. (b) Give participants the opportunity to get feedback regarding their interpersonal skills, particularly their initiation skills.

3. Design. First 5 minutes. Review the session's rationale and goals, especially emphasizing initiation skills.

Next 100 minutes. Give each participant an opportunity to help another participant with a problem.

(a) Have the speaker speak for about three minutes. The helper should interrupt for reflection of thoughts and feelings and/or appropriate disclosure of thoughts, feelings, or experiences.

(b) The helper either attempts a summarizing statement, offering themes or tones, and asks the speaker to confirm that summary, *or* the helper attempts a confronting statement, based on discrepancies detected, and asks the speaker to respond to those discrepancies.

(c) Just before the helper does one of those two things, the helper should seek the advice of the group and the instructors as to the appropriate response. Do *not* at this point consult with the speaker.

(d) After the intervention with an initiation skill, let the speaker and helper go in whatever direction seems appropriate, until their five minutes are up.

(e) Ask both the group and speaker to give the helper feedback.

Proceed with this exercise until all participants have had the opportunity to get feedback and share a problem.

Last 5 minutes. Summarize the exercise, and refer to Chapter Seven to prepare for the next session.

4. *Helpful hint.* You should begin your individual sessions with each participant by evaluating performance in the training so far.

Session 13: Crisis Intervention

1. *Rationale.* Occasionally crises develop with individuals on a residence hall floor that are extremely serious and require that the RA promptly and effectively respond. Usually these crises, such as a severely depressed student, the death of a student's loved one, or a suicidal student, precipitate high anxiety in RAs, unless they have had a chance to prepare for them. The RA's response to a student in crisis should be to provide support and assistance until a referral can be made to persons qualified to help the student.

2. *Goals.* *(a)* Give participants guidelines for dealing with students in crisis. *(b)* Give participants an opportunity to explore their feelings about dealing with students in crisis and practice effective skills in dealing with such students.

3. Design. First 5 minutes. Introduce the session's rationale and goals.

Next 20 minutes. Provide an overview of crisis intervention (refer to Chapter Seven), including the guidelines for helping students in crises. Stress the importance of the ultimate goal of getting the student to persons who can help. Give examples based on your own or other RAs' experiences.

Next 15 minutes. Encourage each participant to discuss personal hesitancies and fears as well as competencies in dealing with students in crises. Participants should discuss any actual past experiences that provide insight into their responses to crisis situations. Instructor self-disclosure is especially important, particularly at first.

Next 15 minutes. Elaborate the severely depressed student as an example of a student in crisis (refer to Chapter Seven for guidelines about how to deal with such a student). Focus not only on guidelines but appropriate interpersonal skills. Role play an interaction with a severely depressed student.

Next 65 minutes. Ask one participant to role play a severely depressed student and another to respond to that crisis. Let the interaction continue for about five minutes, and then allow about five minutes of feedback. Repeat this exercise with five other dyads. Focus on guidelines for dealing with students in crises and appropriate interpersonal skills.

4. Helpful hints. (a) Rehearse the role playing of a severely depressed student in advance of this session. Your role modeling is especially important to the success of the exercise that follows. *(b)* You might use this session to provide information about the campus resources that can be referral sources for students in crises.

Session 14: Feedback and Group Process

1. Rationale. Participants have now spent approximately sixteen hours with one another since the first-impression feedback session. During that time, they have learned about and hopefully more fully developed their interpersonal skills. They have also learned much more about each other, and it is now time to update participants on the thoughts and feelings of others in the group, through another feedback session. This session will give participants a current assessment of their impact upon others and a chance to practice their improved interpersonal skills with each other. However, in this design participants are limited in the amount of feedback they have time to give one another, so they should be asked in advance to give some thought to the *one* most important piece of feedback they have for each group member. Now is also time for another update on how participants are feeling about the group.

2. Goals. (*a*) Give participants updated feedback from each other based on behavior generated in the last few class sessions. (*b*) Give participants an opportunity to practice their interpersonal skills in the feedback situation. (*c*) Let participants comment on their thoughts and feelings about the group to this point in the training.

3. Design. First 5 minutes. Introduce the session's rationale and goals, including a brief review of the rules of useful feedback.

Next 90 minutes. Ask each participant to take about five minutes to receive the one most important piece of feedback from all the other participants. The person receiving the feedback should listen to all the feedback before reacting, but the person can ask for clarification while feedback is being received. The receiver of the feedback then summarizes the feedback and reacts to it regarding thoughts and feelings.

Next 20 minutes. Conduct another group-process checkout, focusing on the following: (*a*) What thoughts and feelings do you have about the group so far? (*b*) How have your thoughts and feelings changed since the last group checkout session? (*c*) What are the group's strengths? (*d*) In what area does the group need improvement?

Next 5 minutes. Assign Floor Characteristics Assessment (refer to Chapter Six in manual), which is due at session 17.

4. Helpful hints. (*a*) Keep the feedback session moving; it should not take more than eight or ten minutes per person. Make sure feedback is understood when initially given, but do not let interpretations or reactions occur at that time. (*b*) When a summarization of feedback is given, make sure the participant has not exaggerated or omitted significant feedback. Make sure these summarizations are accurate and balanced.

Part 4: Group Leadership Development

So far, we have emphasized the one-to-one relationships that RAs establish and maintain with students on their floors. Of the RA's six functions, four (managing and facilitating groups; explaining and enforcing rules; facilitating social, recreational, and educational programs; developing an orderly and quiet atmosphere) require that RAs lead and work with groups of students on their floors. Most RAs feel much more at ease in dealing with a single student than a group of them.

We start from the assumption that RAs must have a basic self-awareness and interpersonal skill level to provide effective group leadership. But leadership on a residence hall floor is very different from other types of student leadership, and thus the typical neophyte RA is not well prepared to assume that leadership. RAs must know and understand their roles and the position's influence and limitations. They must know about the students on their floors as to personal, demographic, and residential characteristics and the floor's group dynamics. Finally, RAs must apply a wide variety of leadership styles, depending on the situation and the floor's maturity level.

In this section, sessions 15 and 16 provide an eclectic model of leadership development and a situational leadership model, respectively, that help RAs decide which style of leadership to apply in various situations. Session 17 is assessing the maturity level of residence hall floors and the bases of power of the RA position. Session 18 covers conflict resolution; session 19 discusses the RA's discipline role. Session 20 is a final feedback session.

Session 15: Introduction

1. Rationale. RAs must function in many group leadership situations. They advise their floor governments, help floors plan and implement social and educational programs, try to create an orderly and quiet atmosphere on their floors, and enforce rules and regulations. While doing these things, the RAs must deal effectively with both formal and informal groups of students. The problem is that RAs are asked to perform as leaders in a very unique group setting, not one in which prior experience is much help. Thus RAs need a different framework within which to look at their leadership with groups on their floors and practice functioning effectively in the various types of group leadership situations they must deal with.

2. *Goals.* *(a)* Introduce an eclectic model of leadership development (refer to Chapter Six). *(b)* Introduce four basic leadership styles and discuss how to apply them to situations that arise on a residence hall floor.

3. *Design. First 5 minutes.* Introduce the session's rationale and goals.

Next 10 minutes. Introduce the eclectic model of group leadership development, focusing on interpersonal skills, the RA position, the residence hall floor, and the situation (refer to Chapter Six).

Next 15 minutes. Elaborate the four leadership styles developed by Hersey and Blanchard (see Chapter Six): telling, selling, participating, and delegating. Stress the importance of defining the maturity level of the persons or groups involved.

Next 30 minutes. Choose a participant who seems to have a good understanding of the four leadership styles. Review with that participant the maturity level of the floor:

The students on this floor are mostly freshmen and sophomores and very active and enthusiastic. In Hersey and Blanchard's terms, however, they are willing but not able to take responsibility.

Introduce the following situation: Students on your floor, especially the house officers, are not responding to your friendly conversation and obvious concern for their problem. A semiformal dinner dance is being planned by the house officers, but they are behind in their planning, missing deadlines, and not attending to the details necessary to make the event happen. It is obvious to you that if something does not happen, the event will fall through.

Give the participant an opportunity to ask further questions about this situation by asking the person:

(a) Do you have all the facts you need?

(b) Do you have a good understanding of the situation?

(c) Do others confirm your understanding of the situation? (In this role playing, this question cannot be answered, but it is a question that should be asked in a real situation.)

(*d*) Who are the key people involved in this situation?

(*e*) What are the possible outcomes of this situation? (Move from the most positive to the most negative.)

Now ask the participant to decide which of the following alternatives he would choose to deal with this situation: (*a*) Call in the officers and give them a very specific plan for pulling off the dinner dance, emphasizing keeping good financial records, confirming necessary arrangements, and so on (telling). (*b*) Inform the house officers that you are available for help if they need it (participating). (*c*) Call in the house officers and help them set goals (selling). (*d*) Do nothing (delegating).

Give the participant the opportunity to state why he chose the alternative he did. Ask other participants to pick an alternative and state why.

Using the Hersey and Blanchard diagram (Figure 1) in Chapter Six of the manual, reveal the most appropriate leadership style, given the maturity level of the floor. (In this instance, selling is the best leadership style.)

Next 25 minutes. Similarly walk a participant through another situation, in the following way:

The students on this floor are a mixture of freshmen, sophomores, juniors, and seniors—a very average floor. In Hersey and Blanchard's terms, they are able but not willing to take responsibility.

Introduce the following situation: Students on your floor have been taking a lot of responsibility for themselves, including setting up a damage committee, running orderly parties, and setting up a tutoring system for helping students who are having trouble academically. However, all these things happen as a result of your (the RA's) initiation and suggestion. You have made your expectations known and have stated that activities of this type will be the future standard.

Give the participant an opportunity to ask further questions (see the previous exercise). Now ask the participant to decide which of the following alternatives she would choose to deal with the situation: (*a*) Maintain informal interaction with the floor, but continue to make sure that all floor members are aware of their responsibilities and your expected standards of performance (telling). (*b*) Support the group, and work toward making the group feel important and involved (participating). *(c)* Emphasize the importance of continued adherence to the rules and the continuation of the status quo (selling). *(d)* Do nothing (delegating).

Give the participant the opportunity to state why she chose the alternative. Ask other participants to pick an alternative, and state why.

Using Figure 1 in the manual, reveal the most appropriate leadership style, given the maturity level of the floor. (In this instance, participating is the best leadership style.)

Next 25 minutes. Similarly walk a participant through another situation:

The students on this floor are active and responsible. In Hersey and Blanchard's terms, they are willing and able to take responsibility.

Introduce the following situation: You have a good, positive relationship with floor members and exhibit a high degree of concern for their welfare. Students on your floor are housed in two separate wings of the building. A decision has been made to allow a fraternity or sorority to take over one of these wings for next year, displacing all current residents. The floor is extremely upset over the decision and confused about what to do about it, but they want to do something. Give the participant an opportunity to ask further questions (see first exercise).

Now ask the participant to decide which of the following alternatives she would choose to deal with the situation: *(a)* Support the group in working on the problem (participating). *(b)* Work with the floor and problem solve with them (selling). *(c)* Do nothing; let the group work it out alone (delegating). *(d)* Move in quickly, act firmly, and redirect their efforts to accepting the decision and living with it (telling).

Give the participant the opportunity to state why she chose the alternative. Ask other participants to pick an alternative, and state why.

Using Figure 1 in the manual, reveal the most appropriate leadership style, given the maturity level of the floor. (In this instance, participating is the best leadership style.)

Last 10 minutes. Summarize the overall mode of leadership, and review once again how an RA decides which leadership style to apply to a given situation.

4. Helpful hints. (a) Make sure participants have a good conceptual understanding of the whole model before you move to the situations. *(b)* Also make sure participants understand each Hersey and Blanchard leadership style and the importance of assessing the general maturity level of the group. *(c)* Pick a fairly perceptive and skillful participant to do the first exercise.

Session 16: Situational Leadership

1. Rationale. Thus far, students have been introduced to an overall model of leadership development and have focused on which leadership style to apply in a given situation, depending on the group's maturity level. Assume that participants will have an opportunity to practice these styles; in other words, once they decide to apply a given style to a given situation, can they pull it off? Do they have the knowledge and skills to provide, for example, a selling style of leadership?

2. Goals. (a) Give participants feedback on how they implement various leadership styles. *(b)* Introduce more comprehensive ways of assessing floor maturity.

3. Design. First 5 minutes. Introduce the session's rationale and goals.

Next 35 minutes. Choose a participant who did not participate in the three exercises in session 15 and ask him to role play the following situation:

As a new RA, you come into a floor that was very tightly controlled by the previous RA. That RA provided lots of structure and exercised a great deal of direct influence and control. As a result, the floor was highly productive in terms of social events, educational programs, and a quiet study atmosphere. You want to maintain a highly productive situation, but you would like to humanize the environment by allowing students to take more responsibility for what is happening.

Situation on the floor: The group responded to the previous RA's task orientation. You are really unsure about whether the floor can learn to take responsibility for its own environment if the RA's strong support is changed. However, you would like to try letting the floor assume more responsibility, but you are not sure just how to do it.

Let the participant ask questions about the situation. Ask the participant to assess the floor's maturity level, based on Hersey and Blanchard's four-part model (unwilling and unable to assume responsibility, willing and able to assume responsibility, willing but unable to assume responsibility, unwilling but able to assume responsibility).

Ask the participant to choose one of the following alternatives to role play the leadership style with other participants: *(a)* Get the group involved in decision making, but see to it that their objectives are met (selling). *(b)* Continue to direct the group the same way as the previous RA, with the hope that they will assume more responsibility (telling). *(c)* Do what can be done to make the group feel important and involved (participating). *(d)* Do nothing (delegating).

Ask the participant to explain why he chose a particular leadership style, and how he assessed the floor's maturity level. Ask the group to comment on these choices, and have the participant and the group agree on the best leadership style.

At this point, ask the participant to leave the room. In this instance, the selling style of leadership is best, based on the Hersey and Blanchard model. Choose five members of the group to role play the floor. If the alternative chosen is the correct one (selling), the floor role players should be cooperative. If the alternative chosen is any of the other styles, instruct the group the following way:

Alternative 2 (telling). Should be supported by the group very actively because they liked the previous RA's style. Any attempt to get the group to assume more responsibility should be resisted. The group should insist the RA stay very involved.

Alternative 3 (participating). The group should resist this approach because the group is not ready for so much responsibility.

Alternative 4 (delegating). The group should be angry over this approach because it is such a drastic change and anxiety about the loss of activities and programs is high.

Bring back the RA role player, and let the role play run for about ten minutes. Ask the observers to be prepared to give feedback to the RA role player about the following questions: *(a)* Did the RA choose the right leadership style? If so, why? If not, why not? *(b)* Did the RA behave consistently with the leadership style chosen? If so, how? If not, how might the style have been better implemented? *(c)* Did the RA practice good interpersonal skills? If so, which ones? If not, where could the RA have improved?

Next 35 minutes. Choose another participant, and ask him to role play the following situation:

You have just returned from an evening at the library to find that your floor is in the midst of a large water battle. There is about an inch of water throughout the bathroom and halls, and residents are sliding down the hallway on their trash cans. Almost everyone on the floor is involved and having a good time.

Situation on the floor: The floor has been an active one and had organized activities and events on its own. They have shown definite signs of assuming responsibility for themselves, but they still have some way to go regarding maturity.

Let the participant ask questions about the situation. Ask the participant to assess the floor's maturity level, based on Hersey and Blanchard's four alternatives (see previous exercise).

Ask the participant to choose one of the following alternatives to role play the leadership style with some other participants: *(a)* Act quickly and firmly to stop the water battle, emphasizing the danger of injury and property damage (telling). *(b)* Work with the group and explain to them what their behavior could lead to. Make all floor members aware of their responsibilities and expected standards of performance (selling). *(c)* Do what you can to let them know their behavior could injure others, but let the group leaders emerge and involve other students in cleaning up (participating). *(d)* Take no definite action (delegating).

Ask the participant to explain why he chose a particular leadership style and how he assessed the floor's maturity level. Ask the group to comment on these choices, and have the participant and the group agree on the best leadership style.

Ask the participant to leave the room. In this instance, telling is the best leadership style, based on the Hersey and Blanchard model. Choose five class members to role play the floor. If the alternative chosen is the correct one (telling), the floor role players should be cooperative, give the RA a little "in jest" resistance, and do what the RA says. If the alternative chosen is any of the other styles, instruct the group the following way:

Alternative 2 (selling). Agree with everything the RA says but continue the water battle because it is so much fun, and assure the RA that no one will get hurt and that the mess will be cleaned up.

Alternative 3 (participating). Agree with everything the RA says, stop the water battle, and get into an argument over who started it and who should clean up.

Alternative 4 (delegating). Some members argue to keep the water battle going because it is all in good fun and support the RA. Others insist that the RA do something because someone might get hurt, damages might occur, and besides, they want to study.

Bring back the role player, and let the role play run for about ten minutes. Ask observers to be prepared to give feedback to the RA role player, based on the questions outlined in the previous exercise.

Next 35 minutes. Choose another participant and ask her to role play a situation in which the RA's ideal response is to do nothing (delegating). Follow the same format as in the previous two exercises.

Next 10 minutes. Review the Floor Dynamics Assessment assignment, in which participants are asked to interview their own RA (or any RA, if they do not have one) according to the format suggested in the manual.

4. Helpful hints

(a) Make sure the group role players behave consistently with the characteristics, interactive dynamics, and maturity level described by the RA role player.

(b) Do not let the group role players get locked into their roles. If the RA makes reasonable suggestions or handles the situation effectively, instruct the role players to be responsive to such RA behavior.

(c) Observe the role playing very carefully, and help the group give the RA role player useful feedback.

(d) When summarizing each role-playing situation, reinforce the basic steps in the model and allow for maximum discussion.

(e) You may run out of time and be able to do only one of the last two situations. Choose the one you think is most relevant to your institution and most frequently encountered by your RAs.

(f) You may want to add or substitute other leadership situations that are more relevant to your campus and residence halls.

(g) Assign the final examination interpersonal skills tape.

Session 17: Floor Assessment and Exercise of Power

1. Rationale. The eclectic leadership development model we presented assumes that RAs have good interpersonal skills, understand their positions, are able to judge their floors' maturity levels, and can implement one of four leadership styles, depending on the situation. Generally, our experience has been that RAs have good interpersonal skills and that they can implement each leadership style suggested by Hersey and Blanchard. We have also found that they can usually define fairly accurately the situations they face.

However, the model is more likely to break down if RAs (1) do not really have a good grasp of their floors' maturity levels and/or (2) do not understand the power bases that underlie their leadership styles. Therefore, it is important for RAs to thoroughly understand their floors' characteristics and dynamics so that they can improve their ability to judge floor maturity in a given situation. It is also important for RAs to know the bases of power they exercise in their position, to more effectively implement the various leadership styles suggested by Hersey and Blanchard.

2. Goals. (a) Provide two specific ways of learning more about a residence hall floor: assessing floor characteristics and assessing floor dynamics. *(b)* Give participants some insight into the typical power bases they use in a position of authority to relate to students.

3. Design. First 5 minutes. Introduce the session's goals and rationale.

Next 20 minutes. Ask participants to comment on their assessment of the floor's characteristics: *(a)* What did you learn about your floor that you did not know previously from just living there? *(b)* What implications does all this information have for your role as an RA? For your judgment about the floor's maturity level?

Summarize the discussion, stressing the insights gained from a collective look at floor members' characteristics and attitudes. Try to relate this information not only to the maturity level of the floor—are they generally willing and able to assume responsibility? Are they unwilling, but able? And so on—but to other RA roles, such as planning relevant programs or dealing with conflicts.

Next 20 minutes. Break participants into dyads, and ask each participant to review with another participant the results of the floor dynamics assessment, based on the RAs she interviewed. Allow each participant about five minutes to discuss the results of the interview and another five minutes for the other participant to react. (Refer to the manual and Chapter Six for the variables discussed.)

Next 10 minutes. Bring the group back together and have them discuss the two assignments. Did these assignments help you gain a better understanding of the floor? If so, how? If not, why not?

Encourage participants to gather this information about their floors early in the year, preferably by the end of the fourth week.

Next 10 minutes. Ask participants to think about how RAs influence what is happening on a residence hall floor. What sources of power or influence does the RA really have? Have participants brainstorm these sources and list them on paper. Essentially, these sources of power should fall into the following five categories (refer to the manual and Chapter Six): *(a) referent power:* influence exerted because of who the RA is as a person. *(b) legitimate power:* influence exerted because of the RA's position, based on rights granted by the institution. *(c) expert power:* influence exerted because of what the RA knows or how the RA's skills are used. *(d) reward power:* Influence exerted because of the rewards or approval the RA can offer. *(e) coercive power:* influence exerted because of punishments or disapproval the RA can offer.

Help participants understand that as RAs they are in a position of authority and must exercise all five types of power if they are to be effective. Power is not a dirty word, and neither is coercive power when exercised openly, directly, rationally, and in the best interests of students.

Next 55 minutes. Introduce participants to the Power exercise: *(a)* Review the situation, presented in session 15:

The students on your floor are mostly freshmen and sophomores and very active and enthusiastic. They are willing but not able to take responsibility. These students, especially the house officers, are not responding to your friendly conversation and obvious concern for their problem. A semiformal dance is being planned by the house officers, but they are behind in their planning, missing deadlines, and not attending to the details necessary to make the event happen. It is obvious to you that if something does not happen, the event will fall through.

(b) Remind participants that the preferred leadership mode was selling: calling in the house officers and helping them set goals.

(c) Ask one participant to leave the room and think about how he would handle this meeting. Ask another few participants to role play house officers; ask the remaining participants to observe.

(d) The RA should think about the five bases of power available to him, and decide which one(s) would most effectively implement a selling leadership mode.

(e) Ask the participants role playing house officers to genuinely respond to the RA's leadership.

(f) Ask observers to comment on what power bases the RA uses, how he used them, and what effect they had on the house officers. In this instance, the RA should have relied primarily on reward and legitimate power, secondarily on expert power.

(g) Repeat this exercise, with different role players, picking any one of the situations and solutions identified in sessions 15 or 16.

Telling leadership modes should rely primarily on coercive and legitimate power. Delegating leadership modes should rely primarily on referent, expert, and legitimate power. Participating modes should rely primarily on expert power, secondarily on referent power.

(h) If time permits, repeat with a different situation.

Last 10 minutes. Review the session, stressing the importance of knowing the floor's characteristics and dynamics as a basis for judging the floor's maturity levels. Tie in the importance of knowing and exercising power in each of the four leadership styles. (Refer to Chapter 6 for relating power bases to leadership styles.)

4. Helpful hints. (a) Make the connection between this session's two goals and the leadership model suggested in sessions 15 and 16. (b) Make sure participants come out of the power exercise with a good notion of which power bases they typically use, which ones they are good at, and which ones they have difficulty with.

Session 18: Conflict Resolution and Third-Party Mediation

1. Rationale. RAs frequently must deal with situations in which one or more individuals or groups are in conflict with one another. As examples, RAs are frequently called on to help roommates resolve their differences; two groups of students on a floor may need help from the RA in getting along with one another. In these situations, RAs must take actions that allow both parties in the conflict to resolve their differences and establish a basis for future relationships. But being a mediator is a very difficult role, and if not handled properly, it could have implications for both the RA's relationship with the conflicting parties and the rest of the floor. Thus RAs need to understand the nature of conflict, the bases for conflict, and, most importantly, how to serve as a mediator.

2. Goals. (a) Help participants understand the nature of conflict and the role of a third-party mediator in resolving conflict. *(b)* Give participants an opportunity to practice their mediator role in situations that RAs must typically handle.

3. Design. First 5 minutes. Review the session's rationale and goals.

Next 15 minutes. Outline the nature and bases for conflict, the role of the third-party mediator, and possible solutions (refer to Chapter Six), stressing that *(a)* Conflict is not a negative concept; it can be handled constructively. *(b)* Assessing the nature of the conflict is the first important step in resolving the situation. *(c)* The role of a third-party mediator is important, difficult, and fraught with all kinds of difficulty.

Now review the guidelines for effective mediation, and then possible solutions.

Next 100 minutes. Ask participants to role play each of the following four conflict situations, with special emphasis on reinforcing the role of the mediator and identifying the best solution.

(a) A student complains to you that she cannot get along with her roommate because the roommate keeps late hours, plays her stereo at all hours of the night and too loudly, entertains disruptive

guests in her room, and makes her leave the room for long periods so she can privately entertain her boyfriend. You decide to call them both in together to discuss the conflict.

(b) You have heard rumors that two roommates are not getting along and are constantly fighting with one another. Neither has complained to you, but the father of one of the men has complained to the Dean that the situation is very bad. You have been asked by the Dean to investigate the situation and try to resolve it. You have little or no information about why the roommates do not get along. You decide to call them both in together to discuss the conflict.

(c) Your floor consists of two cliques with very different ideas about what a residence hall should be. One group, the "bookers," think your floor should be a quiet place in which to study, sleep, and relax. Another group, the "partiers," think the floor should be a place in which to have a good time, let off steam, and party. They think that if someone wants to study, the library is the place. Tensions are escalating between the two groups, and you want to intervene before the situation explodes. You call a house meeting to discuss the situation.

(d) Another RA in your building tells you that there are a group of students on your floor who are very upset with you because of the way you handled a recent disciplinary situation. They feel that you could have handled the situation without making a disciplinary referral, that you were out to get the person you referred. They are putting out the word that you cannot be trusted, that you are really a "hired gun" for the administration. You decide to talk with them.

4. Helpful hints

(a) Do not let the role players get locked into their roles. If the RA makes reasonable suggestions or handles the conflict situation effectively, instruct the role players to respond to such RA behavior.

(b) Be active in giving feedback to the RA role player, stressing the guidelines for effective mediation.

(c) Keep the group focused on mediation skills, and do not let members move to possible solutions too early.

(d) Participants may tend to forget some of the basic interpersonal skills, such as active listening, self-disclosure, and initiation skills, and resort to asking many questions. Reinforce the notion that these skills apply to conflict situations just as importantly as they apply to counseling and leadership situations.

(e) You may want to develop alternative situations, based on your residence hall program's unique needs.

Session 19: Dealing with Discipline

1. *Rationale.* No doubt one thing neophyte RAs worry about most is their role in enforcing institutional rules and regulations. As a result of their disciplinary role, they are asked to step beyond just being students and walk halfway to becoming arms of the administration. At worst, RAs are seen as betraying their fellow students and caring more about institutional rules and expectations than the well-being of the persons on their floors. It is not an easy role to implement, and it is very difficult for many RAs to handle. Some RAs will avoid enforcing rules and constantly look the other way; others will become supermilitant, enforcing rules to the letter and going way beyond the intent of the institution.

However, there are ways RAs can enforce rules and deal effectively with discipline. Everything that has been covered in this training program—including knowing about students' development, having good interpersonal skills, applying good group leadership skills, and having good conflict resolution skills—should help the RA deal with disciplinary situations. But even if RAs have all these things going for them, they may mishandle disciplinary situations because they do not know how to behave within their authority role. Stated another way, they have difficulty exercising power in a coercive way. There are times when RAs must exercise authority-oriented control over a situation and direct students to do something they may not want to do, whether or not they like it. Our assumption is that authoritative messages can be delivered in such a way that students will accept them, given appropriate conditions and good interpersonal skills.

2.   *Goals.* (a) Help participants deal with disciplinary situations and provide guidelines within which such situations should be handled. (b) Give participants the opportunity to practice dealing with some typical disciplinary situations.

3. *Design. First 5 minutes.* Introduce the session's rationale and goals.

Next 15 minutes. Review the guidelines for dealing with disciplinary situations (refer to text Chapter Six), as outlined in Chapter Six of the RA manual.

Next 95 minutes. Ask participants to role play each of the following four disciplinary situations. Allow about five minutes before each role playing for the group to help the role player develop an approach.

(a) You know that what you say to your floor at the beginning of the year about how you are going to handle discipline is very important. You decide to cover this topic in your first house meeting, so that everyone will understand your feelings about this issue. Prepare your remarks, and field any questions the group has.

(b) You walk onto your floor into the middle of a huge water battle. There is about an inch of water on the floor and some damage to the bathroom facilities. It is obvious that everyone involved is having a great time. You must put an end to it because of the damage, the noise, and the potential for injury to those participating.

(c) Parties with alcohol are forbidden in your residence halls. A person knocks on your door and informs you that a party is taking place in a room on your floor and that drinking is occurring, including underage drinking. Such behavior, when reported, typically results in a disciplinary referral. You decide you must go to the room and handle the situation.

(d) Three times you have warned a student on your floor to keep the volume on her stereo at a level that does not disturb others. At this moment you discover that she has turned her stereo speakers facing out the window and is delivering a free concert to the world—it is 11 o'clock at night. You must handle the situation, remembering that the last time you asked her to turn down her stereo, you threatened more drastic action if you had to come to her room again about this issue. In your other three encounters with her, she basically did not feel she was doing anything wrong and that you and others were oversensitive to noise.

Last 5 minutes. Introduce Final Advice assignment (see Session 20). Pass out training and instructor evaluations.

4. *Helpful hints. (a)* Again, make sure the role players do not get locked into their roles. *(b)* Stress the guidelines of dealing with disciplinary situations, but do not let participants forget all their other interpersonal and group leadership skills. *(c)* You may want to develop alternate situations, based on your residence hall program's unique needs.

Session 20: Final Feedback Session

1.   *Rationale.* The training group has been through a lot together, and now it is important for them to develop some closure on the experience. That means many things, including a chance to share their thoughts and feelings about the training, the instructors, other participants, and, most importantly, the future. This session discusses closure and ending the training program constructively and positively.

2.   *Goals. (a)* Let participants share their thoughts and feelings about the training. *(b)* Give participants some constructive advice about their predicted performance as an RA. *(c)* Let participants share their thoughts and feelings about the instructors.

3.   *Design. First 5 minutes.* Introduce the session's goals and rationale, stressing the importance of bringing closure to this experience.

Next 75 minutes. Ask participants to share with each other the advice they developed for them. Have each participant hear all the advice from all other participants; then comment briefly on the two aspects of the advice: *(a)* As an RA, I think you'll be strong on _____ . *(b)* As an RA, I think you'll need to work on _____ . *(c)* The one word I would use to describe you is _____ .

Next 20 minutes. Ask participants to hand in their instructor evaluations and give instructors the following feedback: *(a)* As an instructor, I particularly appreciated your _____ . *(b)* As an instructor, you still need to work on _____ . *(c)* The one word I would use to describe you is _____ .

Next 20 minutes. Ask participants to hand in the evaluation of the training program and share the following: *(a)* What I appreciated most about this training was _____ . *(b)* The most disappointing thing about this training was _____ .

(c) The one word I would use to describe this training is
_____ .

4. *Helpful hints. (a)* Try to keep this session on a positive, upbeat tone. But do not sugarcoat the experiences in this training if they were not all that good for some participants or for the group as a whole. If the experience was more negative than positive, try to focus on how it could be improved. *(b)* Focus on the future!

Abbreviated Versions of Training Program

We presented this training program in its most ideal form. We believe training should be an extension of the selection process and done in advance of students assuming the RA position. We also believe that a great deal of time should be spent on training, and our training program is designed to take about forty hours. Furthermore, we believe that the persons who train RAs should also be the persons who supervise them. Finally, we believe this training model is a basis for further training on specific issues that are important to your institution, your residence hall system, or your resident assistants. We think our training program works best under the circumstances and structure we suggested.

But we recognize that it may not be possible to implement this training program in its ideal form, at least in the short run and maybe even in the long run. So with great reluctance, we outline abbreviated versions of this model, recognizing that the power of the training will be diminished as a result.

Prior Preparation for Abbreviated Training. For a brief format to be successful, participants must be well prepared in advance for the experience. We recommend that they read the manual, especially the first chapters and the introductions to the sections of the training program. We also recommend that they write an autobiography before the weekend or week, to familiarize themselves with student development. We also recommend that they complete the two floor assessment assignments in advance of the training. We recommend some sort of assessment of participant performance in the training, based on Training Program Aids A and B in the manual. It is important for participants to come out of this training, even when it is abbreviated, with some sense of their skills and competencies.

We also recommend that instructors read this entire book as preparation for teaching the model and discuss the training design with professional colleagues. These colleagues might even consider participating directly in the training. We have some ambivalent feelings about involving an experienced RA. On the one hand, an experienced RA can add a lot, as we argued in Chapter Eight. On the other hand, if the RA turns out to be unskilled or ineffective, it may interfere with participant learning. If you decide to use experienced RAs, make sure you have confidence in their ability, and involve them in the preparation for the training program.

Weekend Format. We assume that the autobiography provides some insight into student development, so the weekend sessions should focus on interpersonal skills and leadership development and be an opportunity for participants to get feedback about their strengths and weaknesses. You should review the designs in Part 3, Interpersonal Skills Development, and choose exercises that provide participants with:

1. An introduction to the whole interpersonal skills development model.
2. An opportunity to practice the following interpersonal skills: nonverbal attending, accurate reflection of content and feelings, self-disclosure, concreteness, summarization, and confrontation.
3. An opportunity to practice interpersonal skills in a counseling relationship (session 12 is very helpful).

We recommend that you introduce a particular skill and then let some participants practice the skill. Time limitations will prevent all participants from practicing all skills. You should have completed this part of the training by the end of Saturday evening.

You should then review Part 4, Leadership Development, and then conduct session 15 as an introduction to group leadership development and leadership styles. We recommend you then conduct session 17, floor assessment and the exercise of power by RAs. Session 14 should be the final training session, permitting participants to give feedback to one another and about the group. Sessions 13 (crisis intervention), 18 (conflict resolution), and 19 (discipline) are excellent follow-ups to this weekend training and can be done in two-hour blocks on three separate occasions.

Week-Long Format. You may wish to conduct this training program as part of in-service training during the week prior to students arriving in the fall. Follow the same preparation as outlined for the weekend format. We recommend conducting two or three sessions a day for four or five days, beginning with an opportunity for participants to discuss their autobiographies. We then recommend sessions 7 to 12 from Part 3, Interpersonal Skills Development, and sessions 15 to 17 from Part 4, Leadership Development. Finally, we recommend closing with sessions 4 and 5, enabling participants to give and receive useful feedback.

10

ЛULЛULЛULЛULЛULЛULЛULЛULЛULЛULЛULЛULЛULЛ

Evaluating Participants
for Final Selection

When presenting our selection-training program, we argued that candidates should be screened, trained, and then selected. We believe that observing candidates over extended time in a training program emphasizing the knowledge and skills required of an effective RA is the best selection process. The basic assumption of this approach is that we can fairly and accurately evaluate participant performance in training and then predict, based on that performance, how well a participant will perform as an RA.

But evaluation of participant performance is but one aspect of the issue. We believe, very emphatically, that evaluation is a two-way street; that is, participants should have the opportunity to evaluate their instructors and the training program itself. This chapter reviews our approach to evaluating participant performance in the training model and then offers a framework in which participants can evaluate instructor performance and the training program.

Evaluating Participant Performance

This training program really has three evaluation systems operating at once. The first system, evident throughout the sessions, is the continuous process of participants' getting feedback from other participants and the instructors. Almost every session includes some form of feedback regarding the effectiveness of participants' behaviors. Those sessions near the beginning of the model and at the end are summaries of this feedback and give participants a good idea of their strengths and weaknesses.

The second evaluation system is based on the goals of the training program. There are four parts to the program: student development; self-awareness; interpersonal skills; and leadership skills, including conflict resolution and mediation skills. Instructors evaluate each part according to assignments, class participation, and written examinations. Later in this chapter we more specifically describe how participants are evaluated for each part of the training program.

The third evaluation system is translating training program performance to predicted RA job performance. For example, if a participant is very strong in student development, self-awareness, and one-to-one interpersonal skills but weaker in group leadership and conflict mediation skills, what is the prediction about how that participant will perform in the RA counseling and advising role? Enforcement of rules? Planning programs? Advising groups? Maintaining a good floor atmosphere? Providing information or making referrals? Somehow the skill levels attained as a result of the training program must be translated to the things RAs do on the job. Thus near the end of the training program, instructors must translate participant performance in training to predicted participant performance on the job.

Besides the feedback candidates receive from participating in various exercises, there are several other aspects of the continuous evaluation system. Written comments on assignments give participants feedback about their written work. Sessions 5 and 6 are opportunities for formal feedback on participant performance, both from other participants and instructors. Sessions 14 and 20 also provide that opportunity. We also recommend that instructors meet with participants during the middle of the training to discuss performance to date and progress on how well they might do as RAs.

Participants exhibit their knowledge and skills by writing

assignments, participating in class, and taking a final examination. In each instance, instructors must decide on the quality of the work, which is not easy. Ultimately, in spite of frameworks, models, or numbers, the instructor must make a judgment, based on the evidence presented by the participant. Of course, it helps both the instructor and participant if goals are clearly spelled out in advance, criteria for evaluation of those goals specified, and the judgment is open and honest, timely, and, most of all, well intended.

But ultimately all evaluation is subjective because instructors must draw on their own experiences, knowledge, feelings, and skills to make their judgments. They must guard against the possibility of their own biases and prejudices entering into those judgments. And they must make sure that their judgments are based on what is in the best interests of producing the best possible resident assistant staff, which may not be in the best interests of an individual participant. It is not easy to tell persons that they are not skillful or that, in your opinion, they cannot do the job. But it must be done, if we are to be fully committed to the students in our residence halls. Both participants and instructors must understand that ultimately the evaluation of participant performance is a professional yet subjective judgment.

We chose to evaluate participant performance according to an ABCDF grading scale. When we initially outlined our training program, we said that it should be taught in a way which most closely approximates an academic course for credit, and we recommended, where possible, that it be offered for credit. But regardless of whether or not the program is offered for credit, we learned that evaluating participant performance should be in the form of a traditional grading scale.

We also learned that class attendance is mandatory for a training model based primarily on experience-based learning designs and exercises. Therefore, attendance criteria must be met to earn a grade, regardless of how well a participant performed in the sessions. In short, if students are not there, they cannot learn from their experience. To earn an A, attendance at nineteen or twenty sessions is required. To earn a B, attendance at seventeen or eighteen sessions is required; and so on. Thus, a student taking two cuts is automatically disqualified from an A, regardless of performance in the sessions attended. Because we have made such a big deal about class attendance over the years, we have never had to lower a grade because of absenteeism. But it could become an issue if you are lax about it.

Class Participation. Evaluating class participation and its quality is very difficult and ultimately determined by the instructor's judgment. However, it helps both students and instructors to know, more specifically, what is being evaluated. The following model should be used to evaluate class participation:

1. *Individual skills*
   (a) *Nonverbal communication.* Is the participant aware of personal nonverbal behavior? Does the participant "read" the nonverbal behavior of others?
   (b) *Active listening.* Does the participant accurately reflect others' thoughts and feelings? Is there consistency in such reflections?
   (c) *Self-disclosure.* Does the participant appropriately disclose personal thoughts, feelings, and experiences? Is such disclosure relatively easy or very difficult?
   (d) *Concreteness.* Does the participant develop specificity in others and ask appropriate questions?
   (e) *Confrontation.* Does the participant pick up discrepancies among others' thoughts, feelings, and behaviors?
   (f) *Summarization.* Is the participant able to understand, interpret, and summarize the thoughts and feelings of others and identify alternatives?
2. *Group skills*
   (a) *Group awareness.* Is the participant aware of what is happening in the group? Does the participant understand such group issues as communication patterns, group norms, and influence patterns?
   (b) *Group facilitation.* Does the participant help the group move along and get its tasks accomplished? Does the participant help the group solve a problem?

(c) *Group participation.* Does the participant actively participate in the group? Is the participant willing to learn from
that participation?

(d) *Group presentation.* Does the participant present himself
or herself effectively in the group? Does the participant
speak clearly, have good eye contact, and attend to the
group's reactions when speaking?

(e) *Group acceptance.* Does the group accept the participant
and respect her or his participation?

3. *Feedback skills*
(a) *Giving feedback.* Does the participant give constructive
feedback? Is the participant specific and descriptive
rather than evaluative, timely, and well-intended?

(b) *Receiving feedback.* Does the participant receive feedback
constructively? Does she or he receive feedback nondefensively? Does the participant check out and rephrase
feedback to ensure accurate communication? Does the
participant use the feedback once it is received?

4. *General attitude*
(a) *Cooperation.* Does the participant cooperate and collabo-
rate with class activities? With instructors?

(b) *Involvement.* Does the participant seem involved in the
learning process? Does the participant maintain consistent interest in what is going on?

Our experience has been that if these fifteen variables are
made clear to students at the beginning of the training and used
effectively by instructors, the problem of how to evaluate class participation is minimized. We suggest that class-participation variables be used when evaluating each part of the training and be a
basis for giving students feedback regarding their participation
when the midtraining individual session is held.

Assignments. Evaluating assignments can be equally difficult,
unless guidelines are clearly established. The training model consists of four assignments: the autobiography, First-Impression
Formation, Floor Characteristics Assessment, and Floor Dynamics

Assessment. Each assignment should be evaluated the following way:

1. _Autobiography_ (refer to manual for instructions on this assignment)
   (a) _Format._ Did the participant follow the format suggested in the manual? Were historical events, first collegiate reactions, and current status of each developmental issue written about?
   (b) _Writing._ Did the participant write clearly and in a well organized manner? Did poor writing get in the way of understanding what was trying to be communicated?
   (c) _Insight._ Does the participant have insight into self-development? Can the participant establish deeper self-understandings based on past and present experiences?
   (d) _Feelings._ Does the participant describe the feelings associated with personal development? Are the feeling words used in the right domain and precise?
   (e) _Content._ For each developmental issue, does the participant describe appropriate significant events and experiences? Is the description consistent with the manual's descriptions of these issues?
   (f) _Conceptual understanding._ Does the participant know and understand, overall, personal and academic development? Does the participant know and understand the impact of the collegiate environment on such development?
2. _First-Impression Formation_ (refer to the manual for a description of this assignment)
   (a) _Format._ Did the participant follow the format suggested in the manual? Were all four parts of the assignment completed?
   (b) _Content._ Did the participant adequately describe what he or she was asked to describe for each part of the assignment?
   (c) _Conceptual understanding._ Was the participant able to describe the bases on which she or he forms first impressions?

    (d)   Feelings. Was the participant able to describe how he or she felt about the basis on which he or she forms first impressions?

3. *Floor Characteristics Assessment* (refer to the manual for a description of this assignment)

    (a)   Format. Did the participant get the required number of persons to fill out the floor profile form, and were the answers summarized properly?

    (b)   Interpretation. Was the participant able to interpret the data collected and make inferences regarding the floor's general maturity level?

4. *Floor Dynamics Assessment* (refer to the manual for a description of this assignment)

    (a)   Format. Did the participant have some assessment of each dynamic covered in this assignment?

    (b)   Content. Did the participant present ideas consistent with the definitions of each dynamic covered in this assignment?

    (c)   Interpretation. Was the participant able to interpret the data collected and make inferences regarding the floor's general maturity level?

Final Examination. A final examination is the third way participants show evidence of their performance. We tried several formats for a final and found that traditional ways of formulating final exams do not fit our purposes. We gave class-written finals and take-home finals and tried no finals. We finally hit upon the idea of asking each participant to tape-record a twenty-minute interaction with a student (or another participant) about a matter of importance to that student. We gave participants wide latitude in the content, but we suggested that helping a person solve a problem or deal with an interpersonal issue would be the best opportunity for showing their skills and knowledge. The tape should be evaluated according to the following criteria (further definitions and elaborations are in Chapter Five):

1. *Active listening.* Does the participant accurately reflect the speaker's content and feelings? Are these reflections timely?

2. *Self disclosure.* Does the participant disclose personal thoughts, feelings, and experiences? Are these disclosures appropriate?
3. *Concreteness.* Does the participant develop specificity in the speaker and ask appropriate questions?
4. *Confrontation.* Does the participant point out to the speaker discrepancies among thoughts, feelings, and behaviors?
5. *Summarization.* Does the participant tie together the speaker's thoughts and feelings? Are themes established? Are alternatives spelled out?

Weighting the Evaluations. Instructors must judge participant performance according to class participation, class attendance, assignments, and a final examination. Each section of the course should be evaluated the following way, with these weightings:

1. *Student development.* Participant performance should constitute 15 percent of the final grade, which is based on the autobiography (50 percent) and class participation (50 percent).
2. *Self-awareness.* Participant performance should constitute 15 percent of the final grade, which is based on class participation (85 percent) and the first-impression formation assignment (15 percent).
3. *Interpersonal skills.* Participant performance should constitute 30 percent of the final grade, which is based on class participation (100 percent).
4. *Leadership development.* Participant performance should constitute 30 percent of the final grade, which is based on class participation (75 percent) and the residence hall floor assessment assignment (25 percent).
5. *Final examination.* Participant performance should constitute 10 percent of the final grade, which is based on an evaluation of the tape.

Assume that a 4 constitutes superior performance, a 3 above-average performance, a 2 acceptable performance, a 1 below-average performance, and a 0 unacceptable performance; assign a number for each section, based on class participation and assignments. For example:

Evaluation of participant X

Section	Class Participation	Assignment	Composite
Student development	3 (50%)	3 (50%)	3.0 (15%)
Self-awareness	4 (85%)	3 (15%)	3.8 (15%)
Interpersonal skills	4 (100%)	None	4.0 (30%)
Leadership development	3 (75%)	3 (25%)	3.0 (30%)
Final examination			4.0 (10%)
Class attendance			No penalty
		Final Grade	3.4

In this example, the composite grade for each section was determined by multiplying the number grade by the weighted percentage for both class participation and the assignment and dividing by 100. The final grade was determined by multiplying the composite grade by the weighted percentage for all sections and the final examination and dividing by 100. If there had been a penalty for not attending class, 0.5 would have been subtracted for every two absences.

To convert the final grade from a number to a letter, use the following formula:

3.5 to 4.0 = A   superior performance
3.0 to 3.49 = B   above-average performance
2.5 to 2.99 = C   average performance
2.0 to 2.49 = D   below-average performance
0.0 to 1.99 = F   unacceptable performance

This system of evaluating participant performance may seem a bit complicated and unnecessary, but it has been our experience that when the evaluation system is less structured and less specific, participants lose faith in its validity. In their minds, it leaves too much to the instructor's subjective judgment. Instructors have also found that this structure forces them to give more thought to how they evaluate and why. But more importantly, this system makes translating participant performance in the training to predicted participant performance as an RA a little easier.

We previously discussed the apparent contradiction of evaluating participant performance in an experience-based training program. On the one hand, we are trying to create a nonjudgmental learning environment where participants can experiment with new behaviors, take risks, and learn from both their failures and successes. On the other hand, because the training program is an extension of the selection process, we ask instructors to make a judgment, at the end of the training, about whether participants become resident assistants. The question must be asked: Is this an impossible learning situation?

The answer is theoretically yes but practically speaking, no. We found that if the evaluation issue is dealt with at the beginning of the selection-training process in a very straightforward manner, few problems arise. Here are a few suggestions about how the evaluation issue should be handled:

1. *Deal with the issue immediately.* Participants must know you recognize the evaluation double bind and the potential conflict between your role as facilitator-evaluator. Participants should have an opportunity to express their concerns and instructors a chance to assure participants of the resolvability of the issue.

2. *Make evaluation criteria very clear.* Review the attendance, class participation, assignments, and final examination criteria identified earlier in this chapter. Also review the process of translating participant performance in the training to predicting RA effectiveness on a floor. (You might refer to the manual, Chapter Two, which spells out these criteria.)

3. *When evaluating, have the evidence.* Whether the evaluation is a part of the continuous evaluation process of the exercises and designs, the formal evaluation of participant performance in the training, or the decision to hire or not hire, make sure

there is behavioral evidence, based on performance in the
training program, to back up your judgment. Give examples
and be as specific as possible.

4.   *Most of all, be well intended.* Evaluation should help participants
become the most effective RAs they are capable of being. The
purpose of evaluation is to include as many participants as
possible in the candidate pool, not to exclude as many as
possible. Your approach in conducting any kind of evaluation
should be positive, helpful, supportive, and well intended. Participants must feel you are on their side in this process; if you
are not seen that way, you may well create the double bind you
are trying to avoid.

Prediction of Participant Performance as an RA

Instructors must now judge whether participants will be offered an RA job, declared alternates and used in the event of un-
expected vacancies, or eliminated altogether from consideration as
RAs. In short, the selection process must now be completed. Performance in the training program must in some way be related to
how participants will perform in the various RA roles. Following
are guidelines for translating participant performance in training
to predicted performance as an RA.

RA Role	Most Relevant Sections of the Training
Providing personal help and assistance	Student development, self-awareness, and interpersonal skills
Managing and facilitating groups	Interpersonal skills and leadership development
Facilitating programs	Interpersonal skills and leadership development

Informing and referring students	Student development and interpersonal skills
Explaining and enforcing rules	Interpersonal skills and leadership development
Maintaining floor environment	Leadership development

In the example of participant X, clearly this person had very strong self-awareness and interpersonal skills but weaker student and leadership development skills. The decision to hire or not hire this person depends on three variables:

1. *Emphasis of the RA position at your institution.* If your primary emphasis is on enforcing rules and maintaining a safe, quiet, and orderly floor environment, you should be looking for someone who has strong leadership development skills. On the other hand, if the emphasis is more on personal help and assistance and informing and referring students, you should select someone strong in student development and interpersonal skills. If you have a somewhat even emphasis on all aspects of the RA position, you want someone with a good balance of all skills.
2. *Emphasis of the RA position required in a given location.* If you have a vacancy on a predominantly freshman floor, you may want someone who can provide much personal help and assistance, manage and facilitate groups, and facilitate programs. You should thus look for someone strong in student development, interpersonal skills, and leadership development. If the vacancy is on a predominantly upperclass floor, you may need someone who can maintain a good floor environment and inform and refer students; you should place more emphasis on leadership development and interpersonal skills.
3. *Field from which you have to select.* We found that deciding who should *not* be an RA is easier than choosing from among qual-

ified participants. Mostly you will be trying to decide among several participants who could do the job; your task is to choose the most qualified. In other words, you make a *comparative* judgment. A person whom you might hire one year might not be hired in another year because overall, candidates are stronger in some years than in others.

Getting back to participant X, let us assume you emphasize enforcing rules and maintaining a safe, quiet, and orderly floor environment. Let us also assume the vacancy is on a predominantly upperclass floor. And let us also assume that you have a candidate field that is overall very strong, especially in the leadership development area. In this instance, we would probably *not* recommend participant X because of perceived leadership development weaknesses. On the other hand, participant X might be a stronger candidate for an institution that emphasizes providing personal help and assistance and on a predominantly freshman floor.

We tried to make this whole process a bit clearer by developing evaluation forms that summarize the criteria by which participants are evaluated in the training and show how training performance relates to decisions about selection and placement (refer to Training Program Aids A and B). At the end of training, fill out that form for each participant so there is a written record of the results of the evaluation process, available to both the participant and the person(s) who make final selection decisions. This same form should also be used in the midtraining individual session with participants.

Participant Evaluation of Instructor Performance

We firmly believe that participants should have the opportunity to evaluate the effectiveness of their instructors. Of course, the training sessions are designed for continuous feedback for everyone in the group, including the instructors. Instructors participate in feedback sessions, in reviews of group process, and get feedback when they model various skills and behaviors. So instructors should have a daily basis for knowing how well they are doing, as perceived by participants.

But continuous feedback in the sessions is not enough.

Neither is it enough, in our opinion, to wait until the end of the training for a more formal evaluation. We recommend a mid-training evaluation by participants of instructors. We think this evaluation should be collective rather than individual to guard against the feeling that instructors might use such information against individual participants. Furthermore, instructors should then discuss this evaluation with the group and give the group the chance to clarify and specify their evaluation. We suggest the following criteria for evaluating instructor performance:

1. *Preparation.* Was the instructor adequately prepared for training sessions?
2. *Organization.* Was the instructor well organized in the training sessions? Were sessions orderly and well organized?
3. *Knowledge.* Did the instructor have adequate knowledge for conducting training sessions?
4. *Interpersonal skills.* Did the instructor practice effective interpersonal skills, including nonverbal communication, active listening, self-disclosure, concreteness, confrontation, and summarizing?
5. *Group skills.* Did the instructor practice effective group skills, including group awareness, group facilitation, group participation, group presentation skills, and group acceptance?
6. *Feedback skills.* Did the instructor practice good feedback skills, including giving constructive feedback and receiving feedback nondefensively?
7. *General attitude.* Did the instructor display a positive, constructive attitude, including cooperation and involvement?

Training Program Aid C in the manual describes these criteria in greater detail; participants should use the form at mid-training and at the end of the training program.

Participant Evaluation of the Training Program

As we developed this training program, some of the most valuable feedback we received was from the participants themselves. As we stated in an earlier chapter, only when we really listened to what participants had to say about the training they were getting were we able to develop an effective training model. The revisions of the training model over the past several years were partly based on the written and verbal feedback from hundreds of students who participated in the program.

However, we are not that impressed with feedback from participants *during* the training program. It may sound arrogant, but the participants are not really in a position to evaluate the training until they have gone completely through it and can see each session in total perspective. Even though we recommend that the program be evaluated at its end, there is an argument to be made for evaluating again, about six months after RAs have been on the job. By then, they have a much better idea of whether the training was helpful or relevant to their jobs.

Participants should be given the opportunity to evaluate the training model, based on the following criteria:

1. *Course Content.* To what extent did each part of the training program (student development, self-awareness, interpersonal skills, leadership development) help prepare you for the RA position?
2. *Course methodology.* To what extent were lectures, role playings, feedback sessions, instructor modeling, group process reviews, and skill practice exercises helpful?
3. *Assignments.* To what extent were the autobiography, First-Impression Formation, Residence Hall Floor Assessment assignments helpful?
4. *RA manual.* Did you find the readings and preparations helpful?
5. *Evaluation.* Was the evaluation system fair? Clear?

Training Program Aid D describes these criteria in greater detail; participants should use the form at the end of the training program and approximately six months after they have assumed the RA position.

11

‚Î∏‚Î∏‚Î∏‚Î∏‚Î∏‚Î∏‚Î∏‚Î∏‚Î∏‚Î∏‚Î∏‚Î∏‚Î∏‚Î∏‚Î∏‚Î∏

Supervising
and Evaluating
Resident Assistants
on the Job

According to Belman and Hull (1967), supervision is
" . . . the responsibility and authority that are given to an individual
to plan, direct, control, coördinate, and appraise the work activities
of others" (p. 38). The goal of supervision is to get a job done
effectively, with some degree of satisfaction on the part of those
supervised. This chapter reviews the problems and pitfalls of supervising resident assistants and then defines and discusses what
makes supervisors effective and presents an effective model for
evaluating RA performance.

We found that RAs are only as good as their training and
supervision. If institutions want to strengthen their residence hall
programs, they should start by improving the quality of supervision
RAs receive—it is the most important thing that can be done in
residence halls. However, our experience has been that much of
the supervision of RAs is weak and ineffective. RAs, after they have
been hired, and if they have been trained at all, are relatively free

to do their own thing. As a result, there is little control over their behavior, except in extreme cases, so most residence halls end up being managed from the bottom up. At the other extreme, RAs are supervised very closely and allowed little latitude in interpreting the job. As a result, RAs spend most of their time concealing what they are doing from their supervisors; again, a bottom-up management style results. Most RAs are not properly supervised, and most supervisors have little prior experience with or knowledge about supervision. Thus, many supervisors do not know what they are doing and give RAs inadequate leadership.

That is not to say that the supervision of RAs is easy, even if there is a systematic, continuous, and effective supervisory process conducted by supervisors who know what they are doing. RAs are not usually fully mature adults, and their own developmental issues sometimes interfere with effective performance. Usually the RAs are full-time students and thus unable to devote their full time and energy to the job. And pay and promotion incentives, which are powerful motivators in other organizational settings, are seldom factors in the supervision of residence halls staff. More importantly, there is usually little opportunity for direct observation of RA performance, and outcomes of performance are difficult to define and measure. Many RAs are in their very first position of responsibility in an organization and sometimes naive about how bureaucracies must operate. Finally, the job is unique, and so is the environment.

We believe some of the problems of supervising RAs rest with the supervisors themselves. For example, certain supervisors are very paternalistic and authoritarian, believing that RAs cannot be trusted to work on their own. They believe RAs must be monitored very closely, punished when they do not behave properly, and told what to do, when to do it, and how to do it. It is never possible to cover all situations, and RAs will have to act on their own, at the risk of not doing what is expected. Under this supervisory style, RAs repeatedly attempt to conceal from their supervisors what is *really* going on because the prescribed ways of doing things may not always work on a given floor or in a given situation. An "us and them" RA attitude develops, in which RAs conspire with students to defeat the residence hall administration.

Authoritarian and paternalistic supervisory approaches, however, are not nearly as frequent, in our opinion, as laissez faire approaches, in which RAs are hired and left to do the job on their own. When training is required, it is sporadic and uncoordinated. This approach assumes that only RAs can really determine how to work effectively on their floors because supervisors do not live there and thus cannot possibly know what is going on. If problems develop, the supervisor can be used as a sounding board, but not as a partner in the decision-making process. As long as things are going well, there is no real reason for RAs and supervisors to have much contact. Of course, the result is that it is very easy for an RA to do nothing and get away with it. Also, inconsistencies in approach and effectiveness develop from one RA to another.

Still another approach seems logical and effective: The supervisor becomes the RA's RA. In this approach, the supervisor establishes a warm and supportive personal friendship with the RA, becoming counselor, adviser, and friend. Most of their interactions focus on their relationship and the RA's personal growth and development. The assumption is that the RA will duplicate this relationship with residents and thus will be effective. The problem is that the goal of the supervisor-RA relationship becomes the best interests of the RA, not the best interests of students in the residence halls. Furthermore, someday the supervisor may have to choose between the best interests of the RA (not firing the RA because of some breach of job expectations) and the best interests of the institution (firing the RA for that same breach). In our opinion, the RA's RA approach to supervision does not work.

Residence halls exist for students, not for RAs or supervisors. The best RAs are those that are properly selected, trained, and supervised. RAs should be held accountable for their performance on a floor and supervised in ways that result in effective performance. Supervision should be a collaborative effort, in which the RA and the supervisor work together for the best interests of students and the institution.

Just how is this done? We have found that effective supervision involves two key ingredients: competent supervisors who know and understand their supervisory roles, and a formal system of evaluating RA performance that is open, fair, and valid.

Effective Supervisors

In our experience, the relationship established between the supervisor and the RA is absolutely essential to the effective supervision of resident assistants. Because of their age, lack of experience, and level of maturity, RAs want and need strong leadership from their supervisors. And if the educational potential of residence halls is to be fulfilled, that same strong supervisory leadership is essential. If we were asked what is the one thing a residence hall program could do to improve its effectiveness, we would say, without hesitation, "Start by hiring strong supervisors." We would look for persons who have (1) effective interpersonal skills, (2) knowledge about student development and residential impact, ·(3) good understanding of the supervisory role, (4) effective supervisory techniques, and (5) effective group leadership skills.

Interpersonal Skills. As you might expect, we think supervisors should have the same effective interpersonal skills as the RAs they supervise. They should be attentive to nonverbal behavior; accurately reflect the thoughts and feelings of others; disclose appropriate thoughts and feelings; ask precise, relevant, and open-ended questions; confront discrepancies among thoughts, feelings, and behaviors; summarize interactions; and evaluate alternatives. Supervisors should do all these things at least as well, if not better, than the RAs they supervise.

Student Development and Residential Impact. Supervisors of RAs should thoroughly know and understand students' personal and academic development and the impact of residence halls on it. They should understand that most students are in the process of establishing themselves as autonomous human beings, achieving a sense of independence from childhood influences, and assuming responsibility for their own lives. They should also understand that students are developing a clearer sense of who they are and establishing a sense of ego identity. Supervisors should know that the two processes of autonomy and identity are experienced by students as several specific developmental issues: (1) formulating a personal value system, (2) developing intellectual and academic competence, (3) deciding on a life-style and career, (4) establishing and maintaining interpersonal relationships, and (5) developing a sex-role identity and a capacity for intimate relationships.

Supervisors of RAs should also thoroughly know and understand the residential environment in which they work and its impact on students' personal and academic development. Students in residence halls, compared to those living elsewhere, have clear advantages, particularly during the freshman year: better grades, lower dropout rates, more faculty contact, more participation in student activities, better interpersonal relationships, fewer emotional problems, better parental relationships, and better adjustment to college. Supervisors should know that friends, roommates, and the peer group are major factors in residential impact. Assignment of students, the residence hall staff, and educational and developmental programs are also influential. Supervisors should be experts in residential education and know more about how residence halls influence students than any other persons on campus.

The Supervisory Role. Supervisors of RAs have to know what to do with RAs to help them get their jobs done. The supervisors' first task is to establish an effective interpersonal relationship with those they supervise, one characterized by openness, respect, and trust. Both RAs and their supervisors must be committed to the development of such a relationship and work on it continuously. It is the cornerstone of supervision in residence halls.

Besides developing an effective relationship between him- or herself and RAs, the supervisor must (1) select and train RAs, (2) establish and interpret job functions, (3) provide information, (4) provide advice and support, (5) evaluate RA job performance, and (6) advocate the RAs' and students' concerns. Regarding supervisors selecting and training RAs, we have found very little evidence establishing a relationship between selection procedures and effective RA performance. Thus we recommend combining selection and training, holding the final selection of candidates until after training is completed. We also believe training should be extensive and focus on student development, self-awareness, interpersonal skills, and leadership development.

Supervisors must also establish and interpret job functions. Although institutions vary with respect to specific job functions, most RA job descriptions include (1) providing personal help and assistance; (2) managing and facilitating groups; (3) facilitating social, recreational, and educational programs; (4) informing students or referring them to appropriate information sources; (5) explaining and enforcing rules and regulations; and (6) maintaining a safe, orderly, and quiet residence hall atmosphere. It is up to supervisors to lay out very clearly what is expected of RAs and make sure they understand their roles.

Supervisors must also be a primary source of information about what an RA needs to know. They should keep their RAs informed about everything from how to make a room change to how to apply for a student loan. It is the supervisor's responsibility to make sure RAs have the information necessary to get their jobs done. This never-ending process should never be taken for granted. If supervisors do not know the answers, they should be committed to finding out the information needed to get the answers.

Supervisors must interpret institutional decisions and policies to RAs. Most institutions are continually developing and revising policies and procedures and making decisions that affect students. Supervisors must keep RAs abreast of current happenings and changing institutional policies and decisions so that RAs, in turn, may interpret these things to students. Anyone who has supervised RAs knows they must be prepared to answer the question that starts with "I don't understand why the college is . . . ."

Supervisors must give RAs advice and support. They must be able to offer advice, based on their past experiences, training, and the experiences of other RAs. Supervisors must support their RAs when pressures mount and help them handle the press of being a student, an employee, and a person. Maintaining the RA's mental health is a very important role of the supervisor. Supervisors must also know when to offer advice and support, both when it is asked for and when it is needed but not asked for.

Supervisors must also evaluate RAs' job performances. They must lay out expectations, establish job-performance evaluation criteria, and provide for continuous evaluation. The performance evaluation should help RAs do the best job possible and give students the best possible services and programs. (Later in this chapter we present an evaluation model we have found effective when working with RAs.)

Finally, supervisors must advocate for the RAs' concerns. Because RAs are the persons closest to students, they will probably be the first ones to learn about student issues, problems, and concerns. RAs should be able to use their supervisors as a channel of communication for these concerns as well as a source for dealing with them. Supervisors should know how to untangle bureaucratic red tape and advocate for students when the system is insensitive or unresponsive. Supervisors should also be seen as willing to advocate for issues and problems unique to RAs.

Effective Supervisory Techniques. Just how does a supervisor fulfill all these roles? We believe supervisors must use various supervision techniques: (1) individual conferences, (2) group meetings, (3) training, (4) direct involvement with the RAs' tasks, and (5) informal interaction. Most supervisors use individual conferences with the RAs as the primary method of establishing and maintaining a supervisory relationship. We know some supervisors who meet with each individual RA for two hours every week. We also know some supervisors who have no regularly scheduled individual conferences; they meet only on an "as-needed" basis. Each supervisor must establish the frequency of such conferences, based on the RAs' needs and her or his supervisory style. We advocate regularly scheduled individual conferences, during which time both the supervisor and the RA get a chance to air concerns, discuss problems and issues, and exchange feedback. Too often, "as needed" becomes "never needed," so regularly scheduled meetings should be held.

Group meetings of resident assistants are an efficient way for RAs to share information, air concerns, and discuss problems and issues. If managed properly, it is an opportunity for the supervisor to help RAs help themselves. Unfortunately, some group meetings are simply an opportunity for the supervisor to pass along announcements from the top. Supervisors must work at developing an atmosphere where RAs can get help, support, and advice from one another as well as the supervisor. Some of the group-oriented exercises in the training program might be used to develop this atmosphere, and supervisors might want to consider a feedback session or two during the year, to build group trust and solidarity.

Training sessions are also an opportunity for supervisors to supervise. In addition to the preemployment training we recommended, additional training may be necessary once RAs are on the job. The sessions are excellent opportunities for supervisors to influence RAs and help them succeed on the job.

Supervisors can also work directly with RAs on a task or project, strengthening the supervisory relationship as a result. Supervisors can help RAs plan activities, implement social and recreational programs, act as a resource person for the floor, and work with their floors in other ways. Through direct involvement with RA tasks or projects, the supervisor can observe directly the RA's performance and help the RA do whatever needs to be done.

Supervisors can also spend time with RAs informally. Most RAs appreciate a supervisor who takes a personal interest in them outside the job. We firmly believe supervisors who limit their contacts with RAs to strictly business will not be as effective as those who express their caring with some informal contact. We repeat our caution, however, that supervisors should *not* become close, intimate friends with their RAs, nor should they become their therapists. We believe such relationships compromise the supervisory relationship because of the inevitable conflict between the best interests of the RA and the best interests of students.

All these techniques should be used for one purpose: to help RAs become effective with students on their floors. These techniques should also be used within the context of an open, trusting, and respecting relationship between the supervisor and the RA. We believe that a residence hall professional staff member who supervises ten to twelve RAs is going to spend most of his or her time supervising, if the job is to get done right.

Effective Leadership Skills. Besides effective interpersonal skills, knowledge about student development and residential impact, a good understanding of the supervisory role, effective supervisory techniques, and effective evaluation systems, supervisors must have effective leadership skills. Generally, these are the same leadership skills taught resident assistants in the training program. Supervisors must know a lot about the RAs they supervise, both individually and as a group. They must assess the RAs' maturity level and on that basis determine personal leadership style (telling, selling, participating, or delegating). Supervisors must also know how to respond in a crisis situation, mediate conflicts, and handle disciplinary situations. In short, they must provide leadership to the RAs in much the same way RAs must provide leadership to students on their floors.

Effective Evaluation Systems

The second key ingredient of effective supervision is an open, fair and valid evaluation system. We acknowledge, however, that evaluating RA performance is very difficult, given the nature of the position, the near impossibility of directly observing performance, and the difficulty of defining performance outcomes. Too often these factors are used to avoid the evaluation process altogether or not be committed to it. Effective evaluation systems *can* be developed, and they can be open, fair, and valid. We strongly believe that RAs should be held accountable for their performance, or lack of it, and that there should be consequences for both effective and ineffective job performance.

Too often, it is assumed that doing a good job as an RA is simply a matter of performing effectively on the floor, within the job functions outlined in the RA description. To be sure, this aspect of the job is very important, but other aspects must also be considered. For example, it is important for RAs to establish good working relationships with their supervisors. They should give attention to administrative details and expectations, such as getting reports in on time and following up on administrative tasks. RAs should be good team players and support and assist their fellow RAs. Finally, they should have a positive attitude toward their jobs, the students on their floors, and the institution. These "nonfloor-related" job expectations are very important and should be taken into account when evaluating RA job performance.

We believe the overall purpose of the evaluation process should be to help RAs do their jobs and work effectively with their floors, within the expectations defined by the institution. The purpose should *not* be to root out incompetence or make sure RAs do their jobs, although on very rare occasions it may be necessary to do so. The attitude with which the supervisor approaches the evaluation process is critical to its effectiveness. If the attitude is positive and helpful rather than negative and distrustful, the RAs will view the evaluation process as a very important part of their ability to be effective on the job.

Steps in the Evaluation Process. In our opinion, the evaluation process consists of four steps: (1) providing RAs with a very clear understanding of job functions and expectations, (2) identifying the sources of information that will be used in evaluating RA performance, (3) conducting an initial conference with RAs to review job expectations and the evaluation process, and (4) evaluating the RA on the basis of stated criteria and information collected from all available sources.

The evaluation process should begin with a clear understanding of what is expected of RAs, starting with a clearly written and unambiguous job description. We have resisted the temptation to present a model job description because every institution must develop its own, based on its needs and objectives. However, we think a good starting point is the six job functions identified in Chapter One. If other expectations above and beyond the job description are required, these too should be clearly stated in writing. If RAs are expected to be good team players and establish an effective relationship with their supervisor, these expectations should be spelled out, preferably in advance of assuming the position. We think RAs should have a chance to read what is expected of them and discuss it with their supervisor.

The second step in the evaluation process is to identify what sources of information will be used to evaluate RA performance. Over the years, we have developed three basic sources: (1) students, (2) RAs themselves, and (3) the supervisor. Students who live in residence halls are a primary source of information about and evaluation of RA job performance. The information can be gathered informally, through direct and indirect contact between supervisors and students, and/or formally through written, anonymous evaluations by floor members. Unfortunately, our experience has been that most residence hall programs rely more on informal than formal information sources, and they tend to be haphazard, unrepresentative, and unsystematic and therefore invalid, unreliable, and prejudicial. We believe student evaluations of RAs should be formal, systematic, frequent, written, and anonymous. The evaluation should be tied to the RA job description and administered without RA involvement.

For example, we have used an instrument called Student Evaluation of the Resident Assistant (SERA). The SERA is administered to all students in residence halls toward the end of the first term. It is sent out and collected by floor officers and returned directly to the supervisor. RAs are not involved in its administration in any way, and responses are anonymous. Students are asked to respond to several items by indicating whether they strongly agree, agree, disagree, strongly disagree, or have no basis for evaluation. The items are based on the six functions of the RA identified in Chapter One and include the following:

1. *Providing personal help and assistance*
    (a) My RA has tried to get to know me.
    (b) If I needed someone to help me with social or personal concerns, I could go to my RA.
    (c) My RA is ineffective when I go to him/her for help with social or personal concerns.
2. *Managing and facilitating groups*
    (a) My RA conducts effective house meetings.
    (b) Our floor government is effectively advised by our RA.
3. *Facilitating social, recreational, and educational programs*
    (a) There have been social and athletic activities on our floor.
    (b) My RA is disinterested in our floor's social and athletic activities.
    (c) Educational and culture programs were unavailable for our floor.
    (d) My RA was involved with educational and cultural programs for students on our floor.
4. *Serving as an information and referral source*
    (a) When I need information about the facilities or procedures of the campus, my RA usually knows the answers or will seek them out.
    (b) When I need help, my RA knows where to send me, if she/he cannot help directly.

5. *Explaining and enforcing rules and regulations*
   (a) My RA failed to explain the discipline system and campus rules to students on our floor.
   (b) On our floor, rules and regulations are enforced.
6. *Maintaining a safe, orderly, and quiet atmosphere*
   (a) It is usually too noisy on our floor.
   (b) My RA has tried to help our floor develop an atmosphere where people respect each other's rights and privileges.

The results of this instrument are shared with the RA and serve as one basis for evaluating RA performance. Of course, it is possible to add other questions from time to time, depending on the situation. In addition to using this instrument to evaluate individual RA performance, supervisors can also use it as an overall programmatic assessment. For example, several years ago some faculty complained that students told them that "the dorms are too noisy to get anything done." We produced the results of our latest SERA, which indicated that only 23 percent of students in the halls thought it was "usually too noisy on our floor."

Evaluations by students, even if done the way we have suggested, should be done with caution. We agree with Delworth, Sherwood, and Casaburri (1974) that students "are in the best position to make suggestions or offer alternatives if two conditions exist: (a) personal friendship does not interfere with the objective appraisal, and (b) there is a good understanding of job functions by floor members" (p. 52). We have also found that supervisors should be alert to situational factors that might affect students' evaluations. For example, if an RA broke up a party the night before the evaluations, the supervisor might take that into account and ask for a later evaluation. There also tends to be a "halo" effect among some residents who cannot discriminate among various job functions. For example, if the results of all the items look about the same, supervisors should suspect such an effect. The purpose of the evaluation must be made clear to residents. If floor members like their RA, they may want to overinflate the results in a positive way. Or they may want to use the evaluation as an opportunity to "get" an unpopular RA. Thus it must be made clear that the purpose is to help RAs improve their performance and is but one of several sources of information about RA competence.

A second source of information about RA performance is RAs themselves. Although self-evaluation can degenerate into self-aggrandizement or self-justification, it can, if done well, be a most valuable source of information. One of the most powerful tools a supervisor can use for evaluating RA performance is to compare other sources of information about performance, such as students', with the RA's own self-evaluation. RAs should be asked to predict the results of the student evaluation, to rate themselves on other expectations, and to predict what the supervisor has to say about their performance. They should also be given an opportunity to make some general comments about their overall job performance and how they think and feel about themselves in the position.

A third source of information is the supervisor. The supervisor should have had much direct contact with RAs and with students on their floors. He may have been involved directly with projects or programs and can evaluate other job functions, such as meeting deadlines, participating in staff meetings, relating to other RAs, and having an overall positive attitude. By the way, we do not think RAs should evaluate each other's performance on a floor, but they may provide valuable information about how they relate to each other. In short, the supervisor has many direct and indirect bases for evaluating job performance.

The third step in the evaluation process is to conduct an initial session with each RA in which the job description is reviewed, additional expectations established, and the evaluation process, including sources of information for that process, reviewed and understood. This is also a time when specific expectations are stated relating to the building or floor to which the RA is assigned or to specific programs and activities that will be required. A timetable for the evaluation process is also established. Besides end-of-term or -semester formal evaluations, we recommend more informal evaluations about once a month, or as needed. Frequent contact between RAs and supervisors strengthens the evaluation process and helps it become a positive rather than negative experience for RAs.

The fourth step in the evaluation process is to collect information about RA performance, from all available sources, and collate such information into a formal evaluation. We recommend that

this evaluation occur about eight to ten weeks after the beginning
of the year and again toward the end of the academic year. This
evaluation should occur in an individual conference with the RA,
and a written record of the evaluation should be filed. Of course, it
is quite possible that as a result of the discussion between the supervisor and the RA, the evaluation might be changed, and that is
fine. The ideal outcome would be that both the supervisor and RA
agree on the evaluation. If there is disagreement, the supervisor's
evaluation must stand as the "official" one, but the RA should be
given the opportunity to record objections in writing. There should
also be some source of appeal for an evaluation, preferably to the
immediate superior of the supervisor.

Unacceptable Performance. What if job performance is not acceptable, or questionable? What should be done? We believe that
RAs who are not performing up to expectations should be given all
the help they can in improving their job performance. We also
believe that failure to meet job expectations should be acknowledged in writing and a timetable for improvement established.
"Improvement" should be defined very specifically. For example, if
an item on the student evaluation instrument is particularly low,
the supervisor may establish a minimum percentage of positive
responses the next time the instrument is used. And the supervisor
may decide to administer the instrument sooner than the next
scheduled time, to get a quicker assessment of improved performance. It should also be clear how the supervisor and RA intend to
work together toward improved performance, with the responsibilities of both spelled out very clearly. In most instances, we have
found that when RAs and supervisors work closely together, performance can be improved.

But not always. Sometimes the poor performance continues,
in spite of the supervisor's and the RA's efforts. Termination must
then be considered. It should be used only as a last resort and
should be "threatened" in advance. In other words, the supervisor
should make clear that unless improvement in performance occurs
by a certain date, the RA will be relieved of all responsibilities. The
date should be realistic; that is, there should be enough time for the
RA to have the opportunity to improve performance. Usually, if
things are really going badly and attempts to improve performance

have not worked, the RA will resign voluntarily, but not always. If termination for incompetence is not voluntary, there should be ample opportunity for the RA to state his or her case and appeal to the immediate superior of the supervisor.

Another instance when termination may be the only answer to a problem of performance is "termination for cause." In this instance, the RA may have engaged in some behavior that is clearly unacceptable. It may be job-related behavior, such as physically assaulting a resident without provocation, or it may be behavior unacceptable to the institution and which occurred outside the RA's job responsibilities, such as cheating on an examination. Over the years, we had to dismiss some very competent RAs who did something that was clearly unacceptable to the residence hall program or to the institution. It should be made very clear to RAs just what these unacceptable behaviors are and the consequences for such behaviors. Again, RAs should have an opportunity to defend themselves and appeal the decision to the immediate superior of the supervisor.

We believe if these four steps are followed, the evaluation process will be one that is seen as valid and helpful by both RAs and their supervisors. If your institution has not had an effective evaluating system, you can expect some resistance to establishing one, especially from RAs who have been "doing their own thing" on the job. They may resent closer supervision at first, until they discover the benefits of such supervision.

Evaluating Supervision. We also believe that turnabout's fair play. That is, if the supervisor evaluation of the RA is to have integrity, the RA should have an opportunity to evaluate the performance of the supervisor. We think there should be an occasion where the RA gets to give some direct feedback to the immediate superior of the supervisor, both verbally and in written form. This feedback should be used in the overall evaluation of the supervisor and should be done at least twice a year. It should be based on the supervisor's job description and what is expected by the institution.

We repeat what we said when we opened this section: The key to the whole supervisory process is an effective evaluation system that should be followed in spite of possible difficulty, limitations, and resistance.

Summary

We believe college and university residence halls, if properly managed, can have a powerful influence on the educational and personal development of students. We have reviewed the abundant evidence that supports this belief, including indications that residence halls have positive effects on academic achievement and educational aspirations, as well as on students' interpersonal relations, values, personal adjustment, and satisfaction with college. Depending on how residence halls are staffed, structured, and supervised, these effects can be enhanced or retarded.

An institution's influence is transmitted to its residence halls largely through the residence hall staff. Most residence hall systems rely upon resident assistants (RAs)—part-time paraprofessionals who are also full-time students—to deliver services and programs and develop the educational potential of the residential environment. Consequently, the way RAs are selected, trained, and supervised can have an important influence on what happens to the students in the residence halls.

In this book we have provided the information and models necessary to conduct an effective program of selection, training, and supervision. Our approach is based on ten years of experimenting and learning from our mistakes. It incorporates a rich blend of theory derived from existing literature and research, practical models, and functional advice. We have taken into account the strengths and limitations of residence halls professionals and tailored a program that prepares resident assistants to be skillful and effective.

The key element in a program for resident assistants is the staff doing the selecting, training, and supervising. The models we suggest will work only if administrators are knowledgeable, skillful, and committed to the program. The following items summarize the preparation and skills people need to conduct effective programs.

Understand the residential environment. People who train RAs must recognize the power of the residential environment, know what creates that power, and understand how students' lives are affected by living in residence halls. They must be familiar with person-environment theories and understand the tremendous power of the peer group, in the residential setting. They must never forget how deeply college students need to be liked and accepted and how intensely they influence each other's attitudes and behaviors.

Understand the students. RAs need supervisors who are familiar with theories of student development and with the typical developmental issues students face during their college years. In general, students are moving toward full maturity and developing a sense of identity. They are formulating their values, establishing and maintaining interpersonal relationships, deciding on a lifestyle and career, developing academic and intellectual competence, and developing a sex role identity and a capacity for intimacy. Persons working with RAs need to be familiar with such generalizations.

Know the most effective means of selecting resident assistants. Our experience has taught us that selection and training should be combined and that final selection should not be made until applicants have completed a comprehensive training program. We suggest a seven-step selection and training model:

1. Start the selection process about eight months before applicants will assume their positions.
2. Write a clear and unambiguous job description.
3. Agree upon selection criteria, and make sure interviewers as well as applicants understand those criteria.

4. Screen applicants, eliminating those with poor academic records, recent disciplinary actions, and freshmen.
5. Interview the remaining applicants; assess their personal characteristics, interpersonal skills, and prior relevant experiences, and eliminate applicants who are clearly not qualified. Use students, RAs, and professional staff as interviewers.
6. Place remaining applicants in a comprehensive training program.
7. Make final selections on the basis of performance in the training program. Professional staff, and only professional staff, should make final selections.

Know and be able to use effective training methods. Our experience has taught us that RAs need training for actual situations they will encounter. Specifically, they need the knowledge and skills to provide personal assistance; organize and facilitate groups; implement social, recreational and educational programs; serve as sources of information and referrals; explain and enforce institutional rules and regulations; and maintain safe, orderly, and relatively quiet residence halls. Residence hall staff should conduct training sessions in small groups over several weeks. Training should provide participants with facts about the residential environment and with information about personal and academic development of students, and it should help participants develop greater self-awareness, basic interpersonal skills, and group leadership skills. When possible, training should be offered for academic credit.

Understand and be able to teach basic interpersonal skills. RAs need to be able to respond, be self-disclosing, and initiate. Responding means understanding what a person is thinking and feeling, in a respectful, nonevaluating way, and involves three skills: nonverbal attending, reflective listening, and concreteness. Disclosing means bringing the helper's own thoughts and feelings into the relationship, and involves two skills: appropriate self-disclosure of thoughts and feelings, and appropriate self-disclosure of similar experiences. Initiating means helping the other person bring closure to the interaction, and involves two skills: confrontation and summarization.

Understand group leadership development. In our experience, effective group leadership depends on four variables: (1) the interpersonal skills of the RA, (2) the position of the RA as defined by the institution, (3) the characteristics and backgrounds of floor members and how they interact with one another, and (4) the situations RAs must handle. Based on their assessment of the maturity level of the group with which they are dealing, RAs must decide which of four basic leadership styles to apply ("telling," "selling," "participating," or "delegating"). RAs must also be prepared to handle specific leadership situations, such as intervening in crises, mediating conflict, and handling disciplinary situations.

Be able to conduct a comprehensive training program. Persons selecting, training, and supervising RAs must understand and be able to implement various instructor roles. In the tutor/counselor role, they must help participants understand themselves, their impact on others, and others' impact on them, through the process of giving and receiving constructive feedback. In the facilitator/ trainer role, they must help participants understand group dynamics and behavior and develop group trust. In the instructor/ conceptualizer role, they must communicate effectively the knowledge and concepts necessary to accomplish the learning objectives of the training session. Instructional issues, such as resistance to training, deviant behavior, challenges to the leadership, and the evaluation "double bind" (on the one hand, asking participants to take risks and learn from their mistakes, while on the other hand having such behavior evaluated) must be handled. Instructors must work effectively with coinstructors and, in general, develop a learning environment that accomplishes the objectives of the training program.

Know how to establish clear evaluation criteria and make sound judgments about participant performance. Evaluation criteria need to include the development of individual skills (nonverbal communication, active listening, self-disclosure, concreteness, confrontation, and summarization), group skills (group awareness, facilitation, participation, presentation, and acceptance), feedback skills (giving and receiving constructive feedback), and general attitude (cooperation and involvement). Training performance must be translated into predictions of job performance and decisions made to hire and place RAs. Instructors must be highly committed to a continuous, fair, and open evaluation process throughout training, selection, and hiring.

Be able to provide supervision that enables RAs to perform up to their maximum potential. Our experience has been that RAs tend to be as good as the supervision they receive and, too often, they are undersupervised or oversupervised. Supervisors must have effective interpersonal skills, know and understand student development and residential environments, have a clear definition of their role, use effective supervisory techniques, and practice effective group leadership skills. They must also have practical means of evaluating RA performance that include clear definitions of job functions and expectations, reliable sources of information to be used in evaluating RA performance (including students, other RAs, and the RAs themselves), periodic reviews of job expectations and stated criteria of the evaluation process. Supervisors must also help improve RA performance when it is deficient and be prepared to dismiss RAs whose performance is unacceptable.

As we stated in the Preface, this book reflects what we have learned over the past ten years as we struggled to select, train, and supervise resident assistants. We believe that much of the educational potential of residence halls will remain unfulfilled if RAs lack adequate training and supervision. We also believe that persons who train and supervise RAs can be more effective if they are knowledgeable, and have proven models of supervision and training with the result that RAs, in turn, become more effective and the positive influence of residence halls is enhanced.

Huge amounts of money and resources are *not* needed. The training and supervision models described in this book are designed to work within existing resources of most institutions. What is needed is a commitment to reorganize and reallocate resources and to make the most of what already exists in most residence hall programs. To do anything less is to make a mockery of the avowed goals of a residential education. There is every reason to believe that residence halls at most institutions can become even more powerful an influence on students than the research has shown them to be. Only commitment is necessary.

We hope others will benefit from sharing the knowledge, experience, models, and mistakes we have described. Even as we finish this book, we are in the process of revising and improving our selection/training/supervision models on the basis of our continuing experience. Take what we have started—use it and adapt it to your situation. Good luck!

References

Aguilera, D. C., and Messick, J. M. *Crisis Intervention: Theory and Methodology.* St. Louis, Mo.: Mosby, 1974.

Ainsworth, C., and Maynard, D. "The Impact of Roommate Personality on Achievement: An Exploratory Study and Model of Analysis." *Research in Higher Education,* 1976, *4,* 291–301.

Albrow, M. C. "The Influence of Accommodation Upon 64 Reading University Students—An *Ex Post Facto* Experimental Study." *The British Journal Of Sociology,* 1966, *17,* 403–418.

Alfred, G. H., and Graff, T. T. "Improving Students' Interpersonal Communication." *Journal of College Student Personnel,* 1980, *21,* 155–162.

Allen, E. A. "Paraprofessionals in a Large-Scale University Program." *Personnel and Guidance Journal,* 1974, *53,* 276–280.

Appel, V. H., Berry, M. C., and Hoffman, R. W. "Significant Collegiate Sources of Influence." *Journal of College Student Personnel,* 1973, *14,* 171–174.

Astin, A. W. "The Impact of Dormitory Living on Students." *Educational Record,* 1973, *54,* 204–210.

Astin, A. W. *Four Critical Years: Effects of College on Beliefs, Attitudes, and Knowledge.* San Francisco: Jossey-Bass, 1977.

Bales, Robert F. *Interaction Process Analysis.* Cambridge, Mass.: Addison-Wesley, 1950.

Banning, J. (Ed.). *Campus Ecology, A Perspective for Student Affairs.* Cincinnati: National Association of Student Personnel Administrators, 1978.

Banta, T. W. "Selecting Student Orientation Assistants: A Comparison of Approaches." *Journal of College Student Personnel,* 1969, *10,* 240–243.

Barker, R. G. *Ecological Psychology: Concepts and Methods for Studying the Environment of Human Behavior.* Stanford, Calif: Stanford University Press, 1968.

Barnard, C. *The Functions of the Executive.* Cambridge, Mass.: Harvard University Press, 1938.

Beal, P. E., and Williams, D. A. *An Experiment with Mixed Class Housing Assignments at the University of Oregon.* Association of College and University Housing Officers (ACUHO) Research and Information Committee, 1968.

Belman, H. S., and Hull, T. "Supervisor Development." In R. Craig and L. Bittel (Eds.), *Training and Development Handbook.* New York: McGraw-Hill, 1967.

Bion, W. R. *Experiences in Groups.* New York: Basic Books, 1961.

Bird, C. *Social Psychology.* New York: Appleton-Century-Crofts, 1940.

Blai, B. "Roommate Impact Upon Academic Performance." Unpublished manuscript, Harcum Junior College, 1971.

Blake, R. R., Shepard, H. A., and Mouton, J. S. *Managing Intergroup Conflict in Industry.* Houston: Gulf Publishing, 1964.

Blimling, G. S., and Miltenberger, L. *The Resident Assistant Working with College Students in Residence Halls.* Dubuque, Iowa: Kendall-Hunt, 1981.

Blimling, G. S., and Schuh, J. "Residence Halls in Today's Compartmentalized University." In G. S. Blimling and J. Schuh (Eds.), *New Directions for Student Services: Increasing the Educational Role of Residence Halls,* no. 13. San Francisco: Jossey-Bass, 1981.

Bloland, P. A., and Siegman, A. B. "An Instructional Approach to Student Development." *Journal of College Student Personnel,* 1977, *18,* 174–176.

Bolton, C. D., and Kammeyer, K. C. W. *The University Student: A Study of Student Behavior and Values.* New Haven, Conn.: College and University Press, 1967.

Brammer, L. M. *The Helping Relationship: Process and Skills.* (2nd ed.) Englewood Cliffs, N.J.: Prentice-Hall, 1979.

Brawer, F. *New Perspectives on Personality Development in College Students.* San Francisco: Jossey-Bass, 1973.

Brown, R. D. "Manipulation of the Environmental Press in a College Residence Hall." *Personnel and Guidance Journal,* 1968, *46,* 555–560.

Brown, R. D. "Student Development and Residential Education: Should It Be Social Engineering." In D. DeCoster and P. Mable (Eds.), *Student Development and Education in College Residence Halls.* Washington, D.C.: American College Personnel Association, 1974.

Brown, R. D., Winkworth, J., and Braskamp, L. "Student Development in a Coed Residence Hall: Promiscuity, Prophylactic, or Panacea?" *Journal of College Student Personnel,* 1973, *14,* 98–104.

Bumba, R. P., and others. "Staff Selection and Training: Can the Two Functions Be Combined?" *Journal of College and University Housing,* 1980, *10,* 20–24.

Bushnell, J. H. "Student Culture at Vassar." In N. Sanford (Ed.), *The American College.* New York: Wiley, 1962.

Calia, V. "Systematic Human Relations Training: Appraisal 2nd Status." *Counselor Education and Supervision,* 1974, *13,* 85–93.

Cannon, J. R., and Peterman, J. G. "Functional Selection Indexes for Residence Hall Advisors." *Journal of College Student Personnel,* 1973, *14,* 549.

Carkhuff, R. R. *Helping and Human Relations.* Vols. 1 and 2. New York: Holt, Rinehart and Winston, 1969.

Cartwright, D., and Zander, A. (Eds.). *Group Dynamics: Research and Theory.* New York: Harper & Row, 1968.

Cattell, R. "New Concepts for Measuring Leadership in Terms of Group Syntality." *Human Relations,* 1951, *4,* 161–184.

Cerny, S. M., Zax, M., and Pierce, R. A. "Roommate Compatibility in Freshmen Men and Women." *Journal of the American College Health Association,* 1970, *19,* 108–111.

Chickering, A. W. *Education and Identity.* San Francisco: Jossey-Bass, 1969.

Chickering, A. W. *Commuting Versus Resident Students: Overcoming the*

Educational Inequities of Living Off Campus. San Francisco: Jossey-Bass, 1974.

Clark, B. R., and Trow, M. "The Organizational Context." In T. Newcomb and E. Wilson (Eds.), *College Peer Groups: Problems and Prospects for Research.* Chicago: Aldine, 1966.

Coleman, J. S. "Peer Cultures and Education in Modern Society." In T. Newcomb and E. Wilson (Eds.), *College Peer Groups: Problems and Prospects for Research.* Chicago: Aldine, 1966.

Combs, A. W., Avila, D. L., and Purkey, W. W. *Helping Relationships: Basic Concepts for the Helping Professions.* Boston: Allyn & Bacon, 1971.

Coons, F. "The Developmental Tasks of the College Student." In D. DeCoster and P. Mable (Eds.), *Student Development and Education in College Residence Halls.* Washington, D.C.: American College Personnel Association, 1971.

Corbett, J., and Somner, R. "Anatomy of a Coed Residence Hall." *Journal of College Student Personnel,* 1972, *13,* 215–217.

Danish, S. J., and Hauer, A. L. *Helping Skills: A Basic Training Program.* New York: Behavioral Publications, 1973.

Davidson, M. B. "Educational Outcomes and Implications of Academically and Vocationally Focused Small Groups of Undergraduate Students in a Women's Resident Hall." Paper presented at a meeting of the American Personnel and Guidance Association, Minneapolis, April 1965.

DeCoster, D. "Housing Assignments for High Ability Students." *Journal of College Student Personnel,* 1966, *7,* 19–22.

DeCoster, D. "Effects of Homogeneous Housing Assignments for High Ability Students." *Journal of College Student Personnel,* 1968, *9,* 75–78.

DeCoster, D. "Some Effects of Coordinating Classroom and Residence Hall Assignments for College Freshmen: A Pilot Project." Paper presented at a meeting of the American Personnel and Guidance Association, Las Vegas, April 1969.

DeCoster, D., and Mable, P. "Residence Education: Purpose and Process." In D. DeCoster and P. Mable (Eds.), *Student Development and Education in College Residence Halls.* Washington, D.C.: American College Personnel Association, 1974.

Delworth, U., Sherwood, G., and Casaburri, N. *Student Paraprofes-*

sionals: A Working Model for Higher Education. Washington, D.C.: American College Personnel Association, 1974.

Delworth, U., and Yarris, E. "Concepts and Processes for the New Training Role." In U. Delworth (Ed.), *New Directions for Student Services: Training Competent Staff,* no. 2. San Francisco: Jossey-Bass, 1978.

Doyle, W. W., Foreman, M. E., and Wales, E. "The Effects of Supervision in the Training of Nonprofessional Crisis-Intervention Counselors." *Journal of Counseling Psychology,* 1977, *24,* 72–78.

Egan, G. *The Skilled Helper: A Model for Systematic Helping and Interpersonal Relating.* Monterey, Calif.: Brooks/Cole, 1975.

Egan, G. *You and Me: The Skills of Communicating and Relating to Others.* Monterey, Calif.: Brooks/Cole, 1977.

Erikson, E. *Childhood and Society.* New York: Norton, 1963.

Feldman, K. *College and Student.* Elmsford, N.Y.: Pergamon Press, 1972.

Feldman, K., and Newcomb, T. (Eds.). *The Impact of College on Students.* Vols. 1 and 2. San Francisco: Jossey-Bass, 1969.

Foster, M. E., Sedlacek, W. E., and Hardwick, M. W. "Student Recreation: A Comparison of Commuter and Resident Students." Research report no. 4–77, Counseling Center, University of Maryland, 1977.

French, J. R. P., and Raven, B. "The Bases of Social Power." In D. Cartwright and A. Zander (Eds.), *Group Dynamics.* New York: Harper & Row, 1960.

Gehring, D. D. "Prediction of Roommate Compatibility." *Journal of College Student Personnel,* 1970, *11,* 58–61.

German, S. "Selecting Undergraduate Paraprofessionals on College Campuses: A Review." *Journal of College Student Personnel,* 1979, *20,* 28–34.

Godbold, A. *The Church College of the Old South.* Durham: University of North Carolina Press, 1944.

Gordon, S. S. "Living and Learning in College." *Journal of General Education,* 1974, *25,* 235–245.

Greenleaf, E. "The Role of Residence Educators." In D. DeCoster and P. Mable (Eds.), *Student Development and Education in College Residence Halls.* Washington, D.C.: American College Personnel Association, 1974.

Haldane, M. B. "Leaderless Group Discussion Method as an Effective Procedure for Selecting Residence Hall Counselors." Unpublished doctoral dissertation, Northwestern University, 1973.

Hall, E., and Barger, B. "Some Interrelationships of Living Situations Ratings by College Freshmen." *Student Mental Health Bulletin,* 1966, pp. 1–10.

Hall, R. L., and Willerman, B. "The Educational Influence of Dormitory Roommates." *Sociometry,* 1963, *26,* 294–318.

Hardee, M. "The Residence Hall, A Locus for Learning." Paper presented at the Research Conference on Social Science Methods and Student Residence, University of Michigan, Ann Arbor, November 1964.

Hart, L. E., and King, G. D. "Selection Versus Training in the Development of Paraprofessionals." *Journal of Counseling Psychology,* 1979, *26,* 235–241.

Heath, D. *Growing Up in College.* San Francisco: Jossey-Bass, 1968.

Heath, R. *The Reasonable Adventurer.* Pittsburgh: University of Pittsburgh Press, 1964.

Hellriegel, D., and Slocum, J. *Organizational Behavior.* St. Paul: West Publishing, 1979.

Hersey, P., and Blanchard, K. *Management of Organizational Behavior: Utilizing Human Resources.* Englewood Cliffs, N.J.: Prentice-Hall, 1977.

Holland, J. L. *Making Vocational Choices: A Theory of Careers.* Englewood Cliffs, N.J.: Prentice-Hall, 1973.

Homans, G. *The Human Group.* New York: Harcourt Brace Jovanovich, 1960.

Hutchins, D. E., Yost, M. W., and Hill, D. E. "A Comparison of Undergraduate and Professionally Trained Head Residents." *Journal of College Student Personnel,* 1976, *17,* 510–513.

Insel, P., and Moos, R. "Psychological Environments: Expanding the Scope of Human Ecology." *American Psychologist,* 1974, *29,* 179–189.

Ivey, A. E. *Microcounseling: Innovations in Interviewer Training.* Springfield, Ill.: Thomas, 1971.

Jones, L. M., McCaa, B. B., and Martecchini, C. A. "Roommate Satisfaction as a Function of Similarity." *Journal of College Student Personnel,* 1980, *21,* 229–234.

Kagan, N. *Interpersonal Process Recall: A Method of Influencing Human Interaction.* East Lansing: Michigan State University, Educational Publications Services, 1975.

Kaplan, S., Mann, S. C., and Kaplan, R. "Honors Housing at the University of Michigan." *The Superior Student,* 1964, *7,* 14.

Karlin, R. A., Rosen, L. S., and Epstein, Y. M. "Three into Two Doesn't Go: A Follow-Up on the Effects of Overcrowded Dormitory Rooms." *Personality and Social Psychology Bulletin,* 1979, *5,* 391–395.

Keniston, K. "The Faces in the Lecture Room." In R. S. Morison (Ed.), *The Contemporary University, U.S.A.* Boston: Houghton Mifflin, 1966.

King, P. M. "William Perry's Theory of Intellectual and Ethical Development." In L. Knefelkamp, C. Widick, and C. Parker (Eds.), *New Directions for Student Services: Applying New Developmental Findings,* no. 4. San Francisco: Jossey-Bass, 1978.

Klockars, A. J. "Personality Variables Related to Peer Selection." *Educational and Psychological Measurement,* 1978, *38,* 513–517.

Knefelkamp, L., Parker, C., and Widick, C. "Jane Loevinger's Milestones of Development." In L. Knefelkamp, C. Widick, and C. Parker (Eds.), *New Directions for Student Services: Applying New Developmental Findings,* no. 4. San Francisco: Jossey-Bass, 1978a.

Knefelkamp, L., Parker, C., and Widick, C. "Roy Heath's Model of Personality Typologies." In L. Knefelkamp, C. Widick, and C. Parker (Eds.), *New Directions for Student Services: Applying New Developmental Findings,* no. 4. San Francisco: Jossey-Bass, 1978b.

Kohlberg, L. "Stages of Moral Development." In C. M. Beck, B. S. Crittenden, and E. V. Sullivan (Eds.), *Moral Education.* Toronto: University of Toronto Press, 1971.

Kramer, R. "Moral Development in Young Adulthood." Unpublished doctoral dissertation, University of Chicago, 1968.

Layne, R. G., Layne, B. H., and Schoch, E. W. "Group Assertive Training for Resident Assistants." *Journal of College Student Personnel,* 1977, *18,* 362–398.

Leonard, E. A. *Origins of Personnel Services in American Higher Education.* Minneapolis: University of Minnesota Press, 1956.

Leventhal, A., and others. "Peer Counseling on the University Campus." *Journal of College Student Personnel,* 1976, *17,* 504–509.

Lewin, K. *Field Theory in Social Science.* New York: Harper & Row, 1951.

Linnell, R. *Coeducational Housing at Colleges and Universities.* Los Angeles: Office of Institutional Studies, University of Southern California, 1972.

Loevinger, J. *Ego Development: Conceptions and Theories.* San Francisco: Jossey-Bass, 1976.

Lozier, G. G. "Compatibility of Roommates Assigned Alphabetically Versus Those Assigned According to Educational Goals or Extracurricular Plans." *Journal of College Student Personnel,* 1970, *19,* 108–110.

Lundegren, D. C., and Schwab, M. R. "The Impact of College on Students: Residential Context, Relations with Parents and Peers, and Self-Esteem." *Youth and Society,* 1979, *10,* 227–235.

Mable, P., Terry, M., and Duvall, W. "Student Development Through Community Development." In D. DeCoster and P. Mable (Eds.), *Personal Education and Community Development in College Residence Halls.* Washington, D.C.: American College Personnel Association, 1980.

McCarthy, B., and Berman, A. L. "A Student-Operated Crisis Center." *Personnel and Guidance Journal,* 1971, *49,* 523–528.

Macdonald, D. A. "The Relationship Between Leadership Orientation and Group Productivity and Satisfaction: The Residence Hall Section Adviser and His Section." Unpublished dissertation, Department of Clinical Psychology, University of Florida, 1968.

McGregor, D. *The Human Side of Enterprise.* New York: McGraw-Hill, 1960.

McNeel, S. "Tripling Up: Perceptions and Effects of Dormitory Crowding." Paper read at American Psychological Association, Montreal, 1980.

Madison, P. *Personality Development in College.* Reading, Mass.: Addison-Wesley, 1969.

Magnarella, P. J. "The University of Vermont's Living-Learning Center: A First Year Appraisal." *Journal of College Student Personnel,* 1979, *16,* 300–305.

Meade, C. J. "Interpersonal Skills: Who, What, When, Why." In U. Delworth (Ed.), *New Directions for Student Services: Training Competent Staff,* no. 2. San Francisco: Jossey-Bass, 1978.

Miller, G. D., and Zoradi, S. D. "Roommate Conflict Resolution." *Journal of College Student Personnel,* 1977, *18,* 228–230.

Mitnick, M. M. "A Model for Resident Advisor In-Service Training." *Journal of College and University Student Housing,* 1979, *9,* 25–28.

Moos, R. "Conceptualizations of Human Environments." *American Psychologist,* 1973, *28,* 652–665.

Moos, R., and Gerst, M. *University Residence Environment Scale Manual.* Palo Alto, Calif: Consulting Psychologists Press, 1976.

Moos, R., and Lee, E. "Comparing Residence Hall and Independent Living Settings." *Research in Higher Education,* 1979, *11* (3), 207–221.

Moreno, J. *Who Shall Survive?* Boston: Beacon Press, 1953.

Morishima, J. K. "Effects on Student Achievement of Residence Hall Groupings Based on Academic Majors." In C. H. Bagley (Ed.), *Research on Academic Input: Proceedings of the Sixth Annual Forum of the Association for Institutional Research.* Cortland, N.Y.: State University of New York, 1966.

Morison, S. E. *Harvard College in the Seventeenth Century.* Cambridge, Mass.: Harvard University Press, 1936.

Murray, M. E. "The Effects of Roommates on the Scholastic Achievement of College Students." *Dissertation Abstracts,* 1961, *21.*

Napier, R., and Gershenfeld, M. *Groups: Theory and Experience.* Boston: Houghton Mifflin, 1973.

Nelson, J. P. "Value Changes as a Function of Campus Residence." *Journal of College and University Student Housing,* 1971, *1,* 8–15.

Newcomb, T. "An Approach to the Study of Communicative Acts." In P. Hare, E. Borgatta, and R. Bales (Eds.), *Small Groups.* New York: Knopf, 1962.

Newcomb, T. "The Nature of Peer Group Influence." In T. Newcomb and E. Wilson (Eds.), *College Peer Groups.* Chicago: Aldine, 1966.

Newcomb, T., and Wilson, E. (Eds.). *College Peer Groups.* Chicago: Aldine, 1966.

Newcomb, T., and others. *Persistence and Change: Bennington College and Its Students After 25 Years.* New York: Wiley, 1967.

Nosow, S. "An Attitudinal Comparison of Residential College Seniors with Other Seniors." *Journal of College Student Personnel,* 1975, *16,* 17–22.

Osterhout, S. "Interpersonal Skills Training for Residence Hall Staff Members: Impact on Student Development." *Journal of College and University Housing,* 1977, *6,* 42–44.

Pace, T. "Roommate Dissatisfaction in Residence Halls." *Journal of College Student Personnel,* 1970, *11,* 144–147.

Partham, W. D., and Tinsley, H. E. A. "What Are Friends For? Students' Expectations of the Friendship Encounter." *Journal of Counseling Psychology,* 1980, *27,* 524–527.

Pascarella, E. T., and Terenzini, P. T. "Student-Faculty and Student-Peer Relationships as Mediators of the Structural Effects of Undergraduate Residence Arrangement." *Journal of Educational Research,* 1980, *73,* 344–353.

Perkins, K. "The Effect of Value Similarity on Satisfaction with College Residence Hall Living Groups." *Journal of College Student Personnel,* 1977, *18,* 491–495.

Pervin, L. A. "Satisfaction and Perceived Self-Environment Similarity: A Semantic Differential Study of Student-College Interaction." *Journal of Personality,* 1967, *35,* 623–624.

Pervin, L. A. "The College as a Social System: Student Perception of Students, Faculty, and Administration." *Journal of Educational Research,* 1968a, *61,* 281–284.

Pervin, L. A. "Performance and Satisfaction as a Function of Individual-Environment Fit." *Psychological Bulletin,* 1968b, *69,* 56–58.

Peterman, D., Pilato, G., and Upcraft, M. L. "A Description and Evaluation of an Academic Course to Increase Interpersonal Effectiveness of Resident Assistants." *Journal of College Student Personnel,* 1979, *20,* 348–352.

Peterman, D., Sagaria, M., and Sellers, J. *The Roommate Starter Kit.* State College, Pa.: 1977.

Peters, G. R., and Kennedy, C. E. "Close Friendships in the College Community." *Journal of College Student Personnel,* 1970, *11,* 449–456.

Powell, J. R. "Inservice Education for Student Staff." In D. DeCoster and P. Mable (Eds.), *Student Development and Education in College Residence Halls.* Washington, D.C.: American College Personnel Association, 1974.

Pyle, R. R., and Snyder, F. A. "Students as Paraprofessional Counselors at Community Colleges." In D. G. Zimpfer (Ed.),

Paraprofessionals in Counseling, Guidance, and Personnel Services. Washington, D.C.: American Personnel and Guidance Association Press, 1974.

Rich, H. E., and Jolicoeur, P. M. *Student Attitudes and Academic Environments, A Study of California Higher Education.* New York: Praeger, 1978.

Riessman, F. "Strategies and Suggestions for Training Nonprofessionals." *Community Mental Health Journal,* 1967, *3,* 103–110.

Riker, H. "The Role of Residence Educators." In D. DeCoster and P. Mable (Eds.), *Personal Education and Community Development in College Residence Halls.* Washington, D.C.: American College Personnel Association, 1980, pp. 175–189.

Riker, H., and DeCoster, D. "The Educational Role in College Student Housing." *Journal of College and University Student Housing,* 1971, *1,* 1–4.

Roby, T. B., Zelin, M., and Chechile, R. A. "Matching Roommates by an Optimal Indirect Technique." *Journal of Applied Psychology,* 1977, *18,* 228–230.

Rogers, C. R. *A Way of Being.* Boston: Houghton Mifflin, 1980.

Rudolph, F. *The American College and University, A History.* New York: Vintage Books, 1965.

Sanford, N. "The Developmental Status of Entering Freshmen." In N. Sanford (Ed.), *The American College.* New York: Wiley, 1962.

Sauber, S. R. "College Adjustment and Place of Residence." *Journal of College Student Personnel,* 1972, *13,* 205–208.

Schinke, S. P., and others. "Crisis Intervention Training with Paraprofessionals." *Journal of Community Psychology,* 1979, *7,* 343–347.

Schoemer, J. R., and McConnell, W. A. "Is There a Case for the Freshman Women's Residence Hall?" *Personnel and Guidance Journal,* 1970, *49,* 35–40.

Schroeder, C. C., and Freesh, N. "Applying Environmental Management Strategies in Residence Halls." *Journal of the National Association of Student Personnel Administrators,* 1978, *16,* 51–57.

Schuh, J. "Staff Training." In G. Blimling and J. Schuh (Eds.), *New Directions for Student Services: Increasing the Educational Role of Residence Halls,* no. 13. San Francisco: Jossey-Bass, 1981.

Schuh, J. H., and Williams, O. J. "The Effect of Birth Order on

Roommate Compatibility." *College Student Journal,* 1977, *11,* 285–286.

Selby, T. J., and Weston, D. F. "Dormitory Versus Apartment Housing for Freshmen." *Journal of College Student Personnel,* 1978, *19,* 153–157.

Shapiro, J. G., and Voog, T. "Effect of the Inherently Helpful Person on Student Academic Achievement." *Journal of Counseling Psychology,* 1969, *16,* 505–509.

Shilling, K. "Impact of a Training Course on Personal Development of Resident Assistants." *Journal of the National Association of Student Personnel Administrators,* 1977, *14,* 33–37.

Simon, H. A. "A Formal Theory of Interaction in Social Groups." In P. Hare, E. Borgatta, and R. Bales (Eds.), *Small Groups.* New York: Knopf, 1962.

Smail, M. M., DeYoung, A. J., and Moos, R. H. "The University Residence Environment Scale: A Method of Describing University Student Living Groups." *Journal of College Student Personnel,* 1974, *15,* 357–366.

Smith, A. "Lawrence Kohlberg's Cognitive Stage Theory of the Development of Moral Judgment." In L. Knefelkamp, C. Widick, and C. Parker (Eds.), *New Directions for Student Services: Applying New Developmental Findings,* no. 4. San Francisco: Jossey-Bass, 1978.

Sommer, R. "Study Conditions in Residence Halls." *Journal of College Student Personnel,* 1969, *10,* 270–274.

Stern, G. G. *People in Context.* New York: Wiley, 1970.

Tannenbaum, R., and Schmidt, W. "How to Choose a Leadership Pattern." *Harvard Business Review,* 1960, *36,* 95–101.

Tannenbaum, R., Weschler, I., and Massarik, F. *Leadership and Organization. A Behavioral Science Approach.* New York: McGraw-Hill, 1961.

Taylor, R. G., and Hanson, G. R. "Environmental Impact on Achievement and Study Habits." *Journal of College Student Personnel,* 1971, *12,* 445–454.

Thomas, R. "Personality Variables and Residence Hall Counselor Effectiveness." *Journal of College and University Student Housing,* 1979, *9,* 22–24.

Tibbits, S. "Student Staff Selections: Peer Evaluations May Be

Best." *Journal of the National Association of Student Personnel Administrators,* 1977, *14,* 65–68.

Upcraft, M. L., and Peterson, P. C. "Correlates of Residence Assistant Competence." Unpublished research manuscript, The Pennsylvania State University, 1980.

Upcraft, M. L., Peterson, P. C., and Moore, B. L. "The Academic and Personal Development of Penn State Freshmen." Unpublished manuscript, The Pennsylvania State University, 1981.

Vreeland, R. "The Effects of Houses on Students' Attitudes and Values." In J. Whitley and H. Sprandel (Eds.), *The Growth and Development of College Students.* Washington, D.C.: American College Personnel Association, 1970.

Western Interstate Commission for Higher Education. *The Ecosystem Model: Designing Campus Environments.* Boulder, Col., 1973.

Wetzel, C. G., Schwartz, D., and Vasu, E. S. "Roommate Compatibility: Is There an Ideal Relationship?" *Journal of Applied Social Psychology,* 1979, *9,* 432–445.

White, W. C., and Ottens, A. J. "Crisis Intervention–The Cornell Plan." Paper read at the American College Health Association, Washington, D.C., May 1979.

Whittaker, D. "The Significant Others in the Lives of Sophomore College Students." Paper presented at California Educational Research Association, San Francisco, February 1970.

Widick, C., Parker, C., and Knefelkamp, L. "Douglas Heath's Model of Maturing." In L. Knefelkamp, C. Widick, and C. Parker (Eds.), *New Directions for Student Services: Applying New Developmental Findings,* no. 4. San Francisco: Jossey-Bass, 1978a.

Widick, C., Parker, C., and Knefelkamp, L. "Erik Erikson and Psychosocial Development." In L. Knefelkamp, C. Widick, and C. Parker (Eds.), *New Directions for Student Services: Applying New Developmental Findings,* no. 4. San Francisco: Jossey-Bass, 1978b.

Index

Wilson, E., 80
Win-lose situation, 134
Winkworth, J., 86

X

X type personality, 50

Y

Y type personality, 50–51

Yarris, E., 25
Yost, M. W., 20

Z

Z type personality, 51
Zander, A., 80–81
Zax, M., 84
Zelin, M., 84
Zoradi, S. D., 27